A PRIMER

FOR

PHIGS

A PRIMER
FOR
PHIGS

F. R. A. Hopgood
and
D. A. Duce

Rutherford Appleton Laboratory, UK

JOHN WILEY & SONS
Chichester · New York · Toronto · Brisbane · Singapore

Other Wiley Editorial Offices

John Wiley & Sons, Inc., 605 Third Avenue,
New York, NY 10158-0012, USA

Jacaranda Wiley Ltd, G.P.O. Box 859, Brisbane,
Queensland 4001, Australia

John Wiley & Sons (Canada) Ltd, 22 Worcester Road,
Rexdale, Ontario M9W 1L1, Canada

John Wiley & Sons (SEA) Pte Ltd, 37 Jalan Pemimpin 05-04,
Block B, Union Industrial Building, Singapore 2057

Library of Congress Cataloging-in-Publication Data:
Hopgood, F. R. A. (Frank Robert Albert)
    A primer for PHIGS / F. R. A. Hopgood and D. A. Duce.
      p. cm.
    Include bibliographical references and index.
    ISBN 0 471 93043 1
    1. Computer graphics. I. Duce, David A. II. Title.
T385.H694 1991
006.6—dc20   91-10791
                                 CIP

**A catalogue record for this book is available
from the British Library**

Printed in Great Britain by Biddles Ltd, Guildford

CONTENTS

PREFACE   xi

NOTATION   xiii

1 INTRODUCTION   1
    1.1 HISTORY   1
    1.2 CONCEPTS   2
          1.2.1 Introduction   2
          1.2.2 Language bindings and notation   3
          1.2.3 Device independence and workstations   3
          1.2.4 Output primitives   4
          1.2.5 Coordinate systems and clipping   4
          1.2.6 Appearance control   5
          1.2.7 Structures   5
          1.2.8 Input   6
          1.2.9 Viewing   6
    1.3 PHIGS AND PHIGS PLUS   6
    1.4 REFERENCES   7

2 STRUCTURES   11
    2.1 INTRODUCTION   11
    2.2 STORAGE AND TRAVERSAL   11
    2.3 GRAPHICAL OUTPUT   13
    2.4 STRUCTURE DEFINITION   14
    2.5 POSTING A STRUCTURE   15
    2.6 REOPENING STRUCTURES   17
    2.7 AN EXAMPLE   18
    2.8 LOCAL MODELLING TRANSFORMATIONS   21
    2.9 STRUCTURE EDITING   25
          2.9.1 Edit mode   25
          2.9.2 Absolute editing   26
          2.9.3 Relative editing   29
          2.9.4 Labels   30
          2.9.5 Deleting elements   32
    2.10 POSTING PRIORITY   34

3 OUTPUT PRIMITIVES   37
    3.1 INTRODUCTION   37
    3.2 POLYLINE   39
        3.2.1 The functions   39
        3.2.2 Polyline aspects and registration   40
        3.2.3 Linetypes   41
        3.2.4 Linewidth scale factor   41
        3.2.5 Colour index   42
        3.2.6 Summary   43
    3.3 POLYMARKER   43
        3.3.1 The functions   43
        3.3.2 Polymarker aspects   44
        3.3.3 Marker type   44
        3.3.4 Markersize scale factor   45
        3.3.5 Polymarker colour index   46
    3.4 FILL AREA AND FILL AREA SET   46
        3.4.1 The functions   46
        3.4.2 Definition of interior   48
        3.4.3 Area aspects   49
        3.4.4 Interior style   50
        3.4.5 Pattern aspects   51
        3.4.6 Edge aspects   53
    3.5 TEXT   54
        3.5.1 The functions   54
        3.5.2 Text aspects   55
        3.5.3 Font specification   56
        3.5.4 Defining the text extent rectangle   57
        3.5.5 Orientation   59
        3.5.6 Alignment   59
        3.5.7 Text precision   63

4 ATTRIBUTES   65
    4.1 INDIVIDUAL SPECIFICATION   65
    4.2 PATTERNS   66
    4.3 GEOMETRIC ASPECTS   69
    4.4 BUNDLED SPECIFICATION   69
    4.5 ASPECT SOURCE FLAGS   72
    4.6 COLOUR TABLES   76
    4.7 IDENTIFICATION ATTRIBUTES   78
        4.7.1 Name set   78
        4.7.2 Filters   78
        4.7.3 Rendering   80

5 NETWORKS   83
  5.1 INTRODUCTION   83
  5.2 STRUCTURE HIERARCHY   83
  5.3 MODELLING TRANSFORMATION   84
    5.3.1 Introduction   84
    5.3.2 Global modelling transformation 85
    5.3.3 Picture composition   86
  5.4 A NETWORK EXAMPLE   87
    5.4.1 Introduction   87
    5.4.2 Strategy   87
    5.4.3 Components   88
    5.4.4 Transformations   90
    5.4.5 Define one environment   91
  5.5 GLOBAL TRANSFORMATION RESETTING   98
  5.6 UTILITY FUNCTIONS   100
  5.7 STRUCTURE FUNCTIONS   101
    5.7.1 Introduction   101
    5.7.2 Changing the name of a structure 101
    5.7.3 Changing structure references   102
    5.7.4 Adding elements from another structure 102
    5.7.5 Deleting structures   103
    5.7.6 Emptying structures   104
  5.8 MODELLING CLIP   104
    5.8.1 Introduction   104
    5.8.2 The function   105
    5.8.3 A window clip   106
    5.8.4 Shielding   107
  5.9 APPLICATION DATA   109
  5.10 GENERALIZED STRUCTURE ELEMENT   109

6 VIEWING IN 2D   111
  6.1 INTRODUCTION   111
  6.2 VIEWING   111
  6.3 VIEW INDEX   112
  6.4 METRIC DESK   113
  6.5 VIEW ORIENTATION   114
  6.6 VIEW MAPPING   115
  6.7 VIEW DEFINITION AND CLIPPING   116
  6.8 A COMPLETE EXAMPLE   117

7 3D PHIGS   121
  7.1 INTRODUCTION   121
    7.1.1 Relationship to 2D   121

7.1.2 Coordinate systems   121
7.1.3 3D functions   123
7.1.4 Building transformation matrices   124
7.2 VIEWING   124
7.2.1 Viewing pipeline   124
7.2.2 View example   126
7.2.3 Viewing model   127
7.3 VIEW ORIENTATION   128
7.4 VIEW MAPPING   131
7.5 DEFINING A VIEW   133

8 EXAMPLES   135
8.1 PARALLEL PROJECTION EXAMPLES   135
8.1.1 Introduction   135
8.1.2 View orientation   135
8.1.3 Changing the window to viewport mapping   139
8.2 PARALLEL PROJECTION CATEGORIES   141
8.2.1 Introduction   141
8.2.2 Orthographic projections   141
8.2.3 Oblique projections   142
8.3 PERSPECTIVE PROJECTIONS   142
8.3.1 Orientation   143
8.3.2 Changing the projection reference point   145
8.4 MULTIPLE VIEWS   147
8.5 VIEW CULLING   148

9 INPUT CLASSES   151
9.1 INTRODUCTION   151
9.2 REQUEST MODE   152
9.3 LOCATOR   153
9.3.1 Multiple viewing transformations   156
9.3.2 Overlapping views   157
9.4 STROKE   160
9.5 2D INPUT DEVICES   162
9.6 LOCATOR AND STROKE IN 3D   162
9.7 PICK   162
9.7.1 Pick identifier   165
9.7.2 Pick filters   167
9.8 VALUATOR   170
9.9 CHOICE   173
9.10 STRING   175

10 INTERACTION   177
10.1 MODES OF INTERACTION   177

10.1.1 The PHIGS input model 177
10.1.2 Mode setting 178
10.1.3 REQUEST mode 179
10.1.4 Status 182
10.1.5 SAMPLE mode 182
10.1.6 EVENT mode 185
10.1.7 Mixed input modes 191
10.2 INITIALIZATION OF LOGICAL INPUT DEVICES 194
10.2.1 Initial value 194
10.2.2 Prompt and echo type 196
10.2.3 Echo volume and area 198
10.2.4 Input data record 199
10.2.5 PICK path order 201
10.3 FURTHER INPUT FUNCTIONS 201
10.3.1 Simultaneous events 202
10.3.2 Input queue overflow 202
10.4 INCREMENTAL SPATIAL SEARCH 203

11 WORKSTATIONS 209
11.1 MAIN CHARACTERISTICS 209
11.2 SETTING UP A WORKSTATION 210
11.3 WORKSTATION TRANSFORMATION 210
11.4 DISPLAY UPDATE 212
11.5 WORKSTATION CLOSURE 212

12 ENVIRONMENT 213
12.1 INTRODUCTION 213
12.2 PHIGS OPERATING STATES 214
12.3 PHIGS STATE LISTS 215
12.4 INQUIRY FUNCTIONS 216
12.5 INQUIRIES FOR CSS 218
12.6 ERROR HANDLING 223

13 FURTHER OUTPUT 227
13.1 INTRODUCTION 227
13.2 CELL ARRAY 227
13.3 ANNOTATION TEXT 228
13.4 GENERALIZED DRAWING PRIMITIVE 229

14 ARCHIVES 231
14.1 INTRODUCTION 231
14.2 ARCHIVAL AND RETRIEVAL FUNCTIONS 232
14.3 CONFLICT RESOLUTION 233
14.4 INQUIRY FUNCTIONS FOR ARCHIVES 233
14.5 DELETION FUNCTIONS 234

15 BINDINGS   235
    15.1 INTRODUCTION   235
    15.2 ORGANIZATION OF THE FORTRAN BINDING   235
INDEX   255

PREFACE

PHIGS is the latest of the computer graphics standards. It builds on the earlier standards, GKS and GKS-3D, with the main emphasis on providing a 2D and 3D graphics standard aimed at the person producing highly structured computer graphics or the person who needs to interact with the graphics in a complex way. It has become extremely popular in a short period due to the number of implementations that have been made available on workstations.

This book aims at providing a basic understanding of PHIGS concentrating on those parts which are the most novel, the structure store and the viewing model. It is not an exhaustive description of all the facilities in PHIGS. However, by the end of the book, readers should be capable of writing a wide range of PHIGS programs.

Examples have been written in pseudo-Fortran 77 using the PHIGS names for functions rather than the constrained Fortran 6-character names. The necessary information is provided to convert the examples into genuine Fortran programs. Two major examples, a 2D desk and a 3D object, are used throughout the book. The necessary data is provided to allow the reader to implement these himself and try out further variants of the examples.

Chapters 1 to 4 introduce the PHIGS structure store and the output primitives using mainly 2D examples. Chapter 5 concentrates on the hierarchical structure facilities showing how they can be used to manipulate objects in complex ways. Chapters 6 to 8 describes the viewing facilities available particularly in 3D. Chpaters 9 and 10 discuss the input facilities and how interactive programs are written in PHIGS.

The remaining chapters concentrate on the aspects of PHIGS dependent on the environment in which it is used and the less important features.

While being written as an introductory text, it is hoped that it can also act as a reference guide to the main facilities in PHIGS.

Much of David Duce's contribution to this book was written in Ward 6 of Chapel Allerton Hospital, Leeds, whilst his father was a patient there. The book is dedicated to George Duce, who provides a shining example of what can be achieved by patient determination, and to the doctors, physiotherapists, speech therapist and nursing staff for their skill and loving-care.

The examples have been tested, where possible, using the SUN PHIGS implementation and many of the diagrams have been produced using its CGM workstation. We would like to thank Predrag Popovic for the use of his software for converting CGM to POSTSCRIPT.

We would also like to thank the Yugoslavian Computer Graphics Society whose invitation to give a 2-day PHIGS Tutorial in Dubrovnik in 1990 was the catalyst for the writing of this book.

NOTATION

We have chosen to use the Fortran binding as the basis for the examples in this book. Clearly, the language binding has to comply with the constraints of the language standard itself. In the case of Fortran, this means that all identifiers, such as subroutine names, are limited to six characters. For example, to draw a polyline in PHIGS requires the function:

POLYLINE(point list)

to be executed. The Fortran language binding accesses this function by defining the subroutine:

SUBROUTINE PPL(N, XA, YA)

where the two arrays XA(1 to N) and YA(1 to N) define the (X,Y) points that make up the *point list* in the PHIGS parameter. The POLYLINE name has been abbreviated to PPL. While this particular mnemonic may not be too difficult to remember and relate to the PHIGS function name, some names in the Fortran binding are much harder to remember. For example, the PHIGS function:

INQUIRE SET OF WORKSTATIONS TO WHICH POSTED

has the Fortran subroutine name PQWKPO!

We have compromised in this book by not using the Fortran binding exactly but instead have substituted the full PHIGS function name while retaining the Fortran parameters in the examples. We have also omitted the word CALL throughout. Thus the Fortran subroutine call:

CALL PPL(N, XA, YA)

has been written as:

POLYLINE(N, XA, YA)

in the examples.

The other liberties taken in the examples are to be imprecise as to whether particular parameters are REAL or INTEGER. For example:

```
REAL X(5)
DATA X /0, 1, 2, 3, 4/
POST STRUCTURE(WS, ABC, 0)
```

Strictly speaking, the DATA declaration should have REAL values defined and the third parameter in the POST STRUCTURE function should be a REAL number.

PHIGS also has a number of parameters which enumerate a number of possible options. In Fortran, these are mapped onto integer values from 0 upwards. In the examples, for clarity we have assumed a variable has been set up to have the correct value and the variable name is used instead. For example:

```
SET LINETYPE(DOT)
```

should really be written as:

```
INTEGER DOT
DOT=3
CALL PSLN(DOT)
```

The PHIGS language binding does define a set of names for this purpose. However, these names conform to the Fortran restriction of 6 characters, and to avoid conflicts with variable names used in the application, they start with the letter P. In this book, we have used variable names with more obvious meanings in preference to the defined set and so do not always follow the constraint to 6 characters. The Fortran binding provides the constant PLDOT which could have been used instead of DOT. Some implementations provide an include file with these constants already set up. Some details of the standard names used in implementations is given in Chapter 15.

1 INTRODUCTION

1.1 HISTORY

The emergence of standards in computer graphics was a long time coming. Some standards activities date back to the early 1960s but it was not until the IFIP Seillac Workshop in 1976 in France and the activities of the Graphic Standards Planning Committee in the USA during the 1970s that any real progress was made.

A fundamental decision made at the Seillac Workshop was to concentrate initially on the application programmer interface or *API* initially. The API is the set of function calls required by an application programmer to make use of a substantial graphics system. The main alternative was to attempt to do the initial standardization at a lower level, say the device order code level or the device driver level. The other major decision was to split graphics into two separate parts. The first was concerned with constructing the graphical *scene* to be output while the second was concerned with *viewing* that scene. In 3 dimensions, viewing will require projection of the 3D scene on to a plane producing a *picture* to be rendered on a *display* for the *operator* to look at and interact with. That sentence contains a number of key words that we will use throughout the book to identify specific parts of the graphics system. Early systems had tended to blur the two activities of *modelling* (that is constructing the model of an object from which the scene is generated) and *viewing* often using the same function for two quite distinct purposes. This in turn led to poor understanding of the system by the application programmer.

After Seillac, the decision was made to concentrate initially on a standard that was primarily concerned with displaying a 2D picture. The standardization activities were carried on within the International Organization for Standardization (ISO). This resulted in 1985 in the Graphical Kernel System (GKS) being published [6][10][16] as the first computer graphics standard. Work then continued in a number of separate directions. A standard for the transmission and storage of 2D pictures, the Computer Graphics Metafile (CGM) was actively worked on and resulted in this standard being established in 1987 [2][7][11][17]. This was initially a 2D standard like GKS but work since has extended the functionality and is adding 3D capabilities in a number of Amendments. Work also proceeded in the production of a device level standard called the Computer Graphics Interface (CGI) [2][21].

GKS was followed by two further API standards, GKS-3D [19] and PHIGS [20]. While GKS-3D was a straightforward extension of GKS to 3 dimensions, PHIGS was the first standard aimed at providing facilities for modelling, that is constructing models of objects from which some part could be extracted as a scene of the object and this scene viewed by projection and display.

The three API standards and the related standards have been developed with compatibility in mind. Consequently, the viewing system used by PHIGS is primarily the one developed for GKS-3D with some minor changes. The major area of innovation in PHIGS is the model building. Neither GKS or GKS-3D satisfied the requirement of application programs where modification of the graphical data is required in an efficient manner, where the objects to be displayed consist of geometrically related parts, and where rapid dynamic articulation of graphical entities is required. This is the area addressed by PHIGS and from which the name derives, the *Programmer's Hierarchical Interactive Graphics System.*

Discussion of the process by which international standards are developed would be out of place in this book; for a discussion the reader is referred to the book by Arnold and Duce [3]. The reader should note that prior to 1988 Computer Graphics Standards were published by ISO. Since that date, a joint technical committee of ISO and the International Electrotechnical Commission (IEC), known as ISO/IEC JTC1, has been responsible for standards in the information technology area. This explains why the earlier standards are referred to as ISO standards and the later ones (such as PHIGS) are ISO/IEC standards.

1.2 CONCEPTS

1.2.1 Introduction

The API standards share a set of common concepts. The realization of the concepts varies from standard to standard but the overall concepts remain the same. The aim is to base all three API standards on sound principles. By having common concepts, application program and application programmer portability is also improved. This section will attempt to give an overview to those concepts that are relevant to PHIGS.

1.2.2 Language bindings and notation

All three standards are defined in a language independent way as a set of functions with a description of their meaning that is not dependent on any one programming language [13][14][15][26]. Separate standards exist that *bind* the API standard to a particular language. A language binding defines how the language independent functions and data types described in the PHIGS standard are to be realized as subroutines or procedures and the actual data types of a particular programming language. PHIGS has language bindings for Fortran and Ada. A C language binding standard is expected to be completed during 1991. A Pascal language binding is being worked upon but no dates currently exist for its completion.

In consequence, we have chosen to use the Fortran binding as the basis for the examples in this book. Clearly, the language binding has to comply with the constraints of the language standard itself. In the case of Fortran, this means that all identifiers, such as subroutine names, are limited to six characters. A brief summary of the Fortran language binding is given in Chapter 15. As the ISO Fortran language binding document [14] is 213 pages long, this is inevitably a summary rather than the complete definition. It should be sufficient to allow real PHIGS programs to be written.

The aim is to give an introduction to PHIGS. Inevitably, the user of PHIGS will need to read the manual that comes with his implementation as in many places the richness of the implementation may effect what he decides to do.

1.2.3 Device independence and workstations

The API standards make a clean separation of those parts of the standard that are dependent on the characteristics of the device where output is to appear and input originates and those parts which are the same for all devices.

The key concept providing device independence is the *workstation*. This is not a physical device such as a SUN workstation but all the functions and data that are device dependent. This hypothetical workstation has at most one display surface, a number of input devices and quite a bit of storage space for tables and some intelligence. How it is realized in a specific implementation can be quite varied. For example, an implementation of PHIGS running on a mainframe with an intelligent device such as a physical workstation attached might have the device independent code in the mainframe and the device dependent part (the PHIGS workstation) executing in the physical workstation. Alternatively, PHIGS might run on the mainframe with quite straightforward unintelligent devices attached. In this case, the device driver and device dependent parts would also run on the mainframe. At the other extreme, PHIGS could reside completely in the physical workstation in which case both the device independent and device dependent parts of the system will reside there.

In this book, the word *workstation* will be used to define the device dependent part of PHIGS. An application may use a number of PHIGS workstations at the same time. This could be to provide different views of the scene created or could be to allow the interactive display to be captured on a plotter. The physical realization of this could be two displays and a plotter attached to a mainframe or separate windows on a SUN workstation with an ethernet connection to a laserprinter. Conceptually, PHIGS would treat them the same.

In PHIGS, a scene is created which needs to be seen at the workstation. The device independent scene has to be viewed by the workstation. Each workstation specifies its views independent of any other workstation. Viewing creates a picture of the scene at the workstation. For example, the projection of a 3D scene onto a 2D plane would be performed by the workstation. The 2D picture created must be displayed on the display surface of the workstation. This requires the picture, which is still a set of commands in memory, to be rendered. This can be as simple as ensuring the bits representing a line are turned on in a bit-mapped display or can be quite complex including hidden line or hidden surface removal.

1.2.4 Output primitives

The API standards each define some basic building blocks from which a scene is created and these are called *output primitives*. The simplest output primitive is a polyline which draws a sequence of connected line segments. There is a strong commonality between the output primitives of the three API standards. The major difference is the added complexity of the primitives in 3D compared with 2D. Also, the primitive set has grown as the standards develop. PHIGS has the richest set of primitives of the three standards.

1.2.5 Coordinate systems and clipping

The application needs to define models of objects in coordinate systems appropriate to the application. The scene created when part of the model is to be displayed needs to be defined in a neutral coordinate system that is neither specific to the application nor the device.

The philosophy in all the API standards is to create a scene in some device independent coordinate system (called *world* coordinates in PHIGS). The scene is created from some part of the model defined by the application in coordinates appropriate to the application (called *modelling* coordinates in PHIGS). The world coordinate scene is viewed creating a picture in a device independent coordinate system (called *Normalized Projection Coordinates* in PHIGS). Some part of this picture is displayed on the workstation's display surface using the coordinate system appropriate to the display device (called *Device Coordinates*).

1.2.6 Appearance control

The appearance of output primitives on a display surface is controlled by *aspects* associated with the primitive. The three API standards use the same aspects where appropriate. Aspects can be *global,* that is they are defined in the device independent scene and workstations should present them the same on every display surface. For example, if text is to be output, its height is set globally. All workstations are required to generate text of the appropriate size on the display.

Aspects can be workstation dependent. For example, linestyle may be very dependent on the display's capabilities. The length of the individual dashes in a dashed line or the frequency of dots in a dotted line may be dependent on the device hardware available. For workstation dependent aspects, all three API standards allow the aspect to be bound to the primitive in the device independent scene or to be left partially defined at that stage. In the latter case, the actual binding of the aspects to the primitives is left to the workstation to decide under the control of the application. A set of flags decide what method is used for each aspect. This facility allows, for example, an application to specify that every fifth contour should be differentiated and the workstation can choose whether to do this by changing line thickness, the line style of the contour or its colour or a combination of these.

1.2.7 Structures

A major difference in the API standards is how they store graphical information for later reuse. GKS and GKS-3D provide a low-level segment storage to which only minor changes can be made once it is defined. PHIGS, on the other hand, retains graphical information close to the application level in modelling coordinates in entities called *structures*. These can be linked together into *structure networks*. The scene to be viewed is derived from one or more structure networks that the application wishes to view on one or more workstations.

By providing facilities for editing structures interactively with immediate feedback of the changes on the display, high quality interaction between the operator and the application can take place.

1.2.8 Input

All three API standards have a common model of input. As for output, input is defined in a device independent way. Input is categorized into a set of classes corresponding to the different values provided. The values are associated with the scene. For example, they may be positions in world coordinates, real numbers, integers from a limited range, and so on. The workstation receives input from the physical devices and converts these into virtual input values so that it looks as though the workstation has a number of *logical input devices* attached. There may be no correlation between the workstation's logical input devices and the physical devices provided. For example, a workstation may have a single mouse attached to it which might be used to input values, positions, select from menus and, in general, act like a set of logical input devices. Alternatively, a keyboard and two thumb wheels may be required to input a single position. How physical devices are mapped onto logical input devices is the responsibility of the workstation implementation. The *class* of the logical input device defines the value it delivers to the application.

All three API standards support a range of input styles. The simplest is a dialogue where the operator and application take it in turns to take action. An asynchronous style is provided where the application *samples* logical input values as it requires them. The values are being updated by the operator but the application only takes the new values it requires. The most complex is an *event* driven mode of input where the operator places input values on a queue for the application to deal with. This range of application interaction styles allows applications to be written in PHIGS with styles that are appropriate for the application and the devices that it will interact with.

1.2.9 Viewing

Both GKS-3D and PHIGS, being 3D systems, are capable of producing 3D scenes to be displayed on 2D devices. This requires a *projection* of the 3D scene onto a 2D plane creating a *picture* to be displayed [4]. The way viewing is defined is the same in the two standards and is sufficiently general to provide most of the standard projections in common use.

1.3 PHIGS AND PHIGS PLUS

PHIGS is the ISO/IEC standard number 9592 [20]. It was completed in 1989 and many implementations of the standard were available on the market during 1990 particularly on the range of physical workstations provided by manufacturers such as SUN, DEC, IBM, Hewlett Packard and Stardent.

This book aims to give an introduction to PHIGS concentrating on the major features, the structure store and viewing. However, it contains sufficient description to allow a reader to construct his own PHIGS programs.

A drawback of PHIGS when used on the more sophisticated systems is that it provides little control of sophisticated rendering features such as multiple light sources illuminating an object producing shadows and reflections (see Section 4.7.3). As these can often be provided by the hardware of the more modern devices, some method needs to be provided to accommodate such requirements. To provide this, an extension to PHIGS is being developed called *PHIGS PLUS*. It is hoped that this extension will be completed in 1991 or early in 1992 [22].

Unfortunately, many PHIGS implementations have attempted to add PHIGS PLUS features while the extension is being developed. In consequence, several of the PHIGS implementations contain PHIGS PLUS-like extensions which do not correspond to the standard being developed. It will be necessary for such implementations to be updated to the standard when it is complete.

In this book, no attempt has been made to describe the PHIGS PLUS extensions. At the time of writing (early 1991), it is not possible as the final form of PHIGS PLUS is not known. A more sensible approach is to follow the standard and produce a companion volume when the PHIGS PLUS functionality is frozen.

1.4 REFERENCES

1. S.S. Abi-Ezzi and A.J. Bunshaft (1986), "An Implementor's View of PHIGS", *IEEE Computer Graphics and Applications* **6**(2).

2. D.B. Arnold and P.R. Bono (1988), *CGM and CGI - Metafile and Interface Standards for Computer Graphics,* Springer-Verlag.

3. D.B. Arnold and D.A. Duce (1990), *ISO Standards for Computer Graphics - The First Generation,* Butterworths.

4. I. Carlbom and J. Paciorek (December 1978), "Planar Geometric Projections and Viewing Transformations", *Computing Surveys* **10**(4), pp.465-502.

5. W.H. Clifford, J.I. McConnell, and J.S. Saltz (1988), "The Development of PEX, a 3D Graphics Extension to X11", in *Proceedings of EUROGRAPHICS '88,* ed. D.A. Duce and P. Jancene, North-Holland.

6. G. Enderle, K. Kansy, and G. Pfaff (1987), *Computer Graphics Programming, GKS - The Graphics Standard,* Springer-Verlag. (Second Edition)

7. L.R. Henderson and A.M. Mumford (1990), *The Computer Graphics Metafile,* Butterworths.

8. I. Herman and J. Reviczky (1987), ''A Means to Improve the GKS 3D/PHIGS Output Pipeline Implementation'', in *Proceedings of EUROGRAPHICS '87,* ed. G. Marechal, North-Holland.

9. I. Herman and J. Reviczky (1988), ''Some Remarks on the Modelling Clip Problem'', *Computer Graphics Forum* **7**(4), pp.265-271.

10. F. R. A. Hopgood, D. A. Duce, J. R. Gallop, and D. C. Sutcliffe (1986), *Introduction to the Graphical Kernel System (GKS),* Academic Press. (Second Edition)

11. F.R.A. Hopgood, R.J. Hubbold, and D.A. Duce (Eds) (1986), *Advances in Computer Graphics II,* Springer-Verlag.

12. T.L.J. Howard (1989), ''An Annotated PHIGS Bibliography'', *Computer Graphics Forum* **8**(3), pp.262-265.

13. ISO, ''Information processing systems - Computer graphics - Graphical Kernel System for Three Dimensions (GKS-3D) language bindings - Part 1: Fortran ISO 8806-1 (to be published)'', Part 2: Pascal ISO 8806-2 (to be published), Part 3: Ada ISO 8806-3 (to be published), Part 4: C ISO 8806-4 (to be published), ISO Central Secretariat.

14. ISO, ''Information processing systems - Computer graphics - Programmer's Hierarchical Interactive Graphics System (PHIGS) language bindings - Part 1: Fortran ISO 9593-1 (1990)'', Part 2: Pascal ISO 9593-2 (to be published), Part 3: Ada ISO 9593-3 (1990), Part 4: C ISO 9593-4 (to be published), ISO Central Secretariat.

15. ISO, ''Information processing systems - Computer graphics - Graphical Kernel System (GKS) language bindings - Part 1: Fortran ISO 8651-1 (1988)'', Part 2: Pascal ISO 8651-2 (1988), Part 3: Ada ISO 8651-3 (1988), Part 4: C ISO 8651-4 (to be published), ISO Central Secretariat.

16. ISO (August 1985), ''Information processing systems - Computer graphics - Graphical Kernel System (GKS) functional description'', ISO 7942, ISO Central Secretariat.

17. ISO (1987), "Information processing systems - Computer graphics - Metafile for the storage and transfer of picture description information", ISO 8632, ISO Central Secretariat.

18. ISO (1988), "Procedures for the Registration of Graphical Items", ISO/TR 9973, ISO Central Secretariat, Geneva, Switzerland.

19. ISO (1988), "Information processing systems - Computer graphics - Graphical Kernel System (GKS) for three dimensions (GKS-3D) functional description", ISO/IEC 8805.

20. ISO (1989), "Information processing systems - Computer graphics - Programmer's Hierarchical Interactive Graphics System functional description", ISO/IEC 9592: 1.

21. ISO (1990), "Information processing systems - Computer graphics - Interface techniques for dialogues with graphical devices,", DIS 9636, ISO Central Secretariat.

22. ISO/IEC (1990), "Information processing systems - Computer graphics - Programmer's Hierarchical Graphics System (PHIGS) - Part 4: Plus Lumiere und Surfaces (PHIGS PLUS)", ISO/IEC JTC1/SC 24 N454.

23. M.A. Penna and R.R. Patterson (1986), *Projective Geometry and its applications to computer graphics,* Prentice-Hall.

24. K. Singleton (1987), "An Implementation of the GKS-3D/PHIGS Viewing Pipeline", in *GKS Theory and Practice*, ed. I. Herman and P.R. Bono, Springer-Verlag

25. M.W. Skall (1986), "NBS's Role in Computer Graphics Standards", *IEEE Computer Graphics and Applications* **6**(8), pp.50-57.

26. M. R. Sparks and J. R. Gallop (1987), "Computer graphics language bindings: programmer interface standards", *Computer-Aided Design* **19**(8), pp.418-424.

27. K.M. Wyrwas and W.T. Hewitt (1989), "A Survey of GKS and PHIGS Implementations", *Computer Graphics Forum* **8**(1), pp.49-59.

2 STRUCTURES

2.1 INTRODUCTION

In a low-level graphics system, such as GKS, the production of graphical output consists of a single process. The application requests a polyline to be drawn and the graphical output is generated and appears on the relevant workstation displays as soon as it is required. The advantage of this approach is that not much internal storage is required and the model of the system is easy for the user to comprehend - he asks for a line to be drawn and it appears. The disadvantage of this approach comes when the output generated needs to be modified dependent, say, on some operator input. In this case, each time the graphical output is to be updated, it has to be drawn again. For complex pictures, this can be quite time consuming.

PHIGS is a higher-level graphics system than GKS. Its main purpose is to define computer graphics output that can be easily changed in response to application or operator actions. In order to do this, it must store the information to be displayed internally so that it can be updated efficiently. As it is likely that sets of lines or primitives will be manipulated rather than individual primitives, PHIGS defines a *structure* as the entity to be used for storing graphical output. Structures are stored in a *Central Structure Store (CSS)*. The PHIGS standard itself calls the store the *Centralized* Structure Store but the slightly shorter name will be used throughout this book. There is a close analogy between the CSS of PHIGS and an office filing system. Documents that are created are very similar to the structures in PHIGS. The CSS is very similar to the filing system where the documents are kept. Just as it is possible for documents to have common parts, so several structures can have a common sub-structure.

2.2 STORAGE AND TRAVERSAL

The main concepts of PHIGS are shown in Figure 2.1. To create graphical output, the application needs to define structures that are stored in the CSS. The breakdown of the graphical output into structures would normally be in terms of the requirements of the application. For a circuit design application, structures might be defined for the basic components such as resistors and capacitors. Higher application building blocks, such as an oscillator, could be defined as a structure which referenced the individual component structures. Finally, complete circuits would be defined in terms of the higher level building blocks. The adjective *hierarchical* which is the H in the PHIGS name comes from its ability to define higher level graphics in terms of lower level components. PHIGS structures consist of a sequence of structure elements. Different types of structure elements exist, for example to specify attribute values or create an output primitive.

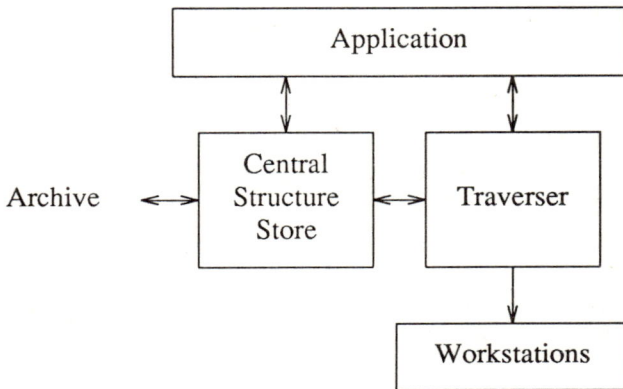

Figure 2.1: *PHIGS Traverser and Central Structure Store*

There is no point in defining structures containing graphical output unless it is possible for these to be displayed on a workstation. This is similar to writing letters or creating documents, putting them in envelopes and leaving them on a desk. This does not provide any communication to your correspondent. When the writer is satisfied with the information to be delivered, it is necessary to post the letter. Similarly, in PHIGS, when a structure that has been created is to be displayed, it must be *posted* to the relevant workstation. The assumption in PHIGS is that it may be possible for the post operation to be extremely fast so that posting can cause the graphical output to appear immediately.

Unlike the posting of a document, the post operation in PHIGS does not actually send the structure. Conceptually, the post operation in PHIGS opens a hatch on the central structure store so that the workstation can see the posted structure. It is as though the postman does not take the letter and deliver it but instead delivers a telescope so that the letter in the filestore can be viewed.

PHIGS describes the display of a structure on a workstation as *traversal*. Posting a structure to a workstation effectively starts the traversal process. Each element in the structure is examined and, if appropriate, the traverser will create some graphical output to be displayed on the workstation equivalent to that structure element. Operations on structures and structure traversal are the most important concepts in PHIGS and, for that reason, they are being described first. However, it is difficult to describe these in graphical terms without knowing something about the graphical output that is allowed. Consequently, at this stage, there will be a short interlude while some minimal features of one output primitive are described. A full description of the main types of graphical output in PHIGS will be postponed until Chapter 3.

2.3 GRAPHICAL OUTPUT

Two types of structure elements are defined in PHIGS for specifying graphical output and the attributes to be associated with the output. For example, an invocation of:

POLYLINE(N, XA, YA)

will create a structure element which, on traversal, will produce graphical output consisting of a sequence of straight lines from (XA(1), YA(1)) to (XA(2), YA(2)) to ... (XA(N), YA(N)). The appearance of the polyline on the display is controlled by attributes. These attributes are also defined by structure elements. Two examples are:

SET LINETYPE(DASHED)
SET LINEWIDTH SCALE FACTOR(THICK)

The polyline has other attributes but the two given above are sufficient for the description of structure operations. The function SET LINETYPE defines the type of line to be displayed for future output. Possibilities are DASHED, DOTTED and SOLID with the last being the default value. The actual parameter is an integer but the mnemonics will be used in this Chapter to make examples easier to read. Similarly, the function SET LINEWIDTH SCALE FACTOR (sometimes written as SET LSF) defines the thickness of line to be displayed for future output. The possible parameter values are NORMAL, THICK and THIN. Actually, there is a whole range of possible values which define the thickness of a line relative to the NORMAL thickness (1.0). A full description of the polyline primitive will be postponed to Section 3.2. It is the main line drawing primitive of PHIGS. Single lines are drawn by specifying a polyline with just two points.

So far, no mention has been made of the coordinates to be used in the definition of graphical output. Suffice it to say, for now, that the application has complete freedom to choose a relevant coordinate system applicable to the problem. In this Chapter, the graphical output will be defined to be 2-dimensional and within the unit square from 0 to 1 in both the X and Y-directions. This happens to be the default settings in place when PHIGS is entered. Consequently, these examples should execute without change on most PHIGS implementations.

2.4 STRUCTURE DEFINITION

A structure definition is started by the function:

OPEN STRUCTURE(ID)

where ID is the name of the structure. In PHIGS, the names of structures are positive integers. Invoking functions that create structure elements will result in these structure elements being added to the structure that has been opened. The structure definition is completed by invoking the function:

CLOSE STRUCTURE

For example:

```
OPEN STRUCTURE(3)
POLYLINE(N, X1, Y1)
SET LINETYPE(DASHED)
SET LINEWIDTH SCALE FACTOR(THICK)
POLYLINE(M, X2, Y2)
CLOSE STRUCTURE
```

will define a structure named 3 with 4 structure elements. When the structure is posted to a workstation, the display will consist of two polylines. The first will have the current default appearance while the second will be dashed and thick.

The form of the central structure store while this structure is being defined is shown in Figure 2.2. The central structure store consists of the set of structures already defined. When a structure is opened initially, the structure state list will have the name of the *open structure* set to point to the structure being defined. The *element pointer* in the structure state list will be set to 0. The *edit mode* will initially be set to INSERT. Invoking the function POLYLINE(N, X1, Y1) will result in the structure state list being examined to find out which structure is open and what elements have already been defined. The element pointer is incremented by 1 and the new structure element stored at that position. While inserting a set of elements into a structure, the element pointer always points to the last structure element inserted. More complex operations on structures will be discussed later. The CLOSE STRUCTURE function resets the structure state list to have null values in the name of the open structure and the element pointer.

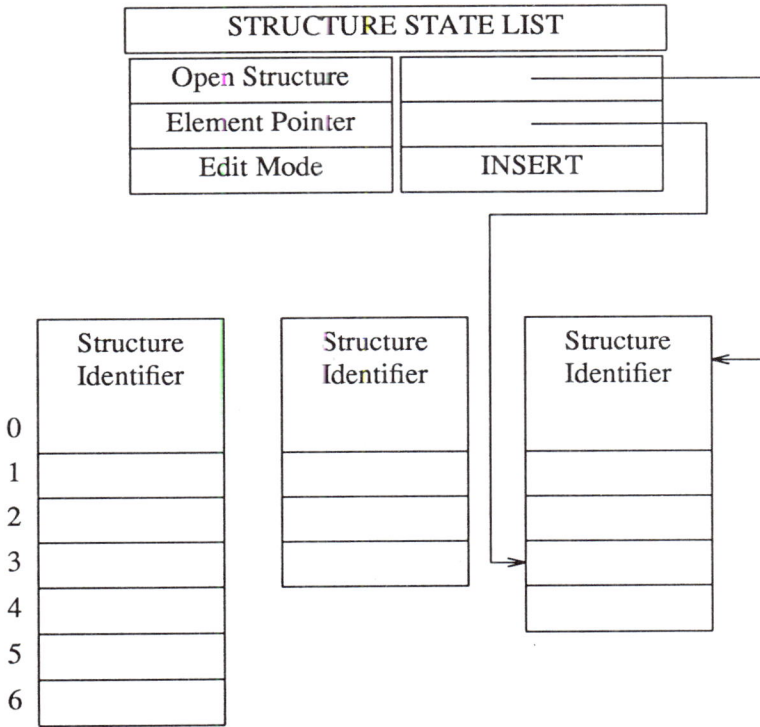

STRUCTURE STATE LIST	
Open Structure	———
Element Pointer	———
Edit Mode	INSERT

Structure Identifier	Structure Identifier	Structure Identifier
0		
1		
2		
3		
4		
5		
6		

Figure 2.2: *Central Structure Store*

2.5 POSTING A STRUCTURE

A structure is posted to a workstation by invoking the function:

POST STRUCTURE(WS, SI, PR)

where WS defines the workstation and SI the name of the structure to be posted. The third parameter defines the priority of the posting which will be described later (see Section 2.10).

The form of the traverser is conceptually shown in Figure 2.3. The traverser will have a set of structures that have already been posted. These are defined in a post list. To this will be added the new posting defined above. It is the function of the traverser to ensure that each workstation has the correct display corresponding to the structures that have been posted to it. Conceptually, the traverser can be thought of as going through the post list one entry at a time interpreting the entries. Once all have been interpreted, it starts again repeating the operation. This is necessary as will be seen later because the structures that have been posted can be changed.

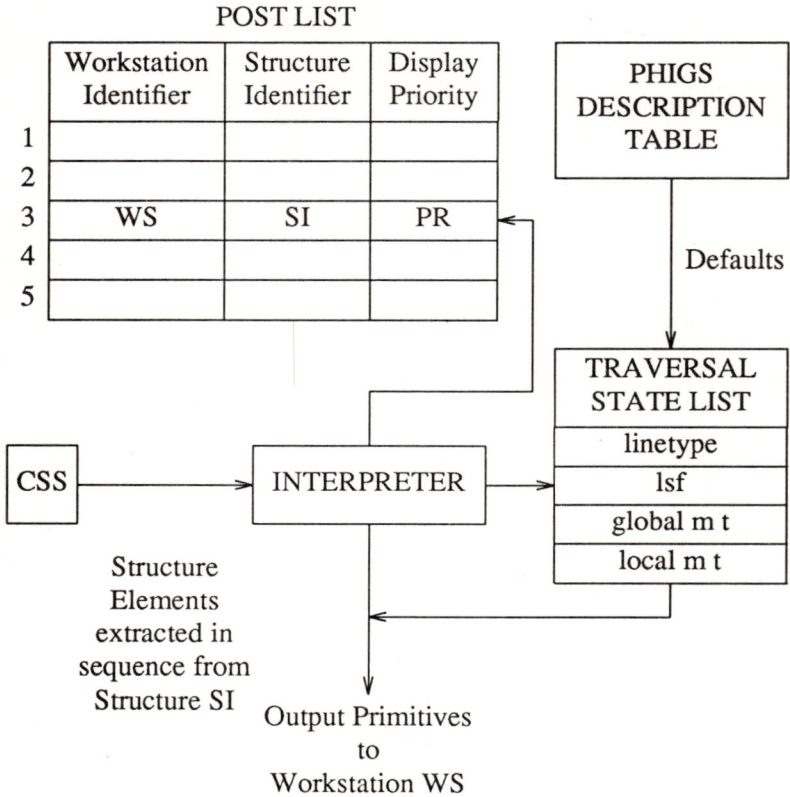

POST LIST

	Workstation Identifier	Structure Identifier	Display Priority
1			
2			
3	WS	SI	PR
4			
5			

PHIGS DESCRIPTION TABLE

Defaults

TRAVERSAL STATE LIST

linetype
lsf
global m t
local m t

CSS → INTERPRETER

Structure Elements extracted in sequence from Structure SI

Output Primitives to Workstation WS

Figure 2.3: *PHIGS Traverser*

Posting the structure defined in Section 2.4 named 3 would cause the traverser to add the structure 3 to its post list. Before each structure is traversed, the traverser initializes the traversal state list from the PHIGS Description Table. This contains all the default values associated with posted structures. The traversal state list has very many values in it. Figure 2.3 just shows the entries for the two polyline attributes and two modelling transformations (to be described later). The default values of the polyline attributes are SOLID and NORMAL. Therefore, the first structure element in the structure 3 will be interpreted as a solid normal polyline. The second entry in the structure is the SET LINETYPE entry. Interpreting an attribute setting element will update the relevant entry in the traversal state list to the value specified (in this case DASHED). Similarly, the interpretation of the third structure element will result in the LINEWIDTH SCALE FACTOR entry in the traversal state list being set to THICK. As a result of these two elements being interpreted and changing the traversal state list, the interpretation of the fourth element will result in a dashed thick polyline being displayed on the workstation.

It should be made clear that this is conceptually how the traverser works. The application cannot enquire the state of the traversal state list nor can it force the traverser to update the displays in a sequential order. As long as the traverser does the job correctly, it can use any technique it likes. Consequently, the traverser could be built in hardware possibly with multiple processors doing the interpretation. It is defined as a black box in PHIGS so that implementations can choose a traversal strategy that best fits the hardware available.

To stop traversal of a structure, the application invokes:

UNPOST STRUCTURE(WS, SI)

This will cause the specified entry in the post list to be deleted and the structure SI will no longer be visible on workstation WS. Using the postman analogy used earlier, the POST function is equivalent to the delivery of a telescope to view the relevant part of the central structure store and the UNPOST function is the removal of the telescope. Neither function changes the central structure store itself. To batch updates to a display, it is sometimes useful to UNPOST, update and POST the structure again.

2.6 REOPENING STRUCTURES

So far, the separation of structure definition and display has not shown up any real advantages over, say, the segment facility in GKS. However, the structure facility in PHIGS is a much richer one. The first difference is that, unlike GKS, the structure is not an entity that is defined once and cannot be changed. Instead, it is a highly dynamic entity that can be under continual change.

The simplest way of changing a structure is to reopen it. If the function:

OPEN STRUCTURE(3)

was invoked a second time, instead of setting the structure state list to have 3 as the open structure and element pointer set to 0, the element pointer is set to point to the last element in the structure. Invoking the POLYLINE function again would cause this structure element to be added to the end of the open structure. Thus:

```
OPEN STRUCTURE(3)
POLYLINE(N, X1, Y1)
CLOSE STRUCTURE
OPEN STRUCTURE(3)
SET LINETYPE(DASHED)
SET LINEWIDTH SCALE FACTOR(THICK)
POLYLINE(M, X2, Y2)
CLOSE STRUCTURE
```

will result in the same structure as before.

Posting a non-existent structure will cause an empty structure to be defined. Consequently:

```
POST STRUCTURE(WS, 3, PR)
OPEN STRUCTURE(3)
POLYLINE(N, X1, Y1)
SET LINETYPE(DASHED)
SET LINEWIDTH SCALE FACTOR(THICK)
POLYLINE(M, X2, Y2)
CLOSE STRUCTURE
```

will have the same final effect as defining the complete structure 3 before posting it. However, the intermediate effect may be different. By posting the structure first, the workstation will start displaying the empty structure. After the first POLYLINE element has been added to the structure, the traverser will attempt to display it on the workstation. Consequently, in this case, intermediate displays may appear depending on the speed and strategy adopted by the traverser. If the traverser is quite slow, there may be advantages in defining the structure before posting it.

2.7 AN EXAMPLE

In this book, a single running example will be used to describe a number of the PHIGS features. PHIGS is both a 2D and a 3D system. To keep the early examples simple, 2D examples are used most of the time. Only when viewing is described is it necessary to use 3D in the examples. The first example consists of displaying an office desk (see Figure 2.4). The desk consists of three parts whose positions are constrained relative to each other. Initially, the parts of the desk can be defined in the coordinates of the unit square. To get the right aspect ratio for the book page, the X-coordinates lie between 0 and 1 while the Y-coordinates lie between 0.333 and 1. Three subroutines DLARGE, DCORNR and DSMALL define the structure element for each desk. The complete structure is defined as DESK. The complete program to display the structure DESK follows.

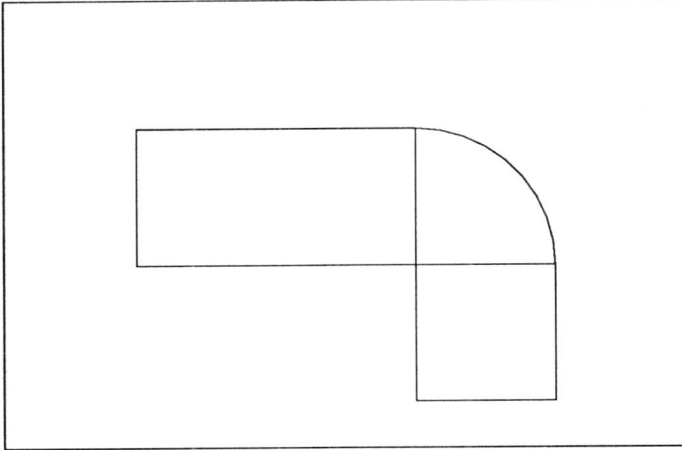

Figure 2.4: *Office desk example*

```
SUBROUTINE DLARGE
REAL XL(5),YL(5)
DATA XL / 0.2,0.2,0.6,0.6,0.2 /
DATA YL / 0.6,0.8,0.8,0.6,0.6 /
POLYLINE(5, XL, YL)
RETURN
END

SUBROUTINE DCORNR
REAL PI, XC(12),YC(12)
INTEGER I
XC(1)=0.6
YC(1)=0.6
XC(2)=0.6
YC(2)=0.8
PI=4.0*ATAN(1.0)
DO 50 I=3,10
XC(I)=0.6+0.2*COS( (11-I)*PI/18.0)
YC(I)=0.6+0.2*SIN( (11-I)*PI/18.0)
50    CONTINUE
XC(11)=0.8
YC(11)=0.6
```

```
XC(12)=0.6
YC(12)=0.6
POLYLINE(12,XC,YC)
RETURN
END

SUBROUTINE DSMALL
REAL XS(5),YS(5)
DATA XS /0.6,0.8,0.8,0.6,0.6/
DATA YS /0.6,0.6,0.4,0.4,0.6/
POLYLINE(5, XS, YS)
RETURN
END

OPEN STRUCTURE(DESK)
DLARGE
DCORNR
DSMALL
CLOSE STRUCTURE

POST STRUCTURE(WS, DESK, PR)
```

The identifier DESK must have a unique value different from other structure identifier names. Either the application has to keep a record of the integer values representing the names already used or a utility has to be defined which converts the identifier DESK into a unique integer.

As was described above, polyline attribute settings remain in force and apply to all subsequent polylines until reset. Consequently, to have the parts of the desk drawn in different linestyles, it is necessary to insert attribute setting functions that establish the required linestyles:

```
OPEN STRUCTURE(DESK)
SET LINETYPE(DASH)
DLARGE
SET LINETYPE(SOLID)
DCORNR
SET LINETYPE(DOT)
DSMALL
CLOSE STRUCTURE
POST STRUCTURE(WS, DESK, PR)
```

This will produce the display in Figure 2.5. Both the attributes linestyle and linewidth could have been defined in the structure. On traversal, the polyline structure element would use the current values of the attributes in the traversal state list when the output primitive was created.

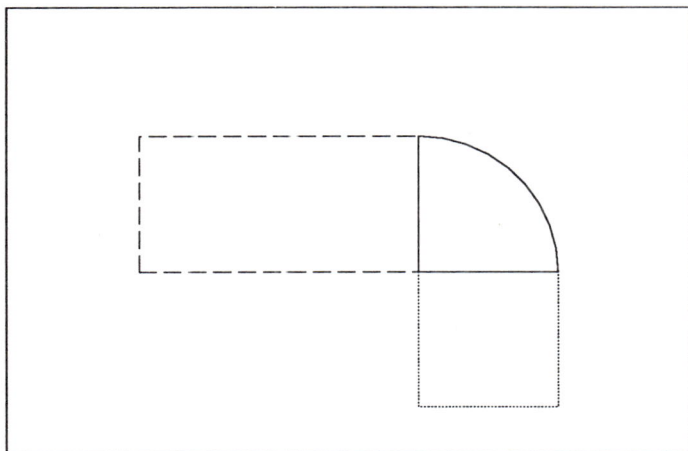

Figure 2.5: *Different linetypes*

2.8 LOCAL MODELLING TRANSFORMATIONS

The coordinates used to define the desk by the application are called
modelling coordinates in PHIGS. As stated earlier, the application can use
a coordinate system appropriate to the application. In the example above,
the desk could have been defined in metres.

PHIGS defines structure elements that provide a coordinate transformation to be applied to all subsequent output in a structure. Similar to the
handling of polyline attributes, the default local modelling transformation is
loaded from the PHIGS description table at the start of a traversal. Its
value is the identity matrix. Resetting the local modelling transformation is
achieved by:

SET LOCAL TRANSFORMATION(MT, TYPE)

where MT is a 3×3 homogeneous matrix and TYPE is one of PRE, POST
or REPLACE. Homogeneous coordinates are ones where a 2D point is
represented by a point in a 3D space. The point (X, Y) is represented by
(XW, YW, W) where X=XW/W and Y=YW/W. In homogeneous coordinates, transformations such as scale, rotate and shift can all be represented
as matrix multiplications. The current local modelling transformation
(CLMT) is stored in the traversal state list. It is applied to all output primitives as they are traversed. As no changes have been made to CLMT in the
examples so far, the identity transformation has been applied which has no
effect. Invoking SET LOCAL TRANSFORMATION updates CLMT as

follows:

$$\text{REPLACE} \quad \text{CLMT}' = \text{MT}$$
$$\text{PRE} \quad \text{CLMT}' = \text{CLMT} \times \text{MT}$$
$$\text{POST} \quad \text{CLMT}' = \text{MT} \times \text{CLMT}$$

Each coordinate (XM, YM) in structure elements traversed is transformed to (XW, YW) as follows:

$$\begin{bmatrix} X \\ Y \\ H \end{bmatrix} = \text{CLMT} \begin{bmatrix} XM \\ YM \\ 1 \end{bmatrix}$$

where XW=X/H and YW=Y/H. To aid in the definition of homogeneous matrices, a utility function is provided:

BUILD TRANSFORMATION MATRIX
  (XF, YF, DX, DY, PHI, SX, SY, ER, MT)

This function builds the matrix MT. The parameter ER is set to 0 if a matrix has been built successfully or to a non-zero error value otherwise. The transformation built can be a mixture of scaling, rotation and shifting. The parameters (XF,YF) define a fixed point which is the origin for scaling and rotation. (DX,DY) define the translation to be applied. PHI defines the anti-clockwise rotation around the fixed point. (SX,SY) scale the coordinates about the fixed point (XF,YF). If all parameters are defined with non-identity transformations, the operations are performed in the order scale, rotate, and shift.

The meaning of PRE multiplication is that the new operation is performed before the existing CLMT while POST multiplication is that it is performed after CLMT. The effect of PRE and POST is, in general, different. The exception is if CLMT and MT are similar operations and have the same fixed point, if appropriate. For example, the desk can be exploded (see Figure 2.6) by:

```
OPEN STRUCTURE(DESK)
DLARGE
BUILD TRANSFORMATION MATRIX(0, 0, 0.03, 0, 0, 1, 1, ER, MT)
SET LOCAL TRANSFORMATION(MT, REPLACE)
DCORNR
BUILD TRANSFORMATION MATRIX(0, 0, 0, –0.03, 0, 1, 1, ER, MT)
SET LOCAL TRANSFORMATION(MT, PRE)
DSMALL
CLOSE STRUCTURE
POST STRUCTURE(WS, DESK, PR)
```

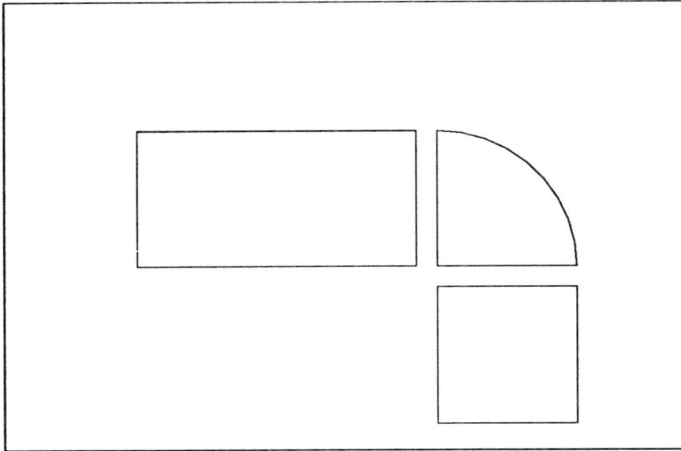

Figure 2.6: *Local modelling transformations*

The REPLACE function could have been PRE or POST equally well as the replaced matrix is the identity matrix. As the concatenated matrices are both shifts, the final transformation could have been POST as well as PRE to give the same effect.

Mixing rotation and scaling will give different effects even about the same fixed point. For example:

```
OPEN STRUCTURE(DESK)
DLARGE

BUILD TRANSFORMATION MATRIX(0.2, 0.6, 0, 0, PI/8, 1, 1, ER, MT)
SET LOCAL TRANSFORMATION(MT, XXX)
SET LINETYPE(DOT)
DLARGE

BUILD TRANSFORMATION MATRIX(0.2, 0.6, 0, 0, 0, 1.25, 1, ER, MT)
SET LOCAL TRANSFORMATION(MT, XXX)
SET LINETYPE(DASH)
DLARGE

CLOSE STRUCTURE

POST STRUCTURE(WS, DESK, PR)
```

Figure 2.7 shows the effect when XXX is PRE and Figure 2.8 when XXX is

POST. The dashed desk is significantly different.

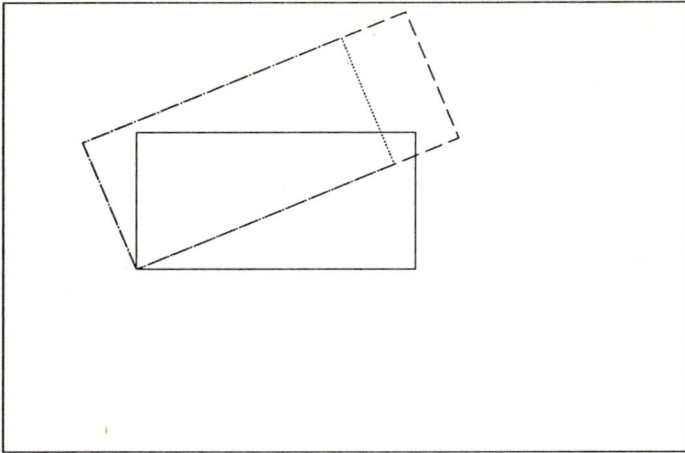

Figure 2.7: *Example of pre-multiplication*

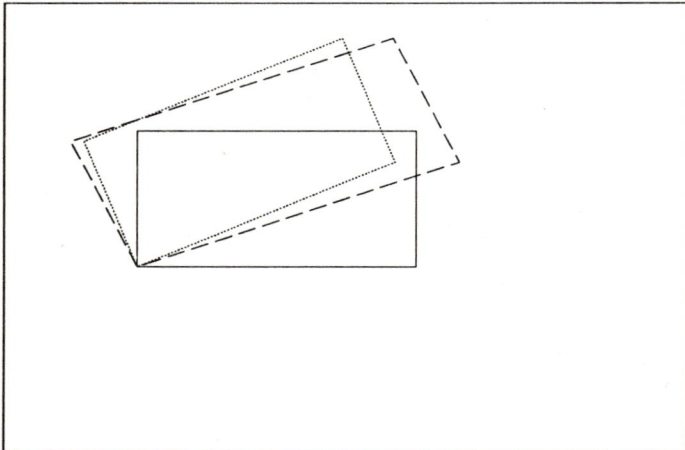

Figure 2.8: *Example of post-multiplication*

For PRE multiplication, the dashed rectangle is expanded about the bottom left hand corner and then rotated. For POST multiplication, the rotation of the rectangle takes place followed by the expansion about the bottom left corner. This produces the parallelogram shown in Figure 2.8. The points to the left of the origin are expanded leftwards while the points to the right of the origin are expanded rightwards.

2.9 STRUCTURE EDITING

PHIGS is designed for use in an interactive environment where the graphical output is likely to be modified as a result of operator action or that of the application. For example, the operator might want to orientate the desk differently or change the positions of the parts making up the desk. Rather than this being achieved by a complete redrawing of the graphical output, PHIGS allows structures to be edited. One example of editing has been described already, the appending of new elements to the end of a structure. PHIGS provides a range of editing facilities which can be classified as absolute, relative and via labels. The third is the easiest to use but the least efficient.

2.9.1 Edit mode

As has been described earlier, structure elements have a position associated with them where 0 is the position before the first element of a structure. For example, the structure:

```
OPEN STRUCTURE(DESK)
POLYLINE(5, XL, YL)
POLYLINE(12, XC, YC)
POLYLINE(5, XS, YS)
CLOSE STRUCTURE
```

can be represented as:

0	DESK
1	POLYLINE(5, XL, YL)
2	POLYLINE (12, XC, YC)
3	POLYLINE (5, XS, YS)

where the element pointer 0 value is pointing before the first element in the structure.

When a structure is opened, the element pointer is set to point at the last element in the structure. When a structure is opened for the first time, no elements exist so the pointer is set to 0. PHIGS has a global switch for the central structure store which is either in INSERT or REPLACE mode. Initially it is set to INSERT mode. In this mode, when a structure element is defined by invoking a function such as POLYLINE, the element pointer is incremented for the open structure and the new structure element is entered there. Consequently, after each insertion, the element pointer points to the element that has been inserted. When the structure is closed, the element pointer becomes undefined until another structure is opened. However, the edit mode remains set to its current value. As the invoking of a function, such as POLYLINE, has very different effects depending on whether the edit mode is INSERT or REPLACE, it is good practice to leave the mode set one way or the other so that the program is more readable. In the examples in this book, we will tend to leave the EDIT MODE set to INSERT. Consequently, if not set explicitly, the assumption made is that the EDIT MODE is INSERT.

In REPLACE mode, a new element is inserted at the element pointer position and the element pointer is not changed. In the special case where the element pointer is set to 0, the new element is inserted at the beginning of the structure. If several elements are defined in INSERT mode one after the other, the effect is as expected and the elements get added to the structure one after the other. If several elements are defined in REPLACE mode one after the other, the effect is that each element overwrites the previous one. This is not always very meaningful. Consequently, in REPLACE mode, it is more normal for the element pointer to be updated between each element replaced.

The PHIGS function for setting the edit mode is:

SET EDIT MODE(XXX)

where XXX can either be INSERT or REPLACE.

The PHIGS function for changing the position of the element pointer is:

SET ELEMENT POINTER(N)

where N is the new position of the element pointer. If N is negative, the element pointer is set to 0. If N is larger than the length of the structure, it is set to point at the last element in the structure. This method of avoiding errors applies to a number of the functions in PHIGS.

2.9.2 Absolute editing

By setting the element pointer to a position other than the end of the structure, it is possible to insert new elements into the structure or replace existing ones.

Given the structure DESK defined in Section 2.9.1, with edit mode set to INSERT, the following functions:

```
OPEN STRUCTURE(DESK)
SET ELEMENT POINTER(0)
SET LINETYPE(DASH)
```

would change the structure to:

0	DESK
1	SET LINETYPE (DASH)
2	POLYLINE (5, XL, YL)
3	POLYLINE (12, XC, YC)
4	POLYLINE (5, XS, YS)

The first thing to notice is that all the element pointer positions for the elements already in the structure have been incremented by 1. The element inserted is numbered 1 and the other element positions are all greater by 1. If the following functions are invoked:

```
SET ELEMENT POINTER(2)
SET LINETYPE(SOLID)
```

the structure changes to:

0	DESK
1	SET LINETYPE (DASH)
2	POLYLINE (5, XL, YL)
3	SET LINETYPE (SOLID)
4	POLYLINE (12, XC, YC)
5	POLYLINE(5, XS, YS)

Note, the user has to keep an update of the element positions in mind each time an edit is done otherwise subsequent edits will be done at the wrong place. The situation can be further complicated by not doing the edits in ascending order. The application can set the element position backwards and forwards if desired. (Actually, doing the edits in reverse order would keep the initial line numbers correct for all the edits!) To change the last polyline to be dotted would require a further edit:

```
SET ELEMENT POINTER(4)
SET LINETYPE(DOT)
CLOSE STRUCTURE
```

The complete structure generated would be as shown below.

0	DESK
1	SET LINETYPE (DASH)
2	POLYLINE (5, XL, YL)
3	SET LINETYPE (SOLID)
4	POLYLINE (12, XC, YC)
5	SET LINETYPE (DOT)
6	POLYLINE (5, XS, YS)

Absolute editing in INSERT mode tends to be used only in well defined situations such as adding elements to the start of a structure or the end of a structure.

The effect of the previous example in REPLACE mode would be completely different. The first edit would still add SET LINETYPE(DASH) to the start of the structure. The second edit would replace the second element giving:

0	DESK
1	SET LINETYPE(DASH)
2	SET LINETYPE(SOLID)
3	POLYLINE(12,XC,YC)
4	POLYLINE(5,XS,YS)

while the third edit would replace the fourth element giving:

0	DESK
1	SET LINETYPE(DASH)
2	SET LINETYPE(SOLID)
3	POLYLINE(12,XC,YC)
4	SET LINETYPE(DOT)

While the invocation of a set of functions that generate structure elements is sensible in INSERT mode as they are added to the structure one after another, it is much less useful in REPLACE mode. If the element pointer is not changed, each new element will overwrite the previous one. Consequently, REPLACE mode is mainly useful in a loop consisting of setting the element pointer position, replacing the element and repeating the pair of functions. Its use in an interactive session will be described later (see Section 9.3). Here, continually updating the same element may be what is required by the application.

2.9.3 Relative editing

If a number of edits are to be made to a structure in INSERT or REPLACE mode, it is often easier if the edits are specified relative to the last one performed. PHIGS provides the function:

OFFSET ELEMENT POINTER(N)

for this purpose. The element pointer is incremented by N where N can have a positive, negative, or zero value. To avoid errors, the same approach is taken as with SET ELEMENT POINTER. If the resulting element pointer is before the start of the structure it is set to 0 and if it is after the end of the structure the element pointer is set to point to the last element in the structure.

Starting from the structure DESK with the three polylines:

0	DESK
1	POLYLINE(5, XL, YL)
2	POLYLINE (12, XC, YC)
3	POLYLINE (5, XS, YS)

The following set of edits in INSERT mode will produce the new structure DESK with the attributes of each of the polylines set differently.

```
OPEN STRUCTURE(DESK)
SET ELEMENT POINTER(0)
SET LINETYPE(DASH)
SET LINEWIDTH SCALE FACTOR(THIN)
OFFSET ELEMENT POINTER(1)
SET LINETYPE(SOLID)
SET LINEWIDTH SCALE FACTOR(NORMAL)
OFFSET ELEMENT POINTER(1)
SET LINETYPE(DOT)
SET LINEWIDTH SCALE FACTOR(THICK)
CLOSE STRUCTURE
```

0	DESK
1	SET LINETYPE (DASH)
2	SET LSF (THIN)
3	POLYLINE (5, XL, YL)
4	SET LINETYPE (SOLID)
5	SET LSF (NORMAL)
6	POLYLINE (12, XC, YC)
7	SET LINETYPE (DOT)
8	SET LSF (THICK)
9	POLYLINE (5, XS, YS)

Each time, the element pointer only has to be incremented by 1 to move over the next POLYLINE element position to achieve the desired effect.

In REPLACE mode, a loop consisting of an element generating function followed by OFFSET ELEMENT POINTER(1) would replace a sequence of structure elements by new ones.

2.9.4 Labels

Neither of the above methods of locating positions in a structure is easy to use for complex edits. PHIGS has a user-defined labelling facility for handling these. Invoking the function:

   LABEL(ID)

creates a structure element that is added to the structure in the normal way. The label ID can be any integer value. On structure traversal, the interpretation of the element has no effect. Its purpose is to provide a position in the structure that can be located other than by remembering the element pointer position. An important point is that the label ID need not be unique. If the same edit is to be applied to several positions in a structure, it may be useful to label each one by the same name.

To set the element pointer at a label, the function provided is:

   SET ELEMENT POINTER AT LABEL(ID)

The structure is searched from the current element pointer position until the label structure element is reached whose name is ID. The element pointer is left pointing at the label structure element. If the search is started from a label structure element with label ID, the search starts from the next element so that the next occurrence of ID is found. PHIGS issues an error message and stops if the label does not exist between the current element pointer position and the end of the structure. For novice PHIGS users, this tends to be a common error. For example:

```
OPEN STRUCTURE(XYZ)
SET ELEMENT POINTER AT LABEL(ID)
```

will always cause an error as the element pointer will be set to the last position in the structure when it is opened. To search the whole structure for the first occurrence of ID requires:

```
OPEN STRUCTURE(XYZ)
SET ELEMENT POINTER(0)
SET ELEMENT POINTER AT LABEL(ID)
```

To do a similar edit to the ones described already, requires labels to be added at the points where edits might be made:

```
OPEN STRUCTURE(DESK)
LABEL(LARGE)
POLYLINE(5, XL, YL)
LABEL(CORNER)
POLYLINE(12, XC, YC)
LABEL(SMALL)
POLYLINE(5, XS, YS)
CLOSE STRUCTURE
```

producing a structure:

0	DESK
1	LABEL (LARGE)
2	POLYLINE (5, XL, YL)
3	LABEL (CORNER)
4	POLYLINE (12, XC, YC)
5	LABEL (SMALL)
6	POLYLINE (5, XS, YS)

Label editing is ideally suited to adding structure elements at defined points in a structure. The element pointer is positioned at the label structure element and, consequently, the inserted elements will be added just after the label element. A similar edit to that in Section 2.9.2 is:

```
OPEN STRUCTURE(DESK)

SET ELEMENT POINTER(0)
SET ELEMENT POINTER AT LABEL(LARGE)
SET LINETYPE(DASH)

SET ELEMENT POINTER AT LABEL(CORNER)
SET LINETYPE(SOLID)

SET ELEMENT POINTER AT LABEL(SMALL)
SET LINETYPE(DOT)
CLOSE STRUCTURE
```

The assumption is that the edit mode is INSERT. This produces the structure:

0	DESK
1	LABEL (LARGE)
2	SET LINETYPE (DASH)
3	POLYLINE (5, XL,YL)
4	LABEL (CORNER)
5	SET LINETYPE (SOLID)
6	POLYLINE (12, XC, YC)
7	LABEL (SMALL)
8	SET LINETYPE (DOT)
9	POLYLINE (5, XS, YS)

2.9.5 Deleting elements

PHIGS provides a number of functions for deleting elements from a structure. The simplest is:

DELETE ELEMENT

which deletes the structure element pointed at by the element pointer. After the deletion, the element pointer is set to the element *before* the element deleted. This has the odd effect that multiple calls of DELETE ELEMENT will delete elements going backwards in the structure from the initial position.

Attempting to delete the element at position 0 in a structure has no effect. Each time DELETE ELEMENT is invoked, the subsequent elements in the structure will have their positions decremented by 1.

To delete a range of elements, PHIGS provides:

DELETE ELEMENT RANGE(EP1, EP2)

All elements between the two positions are deleted including positions EP1 and EP2. The smaller position need not be specified as the first parameter. The effect is the same either way round with the element pointer being left pointing at the element just before the range of deleted elements. If the range specified is larger than from position 0 to the last position in the structure, the deletions are constrained to be within the structure. Given the structure:

0	DESK
1	SET LSF (THICK)
2	SET LINETYPE (DASH)
3	POLYLINE (5, XL,YL)
4	SET LSF (NORMAL)
5	SET LINETYPE (SOLID)
6	POLYLINE (12, XC, YC)
7	SET LSF (THIN)
8	SET LINETYPE (DOT)
9	POLYLINE (5, XS, YS)

the following edits:

```
OPEN STRUCTURE(DESK)
SET ELEMENT POINTER(5)
DELETE ELEMENT
DELETE ELEMENT RANGE(6,5)
DELETE ELEMENT RANGE(1,3)

CLOSE STRUCTURE
```

would produce the following structure. Note how it is quite difficult to work out exactly what the positions of the structure elements are after each edit. As for inserting elements in a structure, performing the deletions in reverse order will preserve the element positions of the earlier entries but this may not always be easy to program.

0	DESK
1	SET LSF (NORMAL)
2	SET LINETYPE (DOT)
3	POLYLINE (5, XS, YS)

The first deletion will remove SET LINETYPE(SOLID). This will decrement the subsequent positions by 1 so that the second deletion will remove the original positions 6 and 7 while the third deletion removes elements 1 to 3.

PHIGS also provides deletions dependent on labels:

DELETE ELEMENTS BETWEEN LABELS(LB1, LB2)

The structure is searched from the current element pointer until LB1 is found at, say, position EP1. Starting from the position immediately after EP1, label LB2 is searched for and found at, say, EP2. The elements deleted are the set between the labels, that is EP1+1 to EP2−1. After the deletion, the element pointer is set to EP1. The label elements are not deleted.

For complex applications, editing and deleting using labels is probably the most sensible approach. However, the application could build its own structure editor (possibly with a display of the structure) and in this case it might be more convenient to do absolute editing. The aim is for PHIGS to provide the basic facilities that satisfy the needs of the application possibly with the introduction of tools built on top of PHIGS.

2.10 POSTING PRIORITY

The PHIGS facilities described so far allow the application to define graphical objects as structures and have them displayed by the POST function. While the structures are being displayed, they can be edited and the traverser is responsible for ensuring that the displayed structure is kept up-to-date with the structure in the central structure store. The POST function has 3 parameters:

POST STRUCTURE(WS, SI, PR)

The first parameter defines the workstation and the second the structure to be posted. The third parameter PR is a value in the range 0 to 1 and defines the priority of the structure posted. A set of structures can be posted to a workstation by multiple calls of the POST function. The traverser will generate a display for each one and keep them all up-to-date.

Ambiguity can occur if the posted structures occupy the same part of the display space. For example, if a red graph is to be drawn over a blue background grid, where two lines cross each other would require the red line to appear over the blue grid line. By defining the two posted structures at different priority values, the traverser is expected to achieve the desired effect. For example:

```
POST STRUCTURE(WS, GRAPH, 0.6)
POST STRUCTURE(WS, GRID, 0.1)
```

The structure with the highest display priority is visible when several posted structures occupy the same part of the display space.

The same effect can be obtained by posting the structures with the same priority but being careful to order the posting operations. If two posted structures have the same display priority, the last posted takes precedence and, in effect, is given a higher priority. The same effect could be achieved by:

```
POST STRUCTURE(WS, GRID, 0.2)
POST STRUCTURE(WS, GRAPH, 0.2)
```

However, this may not always be convenient. Using priority to define which display takes precedence is a much cleaner way of ensuring the display is correct for highly interactive applications making considerable use of the editing, posting and unposting facilities available.

3 OUTPUT PRIMITIVES

3.1 INTRODUCTION

Chapter 2 has given an overview of the structure facilities in PHIGS and how traversal of structures creates graphical output. In Section 2.3, the polyline structure element was described with two of its attributes as the minimum necessary to describe the concept of structure traversal.

This Chapter will describe the output primitives available in PHIGS and their associated attributes.

PHIGS introduces the concept of an *aspect* which describes *how* an output primitive is drawn. For example, linetype and linewidth scale factor are aspects of the polyline primitive. Entries in the PHIGS traversal state list define the *attributes* of the output primitive. The attributes define how the aspects of the output primitive are linked or bound to the output primitive. In the simplest case described so far, the attribute controlled by SET LINETYPE directly controls the linetype aspect. More complex control is possible than in this simple example.

The coordinates used in the definition of structure elements are called *modelling coordinates*. The application can choose the coordinate system most appropriate to its needs. On structure traversal, modelling transformations may be applied to the coordinates so that the coordinates of the output primitive created are different from the coordinates in the structure element. PHIGS calls this coordinate system *world coordinates*.

Structure traversal occurs when a structure is posted to a workstation. The structure traversal creates a graphical *scene* in world coordinates which is viewed by the specified workstation. The viewing process itself is quite complex (particularly in 3D). Suffice it to say that the world coordinate scene is mapped to a *picture* in Normalized Projection Coordinates (NPC) and that picture or some part of it is displayed on the workstation. The transformation of coordinates is shown in Figure 3.1.

This viewing pipeline will be described in more detail in Chapter 7. The simplified 2D viewing pipeline will be described in Chapter 6. The need to describe the viewing pipeline here is related to when attributes are bound to the output primitives. In PHIGS, they can either be bound as part of the world coordinate scene or the binding can be delayed until the *display* is created from the NPC picture.

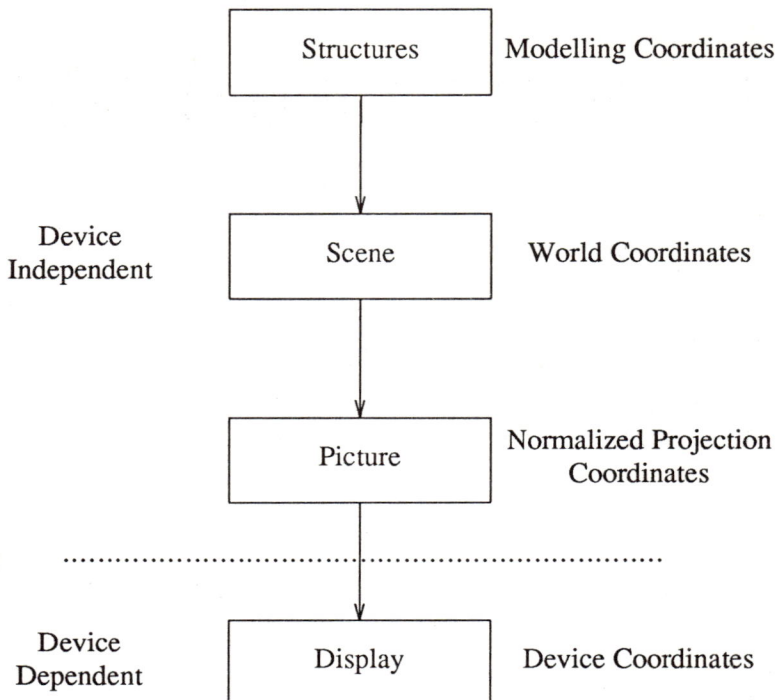

Figure 3.1: *Transformation of Coordinates*

In the following sections, the structure elements associated with output primitives will be described giving the meaning of the output primitive created from the structure element on traversal. The description will be informal in that the function that creates the structure element will be described as though it created the output primitive directly whereas this only happens on traversal.

The output primitives in PHIGS are:

(1) *polyline* : which draws a sequence of connected line segments;

(2) *polymarker* : which marks a sequence of points with a symbol;

(3) *fill area* : which defines the boundary of an area to be displayed;

(4) *fill area set* : which defines the boundaries of a set of areas to be displayed as one;

(5) *text* : which draws a sequence of characters;

(6) *annotation text* : which draws a sequence of characters to annotate a drawing;

(7) *cell array* : which displays an image;

(8) *generalized drawing primitive* : which provides non-standard facilities in a standard way.

For the following examples, the boundary of the figures extends from 0 to 12 in the X-direction and 0 to 8 in the Y-direction. Only the first 5 output primitives will be described in this Chapter. The last 3 are described in Chapter 13.

3.2 POLYLINE

3.2.1 The functions

Two functions are provided in PHIGS:

```
POLYLINE 3(N, XA, YA, ZA)
POLYLINE(N, XA, YA)
```

Each defines an output primitive consisting of a sequence of connected line segments. The second function is a 2D shorthand form of the first as far as the output primitive created is concerned. POLYLINE 3 defines a set of $N-1$ line segments where $(XA(1),YA(1),ZA(1))$ is connected to $(XA(2),YA(2),ZA(2))$. which is connected to $(XA(3),YA(3),ZA(3))$ and so on until $(XA(N-1), YA(N-1), ZA(N-1))$ is connected to $(XA(N), YA(N), ZA(N))$.

POLYLINE defines the same sequence of line segments where it is assumed that the ZA values are all zero. As stated in the previous section, the coordinates are defined in modelling coordinates and are transformed by the traversal and viewing to an equivalent device coordinate form on the workstation. For example:

```
DATA XPL / 2, 4, 6, 8, 10 /
DATA YPL / 1, 5, 2, 6, 4 /

POLYLINE(5, XPL, YPL)
```

On traversal, the polyline generated will be as in Figure 3.2. The assumption is that the polyline defined in world coordinates is mapped onto an area of the display with the same aspect ratio.

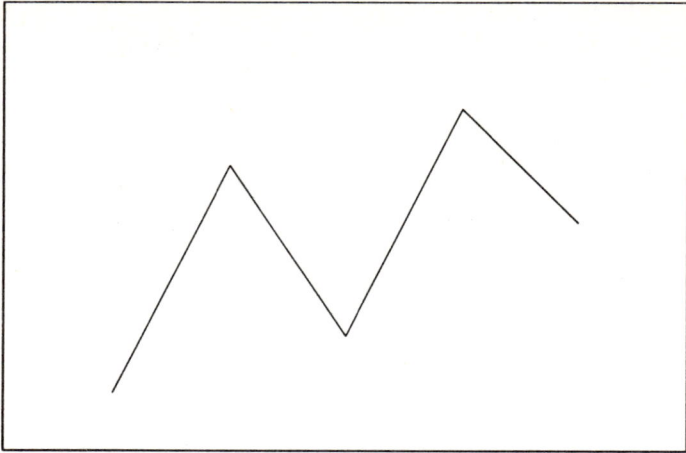

Figure 3.2: *A polyline*

3.2.2 Polyline aspects and registration

The polyline has three aspects to control its appearance on a display and allow two similar polylines to be differentiated. They are *linetype, linewidth scale factor* and *polyline colour index*. The method of setting these aspects will be described in Chapter 4.

PHIGS has a standard scheme for organizing a set of choices of limited number such as linetype. A positive integer value starting at 1 defines the linetypes that are mandated to be available in an implementation. Larger values than this minimum set may be available. If these are defined, there are precise meanings assigned to them. The set of graphics standards (GKS, CGM, PHIGS etc) have a common registration scheme for these [18][25]. For example, the mandatory set in PHIGS is from 1 to 4 with linetype values greater than 4 available in the registered list. At this time, other linestyles are in the process of registration. The number implemented in a PHIGS product is one criterion for choosing between two implementations.

Some hardware will provide linestyles not in the registered list. Also, a PHIGS implementation may be aimed at a specific community where linestyles need to be implemented which are not of general interest. The implementor is allowed to use values less than or equal to zero to define these non-standard linetypes.

Only having 4 linetypes guaranteed in an implementation means that either the application has to be restricted to use only these possibilities or the application may not port from one environment to another. The PHIGS philosophy of not causing unnecessary errors during execution means that a decision needs to be made by an implementation if a requested linetype is unavailable at a workstation. PHIGS implementations default all non-available linetypes to be the same as linetype 1.

3.2.3 Linetypes

The complete table of linetypes for PHIGS is given below:

≤0	implementation dependent
1	solid
2	dashed
3	dotted
4	dashed-dotted
≥5	subject to registration

Examples of the linetypes are shown in Figure 3.3.

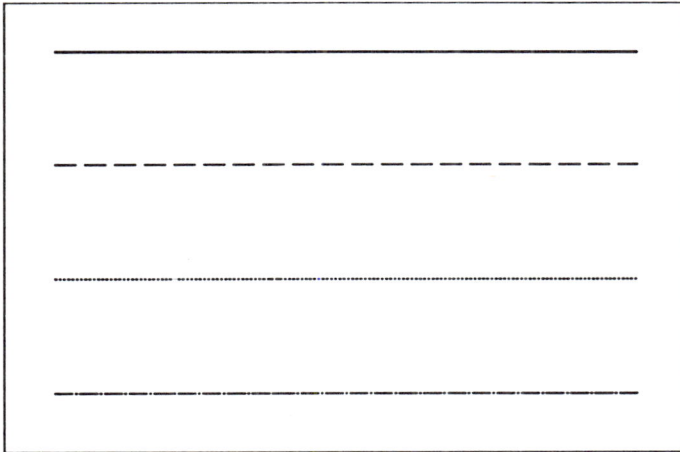

Figure 3.3: *Linetypes in PHIGS*

3.2.4 Linewidth scale factor

Due to the large variability of output devices, PHIGS has taken the decision that it is not feasible to precisely define the width of a line in the modelling coordinates that define the points of the polyline. One problem is that the aspect ratio may be changed which makes it difficult to decide which of the 3 dimensions should be used to specify width. Secondly, several instances of the same set of polylines may be required at different sizes but with the same line thickness. In consequence, line thickness is defined relative to some notional line thickness that is regarded as normal on the device. For a plotter, this is likely to be the line thickness produced by drawing with the standard pens. For a vector refresh display, it would be the standard intensity line. For a raster device, it will be the number of pixels that produce a clear line on the display.

Linewidth is specified relative to this nominal linewidth. The value of linewidth scale factor can be less than or greater than 1 and is a real number. For example, linewidth scale factor can be set to 0.5 of the nominal linewidth or 2.5 times the nominal linewidth. The device is expected to take the nominal linewidth and multiply by the linewidth scale factor and attempt to draw the lines as close to that width as possible. Figure 3.4 gives some examples of linewidths that might be available where the second from the bottom might be the nominal linewidth.

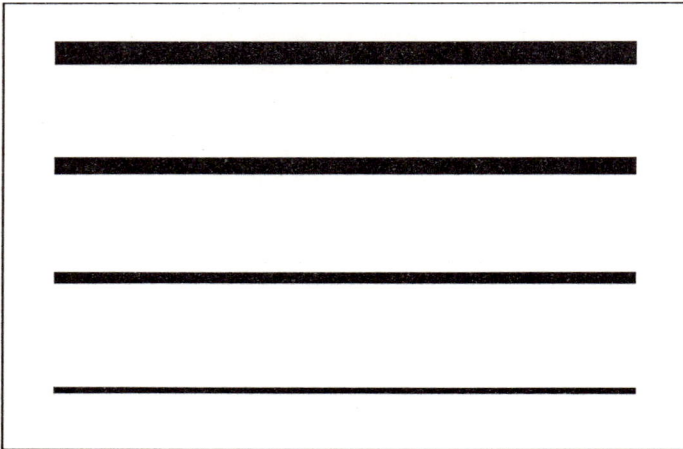

Figure 3.4: *Linewidth scale factors*

3.2.5 Colour index

The third aspect of a polyline is its colour. In PHIGS, colour is specified indirectly by defining a *colour index* that points to a colour description. The *polyline colour index* is the aspect that is associated with polyline output primitives.

Because colour is quite closely connected to the device that will display the output, the table containing the colour descriptions is stored on the workstation. The number of entries in the table will depend on the workstation. Entries 0 and 1 always exist. Entry 0 is defined as the background colour of the display and entry 1 is initially set to the default foreground colour of the display. Individual colours can be specified using a number of different colour models. These are described in Section 4.6.

Initially, the polyline colour index is set to 1 and this will be associated with each polyline output primitive generated on traversal.

As the contents of the workstation colour table may be different on different workstations, a polyline colour index value may produce different colours on different workstations depending on the entries in the workstation colour tables. For the same colour to appear on each workstation for a specified index value, the colour description associated with that polyline colour index value must be the same on each workstation. Even then it will require the workstations to have similar colour displays.

Other primitives have their own colour aspect. For example, polymarkers have a polymarker colour index aspect. As there is a single colour table on a workstation, if the polyline and polymarker colour index aspects are the same, the same colour will be produced on a workstation.

If a polyline colour index value is set to a value that is not available on a workstation, polyline colour index 1 will be used instead.

3.2.6 Summary

Section 3.2 has described the polyline output primitive in some detail together with the three polyline aspects linetype, linewidth scale factor and polyline colour index. Polyline output primitives have other aspects (for example, identification) but as they are the same for all output primitive classes, they will be described later. The three aspects described here are unique to the polyline. However, the third is quite similar to the colour index aspects of other primitive classes.

The following sections will describe the other output primitive classes. Where the similarity with the polyline is close, only a brief description will be given and the fuller details can be inferred by reading the polyline description.

3.3 POLYMARKER

3.3.1 The functions

Two functions are provided in PHIGS:

POLYMARKER 3(N, XA, YA, ZA)
POLYMARKER(N, XA, YA)

The parameters are the same as for the polyline and again define a sequence of points. POLYMARKER is a shorthand for POLYMARKER 3 (see Section 3.2.1). POLYMARKER 3 defines a set of N points to be identified by a marker. A marker is a symbol with a well-defined origin (not necessarily the centre). All N points are marked with the same symbol. As for the polyline, the coordinates of the points are defined in modelling coordinates. Using the same data values defined in Section 3.2.1, the function:

POLYMARKER(5, XPL, YPL)

might, on traversal, generate the polymarker as in Figure 3.5.

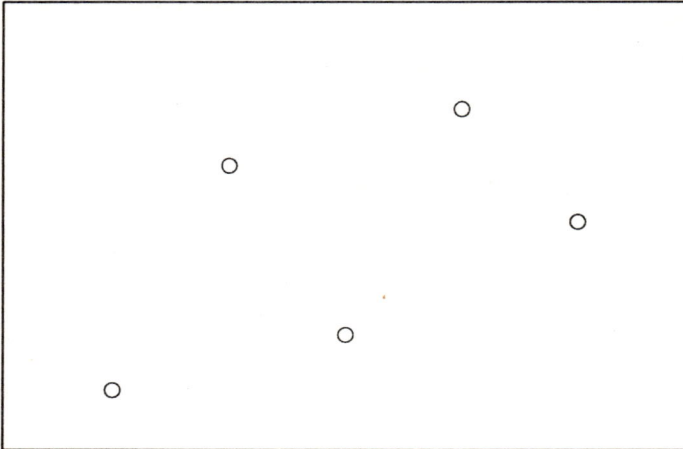

Figure 3.5: *A polymarker*

3.3.2 Polymarker aspects

Polymarkers in PHIGS have three aspects that can control their appearance on a display and allow similar polymarkers to be differentiated. They are *marker type, markersize scale factor* and *polymarker colour index.*

The overall philosophy for defining the aspects is the same as for poly-line aspects (see Section 3.2).

3.3.3 Marker type

The complete table of marker types for PHIGS is given below:

≤ 0	implementation dependent
1	dot
2	plus
3	star
4	circle
5	cross
≥ 6	subject to registration

Examples of the marker types are given in Figure 3.6. This output would
be produced by five separate invocations of the polymarker function each
defining a single point.

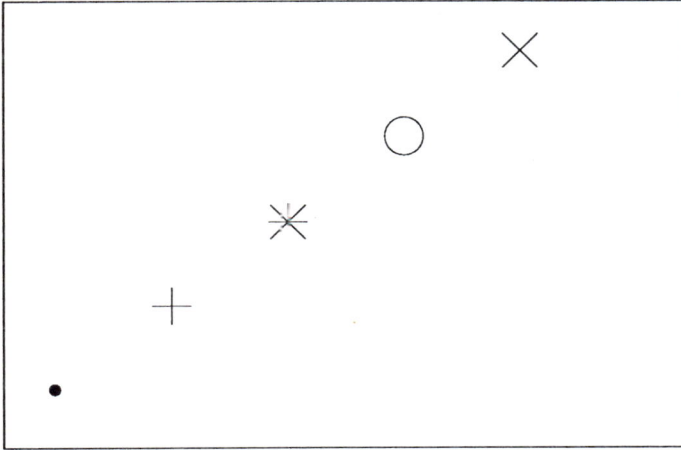

Figure 3.6: *Marker types in PHIGS*

Marker type 1 is the smallest available dot and may well be difficult to
see without looking carefully. We have deliberately increased its size in
Figure 3.6 so that it is visible! Registration and implementation dependent
marker types are handled in the same way as linetypes (see Section 3.2.2).

3.3.4 Markersize scale factor

PHIGS does not treat marker size as a geometric value that is settable in
modelling coordinates. Instead, it is assumed that the device has some
notional size for markers. The aspect markersize scale factor defines the
size of the marker relative to this notional size. Consequently, its definition
is very similar to linewidth scale factor described in Section 3.2.4. Some
examples of different values of markersize scale factor are given in Figure
3.7. These markers are 3, 5, 7, 9, and 11 times the nominal marker size for
this device.

The scale factor can be less than 1. If the implementation has defined
the notional marker size greater than the minimum that it can draw, the
smaller size marker will be output. Because an implementation only has to
approximate to the marker size (some devices may only be capable of
drawing markers at certain sizes), the aspect should not be used when precise sizing is required. In this case, defining the glyph as a structure using

polylines, fill area or fill area set is more appropriate.

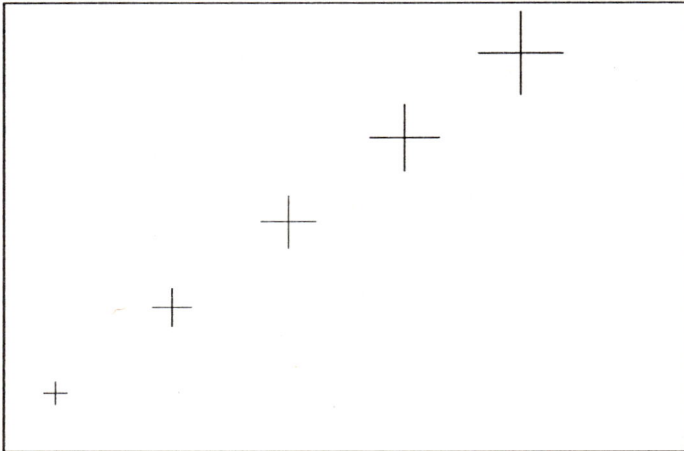

Figure 3.7: *Markersize scale factors*

Again, the display in Figure 3.7 would require five separate polymarker function invocations. All the points in a single polymarker function invocation will have their type and size the same.

3.3.5 Polymarker colour index

This is defined in exactly the same way as polyline colour index (see Section 3.2.5).

3.4 FILL AREA AND FILL AREA SET

3.4.1 The functions

PHIGS provides four functions:

    FILL AREA 3(N, XA, YA, ZA)
    FILL AREA(N, XA, YA)
    FILL AREA SET 3(N, IA, XA, YA, ZA)
    FILL AREA SET(N, IA, XA, YA)

There are two output primitives, fill area and fill area set, each having a shorthand form for the case on the Z=0 plane. Both define an area to be filled with some rendering or pattern. Fill area specifies a single boundary to be filled whereas fill area set specifies a *set* of boundaries. The major reason for including fill area is for compatibility with GKS. However, it is a simpler primitive to use. The two primitives share a set of aspects but fill area set has some additional ones that control the appearance of the boundary edges.

The parameters for fill area are similar to those for polyline and polymarker defining a sequence of points where the last point is normally the same as the first point. If that is not the case, an additional point is added to the sequence at the end which is the same as the first point. This ensures that the sequence of points *always* defines a *closed* boundary.

Whereas polyline and polymarker are true 3-dimensional primitives with no constraints on the points, this is not the case for fill area or fill area set. Both area primitives define boundaries which are in a single plane. If by accident, the application defines a fill area or fill area set where the points are not all in a single plane, the implementation is allowed to interpret it how it likes. For example, it could let the first few points define the plane and project all the other points onto that plane or it could be more sophisticated and attempt to make the best fit by reasoning which points are incorrect.

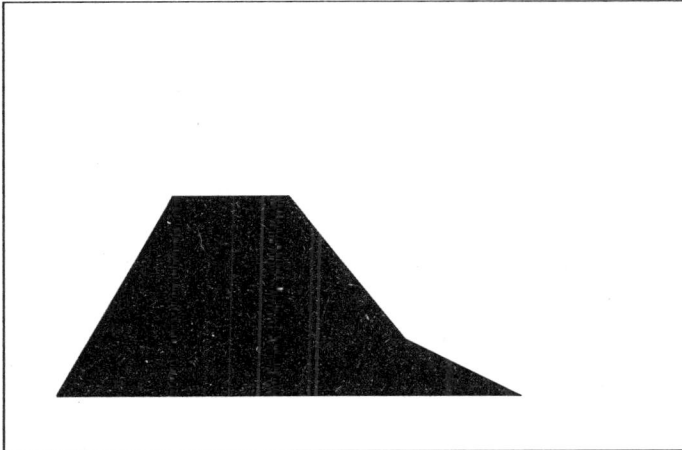

Figure 3.8: *A fill area*

If insufficient points are given to define a plane (less than 3), no error will occur but nothing will be visible on the display either.

A simple example of fill area is:

```
DATA XFA / 1, 3, 5, 7, 9, 1 /
DATA YFA / 1, 4.5, 4.5, 2, 1, 1 /
FILL AREA(6, XFA, YFA)
```

On traversal, the fill area drawn might be as in Figure 3.8. The exact form will depend on the aspect settings defining the interior.

Fill area set has the points (XA(I),YA(I),ZA(I)) for the first area defined by the values I=1 to IA(1). The second area is defined by the points from IA(1)+1 to IA(2) and so on until the last area is defined by the sequence of points from IA(N−1)+1 to IA(N). For example:

```
DATA XFAS / 3, 6, 6, 3, 3, 2, 7, 7, 2, 2, 4, 5, 5, 4, 4 /
DATA YFAS / 23, 23, 18, 18, 23, 16, 16, 9, 9, 16, 7, 7, 4, 4, 7 /
DATA IA / 5, 10, 15 /
DO 10 I=1,5
XFAS(I)=0.333*XFAS(I)
YFAS(I)=0.333*YFAS(I)
10    CONTINUE
FILL AREA SET(3, IA, XFAS, YFAS)
```

Figure 3.9 shows, on the left, the three rectangles defined as a fill area set in the program above. The remaining parts of the diagram are described later. The reduction in size of the coordinates in the example is just to allow integer values to be used in the data declarations.

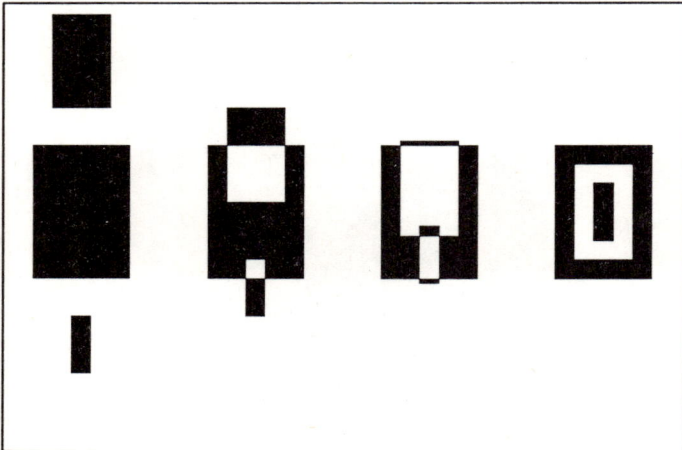

Figure 3.9: *Fill area set example*

3.4.2 Definition of interior

So far, the description has assumed that it is straightforward to decide what is inside the boundary and that is true when the boundary does not intersect itself. However, as soon as that is allowed, and it is in PHIGS, it is necessary to precisely define the inside and outside of the boundary as only the inside will be filled.

PHIGS defines the inside by a rule called the *even-odd* rule. Note that this is not the only rule that could be used and, for example, the X window system has two rules that can be used for specifying the inside.

The even-odd rule states that a point is inside the boundary if a line drawn from infinity to the point hits the boundary an odd number of times. If the line happens to touch the boundary or intersects with the boundary at a point where it crosses itself, care must be taken to make sure the count remains correct. The best solution is to choose a line from infinity that only intersects with the boundary at straightforward positions!

Figure 3.10 shows a reentrant boundary and indicates which points are inside and outside.

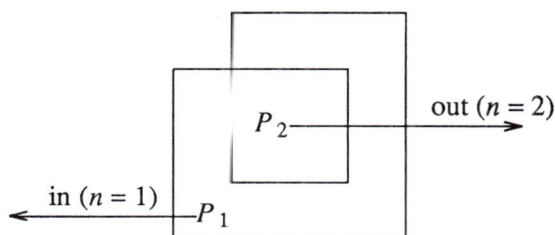

Figure 3.10: *Even-odd rule*

Clearly the even-odd rule works equally well for the multiple boundaries of fill area set. For example, if fill area set defines two boundaries which are concentric circles, the inside is the portion between the two circles. The inside of the inner circle is outside the boundary!

If the three rectangles defined as a fill area set in Section 3.4.1 have the top rectangle moved downwards and the bottom rectangle moved upwards, the effect of the even-odd rule is shown by the area rendered as solid in the other pictures in Figure 3.9.

3.4.3 Area aspects

Fill area and fill area set have six common aspects that control the appearance of the interior of the boundary. The main aspect is *interior style* which defines the type of rendering required. The remaining aspects are appropriate for some subset of the styles.

The area can be rendered in basically three ways, a *solid* colour, a *hatch* style or a *pattern*. The *interior colour index* aspect is used by the first two to define the colour of the solid area or the hatch lines. As both hatching and patterning can be done in a variety of ways, an *interior style index* aspect indicates which style has been chosen. Hatch styles are implementation dependent and the interior style index does not mandate which style is associated with which index. Much more control is defined for patterns. The interior style index for patterns points to a *pattern array* of colour index values to be mapped onto the area to be filled. Thus it does not use the interior colour index value. The three aspects *pattern size, pattern reference point* and *pattern vectors* define the size and orientation of the pattern. These apply to all pattern styles but are not used by solid or hatch styles.

The interior colour index aspect and the entries in the pattern array are defined in the same way as the colour index values for polylines and polymarkers. Each workstation provides a colour description for each index value.

3.4.4 Interior style

The interior style aspect has the values HATCH and PATTERN to specify which filling is required. The hatching used is specified by the interior style index. Figure 3.11 gives some examples of possible hatch styles. None are mandated and the style available in an implementation for a specific interior style index is not defined. The user must therefore consult the reference manual for the PHIGS product he is using.

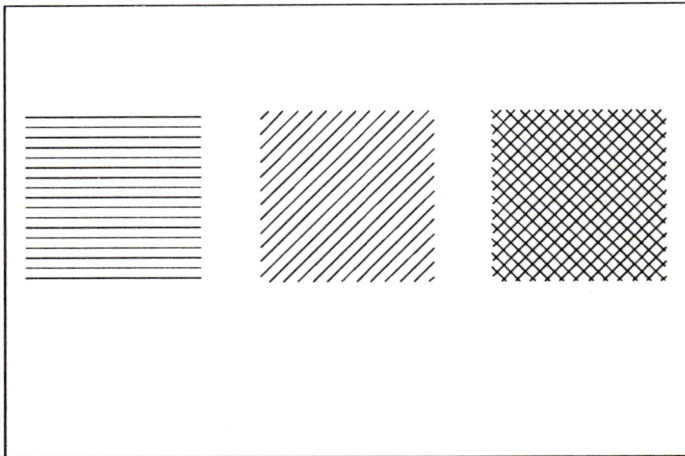

Figure 3.11: *Hatch styles in PHIGS*

The solid colour is specified by the interior style aspect having one of the values HOLLOW, SOLID or EMPTY. SOLID fills the interior with a uniform colour defined by the colour index value. HOLLOW is a quick and dirty rendering which just draws the outline of the fill area. It is provided as a quick debug aid. The way the boundary line is represented is up to the workstation or implementation to define. There is no necessity for it to take account of, say, the polyline aspects like linetype. If the aspect is defined as EMPTY, no filling occurs and no boundary line is drawn. Its only use is if there is an HLHSR method (see Section 4.7.3) defined which allows the fill area to occlude parts of a picture behind this fill area.

The most complex fill area style is interior style PATTERN. In this case, the type of pattern is defined by the interior style index which points to an array of colour indices.

3.4.5 Pattern aspects

For interior style PATTERN, the interior style index, sometimes called the pattern index, is a pointer into a pattern table which defines the set of patterns available to render the area to be filled.

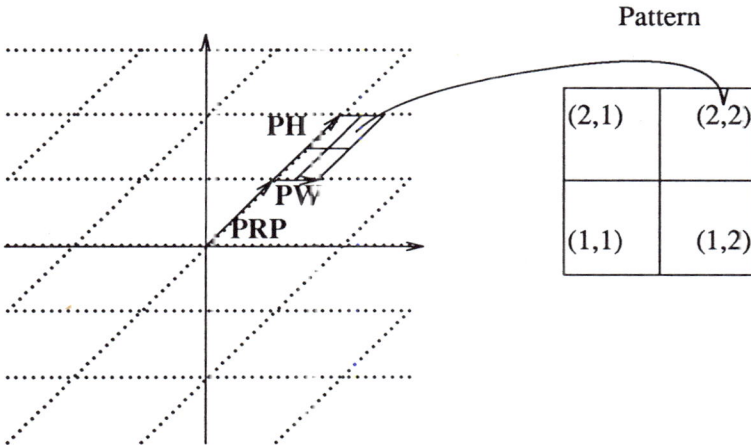

Figure 3.12: *Pattern size and origin*

The pattern is a 2-dimensional array of colour index values which define the repetitive pattern with which to render the area. Clearly, this does not completely define the form of the rendering as it is necessary to specify the origin from which the pattern is to start and the size of the pattern cells.

The size of the pattern is defined by:

SET PATTERN SIZE(PW, PH)

This specifies the size of the rectangle in modelling coordinates that is to be rendered with one colour in the pattern. As the modelling coordinates can be transformed on traversal, this can be a quadrilateral in normalized projection coordinates.

The 2D shorthand form for the definition of the origin is:

SET PATTERN REFERENCE POINT(PRPX, PRPY)

The pattern is assumed to be parallel to the X and Y-axes in modelling coordinates thus PRP is the origin of the pattern and (PW,PH) defines its size as shown in Figure 3.12. In 3 dimensions, it is necessary to define both the origin for the pattern and the directions of the X and Y axes in the pattern of the fill area. The function provided is:

SET PATTERN REFERENCE POINT AND VECTORS
(PRPX, PRPY, PRPZ, PAX, PAY, PAZ)

The origin is defined by (PRPX, PRPY, PRPZ). The orientation of the pattern is determined by the two pattern reference vectors. The X-direction (width) is defined by the points (PRPX, PRPY, PRPZ) and (PRPX+PAX(1), PRPY+PAY(1), PRPZ+PAZ(1)). The Y-direction (height) by (PRPX, PRPY, PRPZ) and (PRPX+PAX(2), PRPY+PAY(2), PRPZ+PAZ(2)). The pattern width and height specified by SET PATTERN SIZE are measured along these directions. Mapping pixels on the display to a particular colour is defined as follows. If the centre of a pixel is within a pattern cell, the colour appropriate to that cell is used. An example of setting up a pattern is as follows:

```
DATA XFA / 2, 8, 8, 2, 2 /
DATA YFA / 6, 6, 2, 2, 6 /
DATA ZFA / 0, 0, 0, 0, 0/

DATA PAX / 1, 0 /
DATA PAY / 0, 1 /
DATA PAZ / 0, 0 /

SET PATTERN SIZE(3, 2)
SET PATTERN REFERENCE POINT AND VECTORS(3, 3, 0, PAX, PAY, PAZ)

FILL AREA 3(5, XFA, YFA, ZFA)
```

Even if the same pattern is used, the same area can have significantly different rendering depending on the size of the pattern cell and how its origin relates to the area to be filled as can be seen in Figure 3.13.

The main problem in the definition occurs if the origin or vectors do not occur in the plane of the fill area or fill area set. In this case, the points are projected onto the fill area or fill area set plane along a normal to that plane. Again, this ensures that it is difficult in PHIGS to generate an error in the definition of the pattern.

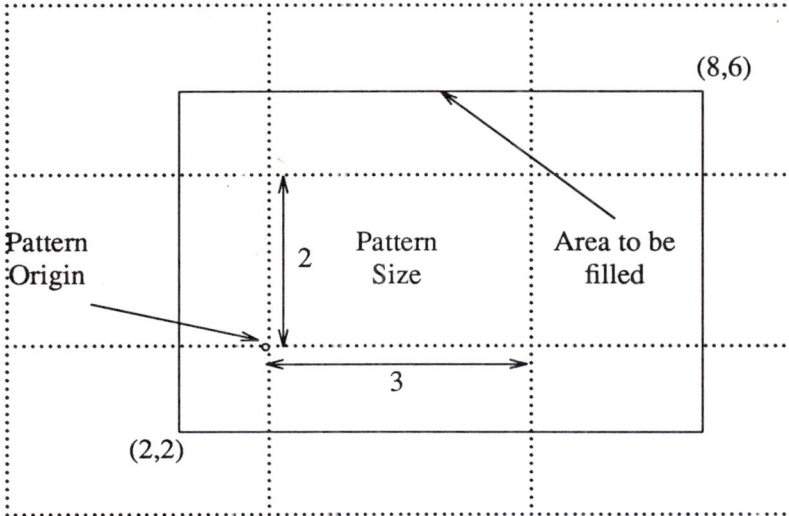

Figure 3.13: *Example pattern size and reference point*

3.4.6 Edge aspects

The major difference between fill area and fill area set is that fill area set has aspects which define how the boundary of the fill area set is rendered. For fill area, no boundary is drawn unless fill area style HOLLOW is specified.

For fill area set, additional aspects provided are *edge flag, edgetype, edgewidth scale factor* and *edge colour index*. The edge flag can be set to ON and OFF. If set ON, the edge is rendered according to the other aspects. The meaning of these is similar to the meaning of the polyline aspects. Edgetype corresponds to linetype, edgewidth scale factor to linewidth scale factor and edge colour index to polyline colour index.

Edges are drawn on top of the interior. Conceptually, the two are disjoint. Thus, an edge drawn as a dashed line may be displayed with the boundary of a HOLLOW fill area being visible between dashes. If a fill area set is clipped with the edge flag set to ON, the new edges generated by the clipping will not be rendered. It is only those unclipped parts of the original boundary that will be rendered.

While it is quite easy to draw a polyline around a fill area by just one extra function invocation, it may require a series of polyline functions to do the same for fill area set. This is one of the reasons for adding the edge boundary to fill area set.

3.5 TEXT

3.5.1 The functions

PHIGS provides two functions:

TEXT 3(PX, PY, PZ, TDXA, TDYA, TDZA, CHARS)
TEXT(PX, PY, CHARS)

Each defines output consisting of a sequence of characters, specified by CHARS, located with reference to a point called the *text position*. The second function is a 2D shorthand form of the first where output is with reference to the text position (PX,PY,0) in the Z=0 plane. Depending on the attribute settings, the text position could be the start, centre or end of the text string and the text could be orientated at any angle. A simple example, producing Figure 3.14, is:

TEXT(1, 3, 'Example String')

Figure 3.14: *Simple text example*

The greater complexity of the TEXT 3 function is because, in 3D, it is necessary to specify the plane on which the characters are to be output. The text position (PX,PY,PZ) is a point in this plane. The direction vector (TDXA(1), TDYA(1), TDZA(1)) defines the positive X-axis and (TDXA(2), TDYA(2), TDZA(2)) defines the positive Y-axis in the plane. As it is possible to define direction vectors that are not quite perpendicular to each other, the PHIGS system assumes that the two direction vectors are used to define the plane through (PX,PY,PZ). Once this is established, the first direction vector defines the X-axis. The positive Y-axis is then defined as the axis in the plane perpendicular to the X-axis that is nearest in direction to the second direction vector. The size and orientation of text in this plane is defined using a *Text Local Coordinate* system with the same metric as modelling coordinates. CHARS defines the string of characters to be output. An example of output from TEXT 3 would be:

```
TDXA(1)=COS(0.3*PI)
TDYA(1)=0
TDZA(1)=-SIN(0.3*PI)
TDXA(2)=0
TDYA(2)=1
TDZA(2)=0
TEXT 3(X, Y, Z, TDXA, TDYA, TDZA,'3D String')
```

which, on traversal, would produce the output shown in Figure 3.15 if viewed in perspective slightly from above.

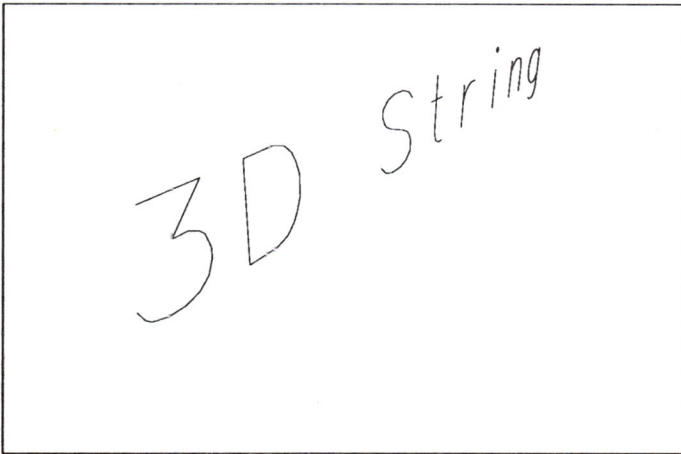

Figure 3.15: *Example of TEXT 3*

If the second direction vector had TDYA(2) set to −1, the Y-axis would have been in the opposite direction and the output would have been inverted as shown in Figure 3.16.

3.5.2 Text aspects

Text is the most complex of the output primitives in PHIGS with nine aspects to control the appearance on the display. Five aspects, *character height, character expansion factor, character spacing, text path* and *text font* define a *text extent rectangle* that encloses the character string in the text plane. The coordinates of the text extent rectangle are defined in the text local coordinate system. The aspect *character up vector* specifies the orientation of this text extent rectangle relative to the text local coordinate system axes. The aspect *text alignment* positions the text extent rectangle relative to the text position. Finally, *text colour index* defines the colour in the same way as polyline colour index (see Section 3.2.5). The *text precision* aspect allows some of the above aspects to be ignored.

Figure 3.16: *Inverted text by changing Y axis direction*

The text extent rectangle in the text plane will be transformed by any modelling transformations defined during traversal and will be clipped as required. In consequence, the most general case will be that the text extent rectangle is transformed to a parallelogram by the modelling transformation. This may result in the text being sheared.

3.5.3 Font specification

Any PHIGS implementation will provide the user with a number of differentiable character fonts. The font designer specifies the shape of each character relative to some local 2D coordinate system. Fonts can either be monospaced (all characters have the same width) or proportional (width depends on the character form). The font designer must specify a number of positions for each character in the font as shown in Figure 3.17.

The height of a character is defined as the distance from the base line to the cap line. The width of a character is defined as the distance from the left line to the right line. Normally, the font will be defined such that characters abutted together will have sufficient space between them for comfortable reading. Thus the width is usually greater than the width of the character form itself.

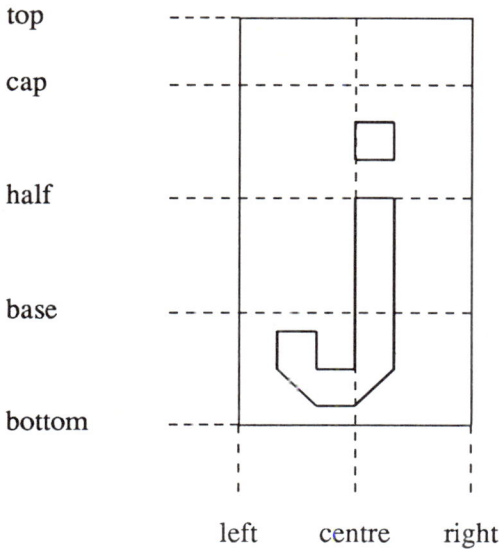

Figure 3.17 Character definition within a font

The text font aspect is a number which specifies the font to be used on a workstation to draw the characters. Fonts numbered 1 and 2 have to be provided. Fonts numbered greater than 2 are subject to the Registration scheme. An implementation can define any number of fonts using zero or negative numbers that are local to the implementation. Implementations frequently have a large number of fonts available (40 or more) so it is a point to look at when choosing an implementation. Font number 1 has to be a monospaced font and font number 2 must be differentiable from it. Both must define the characters in the ISO 646 standard. The requirements for both fonts 1 and 2 to be available was a late addition to the standard and earlier implementations of PHIGS sometimes do not comply with this requirement.

3.5.4 Defining the text extent rectangle

The TEXT or TEXT 3 function defines the sequence of characters to be output on the display. The text font aspect defines the font to be used. Different fonts define the relative widths of characters differently so it is necessary to define the text font to be used in order to identify the precise character bodies of the characters in the text string to be displayed.

The character height aspect defines the height of the character bodies to be displayed. The character body in the font description is expanded equally in both the X and Y directions until the specified character height is obtained.

The character expansion factor aspect provides additional expansion in the X-direction. If a value of 2.0 is specified, the width of the character body is doubled while leaving the height the same. Examples of different character expansions are given in Figure 3.18.

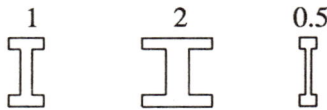

Figure 3.18: *Character expansion factor*

The character spacing aspect specifies how much additional spacing is required between two adjacent character bodies. A positive value will insert additional spacing as a fraction of the character height. A negative value of character spacing will cause the adjacent character bodies to over-lap. Whether the spacing is applied in the top-bottom or left-right direction of the characters depends on the setting of the text path aspect. Examples of different character spacing are given in Figure 3.19.

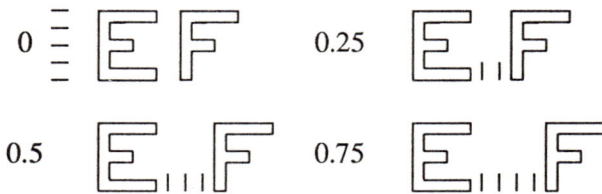

Figure 3.19: *Character spacing*

If the text path aspect is set to RIGHT, the second character body in the sequence of characters to be displayed is placed to the right of the first character body with the additional spacing in between if defined. The third character is placed to the right of the second and so on. If the text path aspect is set to LEFT, the second character body is placed to the left of the first character body and so on. In both cases, the height of the text extent rectangle is defined by the character height and extends from the top line to the bottom line. The width of the text extent rectangle extends from the left line of the left-most character to the right line of the right-most character.

If the text path aspect is set to DOWN, the second character body is placed below the first character with the additional spacing, if defined, in between. The third character body is placed below the second and so on. If the text path aspect is set to UP, the second character body is placed above the first character body and so on. In both cases, the height of the text extent rectangle is from the top-line of the top-most character to the bottom-line of the bottom-most character. The width is the same as the width of the widest character to be displayed.

As the fonts are defined separately on each workstation, the size of the text extent rectangle can be different on each workstation. This clearly causes problems if the application, say, is trying to surround the text with a rectangle drawn as a polyline. To ensure that this is possible, PHIGS insists that font number 1 is a monospaced font and that the aspect ratio for all the characters is the same for every workstation in the implementation. Consequently, if font number 1 is used, the rectangle around the text will appear the same on every workstation. If any other font is used, there is no guarantee, say, that the output on the display is the same as the output on an associated plotter which could have a different set of fonts defined.

3.5.5 Orientation

The character up vector aspect defines the orientation of the text extent rectangle (and the enclosed text) to the local text coordinate system in the plane by specifying the direction of the rectangle's height with respect to the local text coordinate system. For example, if the character up vector is set to (0,1), the vector is along the Y-axis of the local text coordinate system and so the text extent rectangle is aligned with the axes of the local text coordinate system. If the character up vector is set to (1,0), the up direction is along the X-axis of the local text coordinate system so the text extent rectangle is rotated by 90^c clockwise.

It should be remembered that just by setting the character up vector aspect to (0,1) does not guarantee that the text will be in its normal orientation. The text plane defined may be at an angle to the horizontal and a modelling transformation applied at traversal may also rotate the text.

3.5.6 Alignment

The text primitive defines the text position. The text alignment aspect defines the position in the text extent rectangle that coincides with the text position. The alignment is relative to the coordinate system of the text extent rectangle, that is the Y-direction is the direction of the character up vector.

The text alignment aspect has a pair of values that control the positioning in the X and Y-directions. The X-component has four possible values, LEFT, CENTRE, RIGHT and NORMAL. The Y-component has six possible values, TOP, CAP, HALF, BASE, BOTTOM and NORMAL.

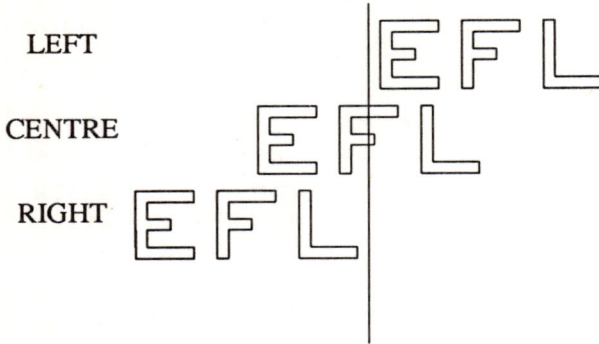

LEFT

CENTRE

RIGHT

Figure 3.20: *Horizontal text alignment*

If the X-component has value LEFT, the left side of the text extent rectangle coincides with the text position. For RIGHT, the right side of the text extent rectangle coincides with the text position while for CENTRE the text position lies midway between the left and right sides of the text extent rectangle. Examples of alignment horizontally are given in Figure 3.20.

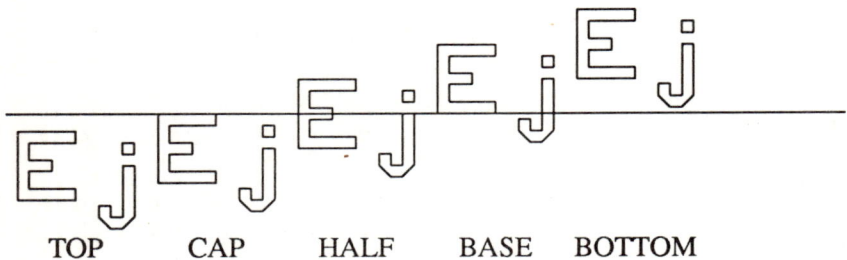

TOP   CAP   HALF   BASE   BOTTOM

Figure 3.21: *Vertical text alignment*

If the Y-component has value TOP, the top of the text extent rectangle coincides with the text position and similarly if it has value BOTTOM, the bottom of the text extent rectangle coincides with the text position. The values CAP, HALF and BASE are really only useful for text defined with text path LEFT or RIGHT. However, they are defined in such a way that they are also well defined for text path UP and DOWN. If CAP is defined, the text position coincides with the cap-line of the top-most character (for LEFT and RIGHT paths this is all the characters). If BASE is defined, the text position coincides with the base-line of the bottom-most character. If HALF is defined, the text position coincides with the line half way between the half-lines of the top and bottom-most characters. In consequence, for text defined with text path set to LEFT or RIGHT, CAP, HALF, and BASE have their obvious meanings. Examples of vertical alignment are given in Figure 3.21. The NORMAL X and Y-alignment values define the most appropriate text alignment depending on the text path defined. The table below gives the values of NORMAL for the possible text paths.

TEXT	NORMAL Alignment	
PATH	HORIZONTAL	VERTICAL
RIGHT	LEFT	BASE
LEFT	RIGHT	BASE
UP	CENTRE	BASE
DOWN	CENTRE	TOP

Character expansion factor = 2

Character spacing = −0.86

Up Vector

Text Origin

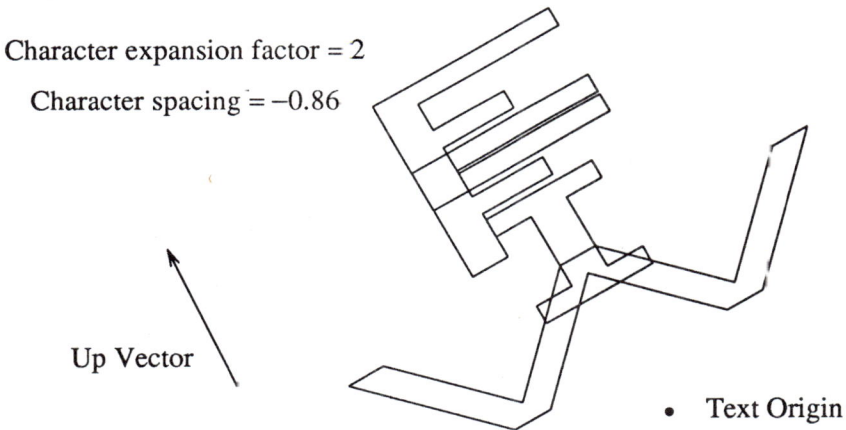

Figure 3.22: *Several text aspects specified together*

Figure 3.22 shows an example where several text aspects have been set together. Figure 3.23 shows the effect of a modelling transformation which does an expansion in the X-direction and a contraction in the Y-direction on a text primitive when the character up vector is set to (−1,1). Note that this can distort the character forms even in 2D. It also places quite a demand on the workstation which has to render the text primitive on the display.

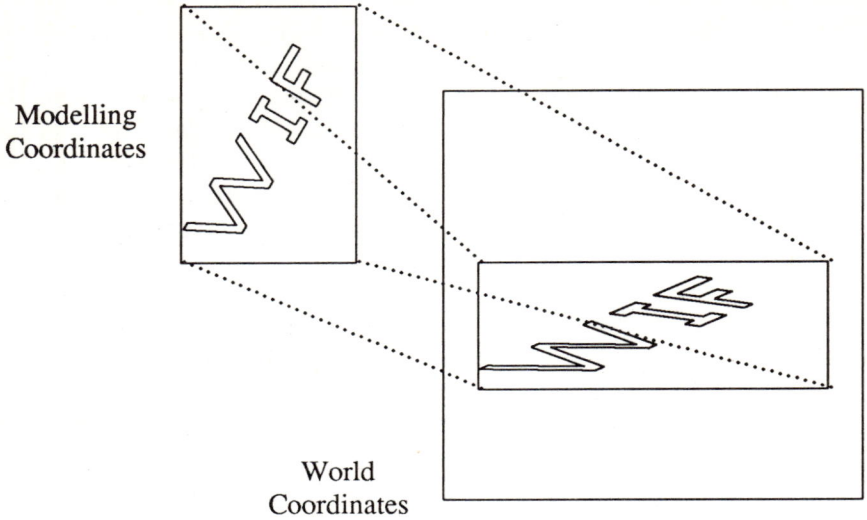

Figure 3.23: *Effect of modelling transformation on text*

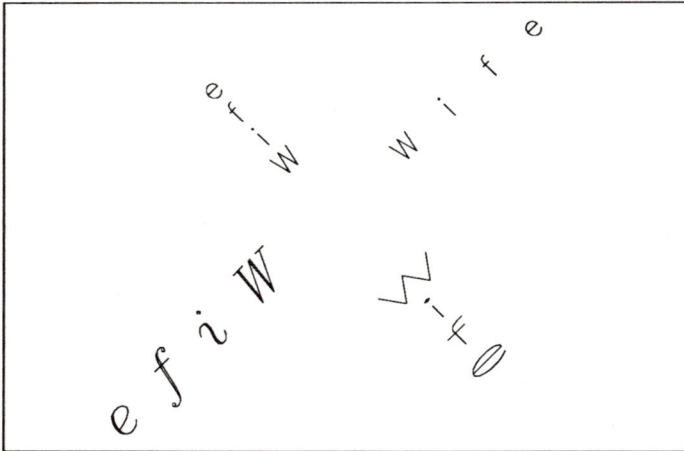

Figure 3.24: *Different text paths and aspects*

Figure 3.24 shows the same text string *Wife* output with text position set to the four corners of a central square with the letter W at the corners. The character up vector aspect is set to (−1,1) throughout. The top left text string is defined with text path set to UP. The top right is with text path set to RIGHT and character spacing set to 2.0. The bottom right has the text

path set to DOWN and character expansion set to 3.0 while the bottom left
has the text path set to LEFT, the character height double the others and a
different font selected.

3.5.7 Text precision

It is possible that a workstation will have difficulty in reproducing all the
text aspects described above. For example, hardware fonts on workstations
very rarely allow character shearing. On some simple workstations, it is
only possible to output text horizontally.

The text precision aspect in conjunction with the text font aspect
specifies how closely the workstation can represent the text output. If the
text precision aspect is set to STROKE, the workstation is expected to use
all the aspects correctly. In some cases, this may mean that the characters
have to be output by software line drawing or area filling.

If the text precision aspect is set to CHAR, the text extent rectangle and
the individual character bodies are calculated precisely. However, the individual characters may not be precisely defined within the character body.
For example, the correct character height may be used for the character but
the character will be vertical irrespective of the value of the character up
vector. If the text precision is set to STRING, a text string of approxi-
mately the right height and width is output but its alignment, orientation
and path direction may be incorrect. This quick and dirty text can be used
in debugging when the STROKE precision text is expensive to produce.
STRING precision text is frequently used for error messages and operator
prompts that do not form a major part of the graphical output and where
precision is less necessary as long as it is readable.

Every workstation must support at least two STROKE precision fonts
(numbers 1 and 2). It is also assumed that CHAR and STRING precision is
available for these fonts (not difficult as drawing at STROKE precision is
an allowable definition). For other fonts, there is no guarantee that all pre-
cisions are supported. If a requested font is not available, text font 1 will be
used at STRING precision.

4 ATTRIBUTES

4.1 INDIVIDUAL SPECIFICATION

In PHIGS, the appearance of a primitive on a display is defined by its aspects. The simplest method of defining such aspects is to have an *individual* attribute for each aspect. The attribute is a value in the traversal state list which, on traversal, is bound to the primitive. The polyline primitive has three aspects for controlling its appearance, linetype, linewidth scale factor and polyline colour index. The traversal state list has entries for the three attributes that specify these aspects. The three functions:

    SET LINETYPE(LTYPE)
    SET LINEWIDTH SCALE FACTOR(LWIDTH)
    SET POLYLINE COLOUR INDEX(COLI)

define structure elements that are added to the open structure. On structure traversal, attribute setting structure elements of this type cause the corresponding entry in the traversal state list to be updated with the new value. When a polyline structure element is traversed, the polyline primitive generated has the aspects associated with it set to the current values of the entries in the traversal state list. It is the workstation's responsibility to provide as close a display as possible to the values of the aspects specified. The examples so far have used aspects defined by individual specification.

Attribute setting functions exist for all the aspects described in Chapter 3. These are:

Polyline
    SET LINETYPE(LTYPE)
    SET LINEWIDTH SCALE FACTOR(LWIDTH)
    SET POLYLINE COLOUR INDEX(COLI)

Polymarker
    SET MARKER TYPE(MTYPE)
    SET MARKER SIZE SCALE FACTOR(MSZSF)
    SET POLYMARKER COLOUR INDEX(COLI)

Fill area and fill area set
  SET INTERIOR STYLE(STYLE)
  SET INTERIOR COLOUR INDEX(COLI)
  SET INTERIOR STYLE INDEX(ISTYLI)
  SET PATTERN REFERENCE POINT(RFX, RFY)
  SET PATTERN REFERENCE POINT AND VECTORS
    (RFX, RFY, RFZ, RFVAX, RFVAY, RFVAZ)
  SET PATTERN SIZE(SZX, SZY)
  SET PATTERN REPRESENTATION
    (WS, PI, DIMX, DIMY, SX, SY, DX, DY, COLIA)
  SET EDGE FLAG(EDFLAG)
  SET EDGETYPE(EDTYPE)
  SET EDGEWIDTH SCALE FACTOR(EWIDTH)
  SET EDGE COLOUR INDEX(COLI)

Text
  SET CHARACTER HEIGHT(CHH)
  SET CHARACTER EXPANSION FACTOR(CHEF)
  SET CHARACTER SPACING(CHSP)
  SET TEXT PATH(TXP)
  SET TEXT FONT(FONT)
  SET CHARACTER UP VECTOR(CHUX, CHUY)
  SET TEXT ALIGNMENT(TXALH, TXALY)
  SET TEXT PRECISION(PREC)
  SET TEXT COLOUR INDEX(COLI)

4.2 PATTERNS

The only unusual attribute setting function is SET PATTERN REPRESEN-
TATION. All the others apply to every workstation in use and it is the
workstation's responsibility to make as close a match to what is required as
possible. For interior style PATTERN, the style index points to a pattern
which is defined separately for each workstation. Thus, SET PATTERN
REPRESENTATION sets the style index entry PI on workstation WS to
the specified pattern.

The colours of the pattern cells are defined in the array COLIA which
has dimensions DIMX and DIMY. The definition of this pattern starts at
the entry COLIA(SX, SY). The next entry in the X-direction is
COLIA(SX+1, SY) and the next entry in the Y-direction is COLIA(SX,
SY+1). This allows a number of patterns to be stored in the same array and
for sub-parts of a pattern to be used. For example:

```
INTEGER COLIA(10, 20)
DATA XFA/2, 8, 8, 2, 2/
DATA YFA/6, 6, 2, 2, 6/
COLIA(4, 3)=0
COLIA(4, 4)=1
COLIA(4, 5)=1
COLIA(5, 3)=1
COLIA(5, 4)=0
COLIA(5, 5)=1
SET PATTERN SIZE(DX, DY)
SET PATTERN REFERENCE POINT(X, Y)
SET INTERIOR STYLE(PATTERN)
SET INTERIOR STYLE INDEX(4)
SET PATTERN REPRESENTATION(WS, 4, 10, 20, 4, 3, 2, 3, COLIA)
FILL AREA(5, XFA, YFA)
POLYLINE(5, XFA, YFA)
```

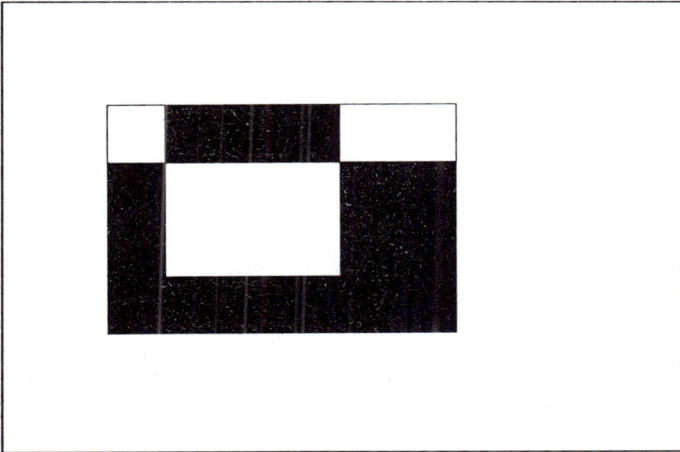

Figure 4.1: *Patterned fill area*

This defines a rectangular area to be filled stretching from 2 to 8 in the X-direction and 2 to 6 in the Y-direction (defined by XFA,YFA). The 4th pattern starts at entry (4, 3) in the COLIA array which has dimensions (10, 20). The number of elements in this pattern are 2 in the X-direction and 3 in the Y-direction. The elements in the COLIA array point to the colour table and we will assume that 0 represents the background colour (white) and that colour table entry 1 on workstation WS defines a black colour. If (X, Y) is set to (3, 3) and (DX, DY) is set to (3, 2) the fill area will be as shown in Figure 4.1. A polyline has been drawn around the boundary of the area to be filled.

Figure 4.2: *Pattern with same aspect ratio but smaller in size*

Figure 4.3: *Same pattern with more repeats in X and less in Y*

The pattern is so large that a complete cycle of the pattern is not visible. With the origin some way in from the bottom left corner, bits of the previous pattern repeat are visible to the left and below.

If (X, Y) is set to (2.5, 2.5) and the same aspect ratio is used for the pattern but it is made smaller in size, the effect is shown in Figure 4.2. The appearance of the pattern can be changed significantly by a change in aspect ratio. Putting the origin back to (3, 3) and changing (DX, DY) to (0.6, 1.0) gives a pattern repeating more frequently in the X and less in the Y as shown in Figure 4.3.

4.3 GEOMETRIC ASPECTS

Some of the aspects described so far effect the geometry of the picture on the display as well as how it is rendered. Consequently, it is only sensible that these are defined individually as above. However, other aspects are mainly to provide differentiability between primitives (for example, linestyle). In this case, it is not unreasonable for these to be defined differently on each workstation in order to achieve maximum differentiability on a particular workstation.

To some extent the division into two classes is rather arbitrary as all aspects have some effect on the geometry of the picture, even the text font used does. The decision, in some cases, reflects the types of workstations around when PHIGS and the earlier graphics standards were defined. The set of aspects that can only be controlled globally are:

  character height
  character up vector
  pattern size
  pattern reference point and vectors

All the other aspects can be set differently on each workstation using the *bundled* mode of aspect setting.

4.4 BUNDLED SPECIFICATION

The aspects for a primitive such as polyline can be defined differently on each workstation. This is achieved by having on each workstation a table which contains values for all the aspects that can be set either individually or bundled. The table will have a number of entries which define different combinations of the aspects. The index into the table is called the *polyline index*.

Figure 4.4 shows the form that the table will have on a workstation with the values for table position 2 filled in. These entries can either be predefined or set by the application.

POLYLINE INDEX	LINE TYPE	LINEWIDTH SCALE FACTOR	COLOUR INDEX
1			
2	SOLID	2.0	4
3			
4			
5			

Figure 4.4: *Polyline bundle table*

If the aspects of a primitive are being defined by a bundle table on the workstation, the attribute controlling the appearance is the index into the bundle table. Thus index attributes are defined as follows:

polyline index
polymarker index
text index
interior index
edge index

and entries for each of these appear in the traversal state list. The aspects of fill area primitives are controlled by the interior index, whereas the fill area set aspects are determined by two indices, the same interior index and also the edge index. Each index has an associated attribute setting structure element defined by:

SET POLYLINE INDEX(I)
SET POLYMARKER INDEX(I)
SET TEXT INDEX(I)
SET INTERIOR INDEX(I)
SET EDGE INDEX(I)

A PHIGS implementation will have a number of bundle table entries already defined so that a structure containing:

```
SET POLYLINE INDEX(1)
POLYLINE(N, XA1, YA1)
SET POLYLINE INDEX(2)
POLYLINE(M, XA2, YA2)
SET POLYLINE INDEX(3)
POLYLINE(P, XA3, YA3)
```

will, on traversal, display three polylines on each of the active workstations and the workstations are likely to have been initialized so that the polyline aspects for these 3 index values are differentiable on each of the workstations. The entries in the table will depend on the PHIGS implementation, no guidance is given in PHIGS itself. For example, a monochrome workstation might be initialized with the first 3 bundle table rows for polyline set to normal thickness, black lines but with different linestyles. The same PHIGS implementation might, on a colour workstation, set the first three rows to normal thickness, solid lines but with different colours set. The aim will be to choose settings that give maximum differentiability on that workstation.

The user is able to tailor the workstation bundle table entries to his own requirements by defining the aspects associated with a particular index value. The form of the function is:

SET XXX REPRESENTATICN(WS, INDX, ...)

The XXX defines the bundle table to be set, the WS parameter defines the workstation on which the bundle table occurs and INDX defines the row of the table to be updated. The subsequent parameters in the function define the aspect values to be entered into that row of the table.

The parameters of the SET REPRESENTATION functions are:

POLYLINE	(WS, PLI, LTYPE, LWIDTH, COLI)
POLYMARKER	(WS, PMI, MTYPE, MSZSF, COLI)
TEXT	(WS, TXI, FONT, PREC, CHXP, CHSP, COLI)
INTERIOR	(WS, INI, INTSTY, STYLI, COLI)
EDGE	(WS, EDI, EDFLAG, EDTYPE, EWIDTH, COLI)

Note that these tables are similar to the SET PATTERN REPRESENTATION table. The main difference is that the aspects above can also be set globally whereas patterns have to be defined separately for each workstation.

An example of the text bundle table is given in Figure 4.5.

INDEX	TEXT FONT	TEXT PREC.	CHAR EXP. FACT.	CHAR SPAC.	COL. INDEX
1					
2	−3	STROKE	2.0	0.0	3
4					

Figure 4.5: *Text bundle table*

The font number specified is −3 which is an implementation specific font for this particular workstation.

Figure 4.6 gives an example of the interior bundle table used by both the fill area and fill area set primitives. Note that some table entries are blank. For interior styles HOLLOW and SOLID, there is no need to specify the style index as it is not used. For interior style PATTERN, the colour index is not used.

INDEX	STYLE	STYLE INDEX	COLOUR INDEX
1	HOLLOW		1
2	SOLID		2
3	PATTERN	2	
4	PATTERN	1	
5	HATCH	1	3

Figure 4.6: *Interior bundle table*

Figure 4.7 gives an example of the edge bundle table used by the fill area set primitive. Note that the entries are very similar to the polyline bundle table. The first entry specifies whether edges will be drawn or not.

EDGE INDEX	EDGE FLAG	EDGE TYPE	EDGEWIDTH SCALE FACTOR	COLOUR INDEX
1	ON	SOLID	1.0	2
2				

Figure 4.7: *Edge bundle table*

The number of entries in these tables is, again, implementation dependent although there are some minimum requirements defined by PHIGS. The size of the bundle tables must be at least 20 in length and there must be at least 5 predefined values (in the case of text it is 6). The pattern table has to have at least 10 entries but only 1 needs to be defined. An implementation will normally set up a minimum set of differentiable table entries for each workstation. An implementation can choose not to implement hatch styles at all but, if it does, it must implement at least 3.

4.5 ASPECT SOURCE FLAGS

So far, two different methods of setting aspects have been described. For example, the aspects associated with a polyline primitive can be defined by:

```
SET LINETYPE(SOLID)
SET LINEWIDTH SCALE FACTOR(3.0)
SET POLYLINE COLOUR INDEX(5)
POLYLINE(6, XA, YA)
```

or by:

```
SET POLYLINE INDEX(4)
SET POLYLINE REPRESENTATION(WS, 4, SOLID, 3.0, 5)
POLYLINE(6, XA, YA)
```

Both have the same effect on the workstation WS. What has not been explained is what happens if the application defines:

```
SET LINETYPE(SOLID)
SET LINEWIDTH SCALE FACTOR(3.0)
SET POLYLINE COLOUR INDEX(5)
SET POLYLINE INDEX(4)
SET POLYLINE REPRESENTATION(WS, 4, DOTTED, 1.0, 7)
POLYLINE(6, XA, YA)
```

On traversal, is the polyline on workstation WS to be drawn as SOLID or DOTTED? Is the linewidth scale factor to be set to 3.0 or 1.0? Is the polyline colour index to be set to 5 or 7?

In PHIGS, it is possible for the application to specify that all the aspects are defined by the individual specification values in the traversal state list or all the aspects are defined by the workstation polyline bundle or a mixture of the two.

For each aspect, the traversal state list has an entry called the *aspect source flag* which specifies whether the value in the traversal state list is used (flag set to INDIVIDUAL) or the value in the bundle table on the workstation (flag is set to BUNDLED). The function defining the setting of aspect source flags is:

SET INDIVIDUAL ASF(ID, VAL)

The first parameter defines the aspect to be controlled and VAL is the new value for that aspect. For example:

SET INDIVIDUAL ASF(LINETYPE, INDIVIDUAL)

will set the LINETYPE aspect to INDIVIDUAL as shown in Figure 4.8. The complete set of ASFs is linetype, linewidth scale factor, polyline colour index, marker type, marker size scale factor, polymarker colour index, text font, text precision, character expansion factor, character spacing, text colour index, interior style, interior style index, interior colour index, edge flag, edgetype, edgewidth scale factor, and edge colour index.

The setting of the ASFs initially is likely to be to INDIVIDUAL especially if the PHIGS system is of USA origin. The standard allows either initial setting. Figure 4.8 and Figure 4.9 show how the system works. The traversal state list has entries for the 3 linetype attributes: linetype, linewidth scale factor (abbreviated to SF) and polyline colour index. It also has entries for the 3 associated aspect source flags (ASFs). Finally, it has an entry for the polyline index that points to an entry in the polyline bundle table. The following program would set up the entries in Figure 4.8 and Figure 4.9:

```
SET LINETYPE(SOLID)
SET LINEWIDTH SCALE FACTOR(1.0)
SET POLYLINE COLOUR INDEX(2)
SET POLYLINE INDEX(1)
SET INDIVIDUAL ASF(LINETYPE, INDIVIDUAL)
SET INDIVIDUAL ASF(LINEWIDTH SCALE FACTOR, BUNDLED)
SET INDIVIDUAL ASF(POLYLINE COLOUR INDEX, INDIVIDUAL)
SET POLYLINE REPRESENTATION(WS, 1, DOTTED, 3.0, 1)
POLYLINE(5, XA, YA)
```

Traversal State List	
Linetype ASF	INDIVIDUAL
Linetype	SOLID
Linewidth SF ASF	BUNDLED
Linewidth SF	1.0
Colour index ASF	INDIVIDUAL
Colour index	2
Polyline index	1

Polyline primitive created			
Linetype	Linewidth Scale factor	Colour Index	Polyline Index
SOLID		2	1

Figure 4.8: *Aspects bound before workstation*

On traversal, the polyline primitive created will have the aspects bound to it from the traversal state list entries if the associated ASF is set to INDIVIDUAL. In the example, the linetype and polyline colour index ASFs are set to INDIVIDUAL, so the polyline primitive created will have linetype set to SOLID and polyline colour index set to 2 from the traversal state list entries. The linewidth scale factor entry is left empty.

Polyline Bundle Table			
Index	Linetype	Linewidth Scale Factor	Colour Index
1	DOTTED	3.0	1

Aspects of displayed polyline		
Linetype	Linewidth Scale Factor	Colour Index
SOLID	3.0	2

Figure 4.9: *Aspects bound at workstation*

If all aspects are bound to the primitive, that is all the ASFs are set to INDI-VIDUAL, the polyline primitive is completely defined and it is sent to the workstation for rendering on the display. There is no need to send the poly-line index in this case. If some aspects have not been bound to the primi-tive, at least one ASF is set to BUNDLED, the polyline index is bound to the primitive as well and the workstation is left to define the remaining aspects from the relevant entry in the polyline bundle table.

As the linewidth scale factor ASF is set to BUNDLED, the polyline index is bound to the primitive (value 1). The workstation will extract the linewidth scale factor value (3.0 in this case) from the bundle defined in position 1. This results in the aspects bound to the primitive being linetype SOLID, linewidth scale factor 3.0, and polyline colour index 2.

If the application is associated with a single workstation, specifying the aspects individually may be appropriate. If the application is to run on a range of workstations, or if it uses several workstations together, and the aim is maximum portability, the bundled mode of working may be prefer-able. The choice depends on the types of workstation in use and whether the application is aiming for maximum differentiability or closeness to a virtual specification of the graphics. Both are valid aims. Applications need to decide whether maximum differentiability or closeness of realiza-tion is the aim.

If the display is required to be made up of blue and turquoise lines, and the display cannot produce differentiable colours, are red and blue lines acceptable or would all blue lines be preferable? The answer to this ques-tion is application specific and will influence which mode of working is chosen.

4.6 COLOUR TABLES

Each workstation has its own colour table, the entries in which are pointed at by all the primitive's colour index aspects. A typical form of the colour table is shown in Figure 3.34.

INDEX	C1	C2	C3
0			
1	0.1	0.4	0.1
2			
3			

Figure 3.34: *Colour table*

Note that, unlike the other tables, an index 0 entry is specified, which is the background colour.

The colour index points to a row of the table which defines 3 colour components C1, C2 and C3. The colour that these specify depends on the *colour model* in use. PHIGS allows the workstation to define colour using one of the following colour models:

(1) *RGB* : red, green and blue components;

(2) *CIELUV* : the universal colour definition system;

(3) *HSV* : hue, saturation and value components;

(4) *HLS* : hue, lightness and saturation components.

It is possible for other colour models to be specified. As before, values greater than 4 are subject to the Registration mechanism while values less than or equal to 0 can be used by the implementation to define implementation ones.

Every workstation must support colour specifications using the RGB and CIELUV models. The other two are optional. The requirement to support the CIELUV model was a late addition to the definition of PHIGS. Consequently, some early implementations still do not support the CIELUV model even though it is mandatory.

A full description of colour models is outside the scope of this book. The reader should consult any of the standard text books in Computer Graphics, such as Foley, van Dam, Feissier and Hughes. Suffice it to say:

(1) *RGB* : the individual components are in the range 0 to 1 and give the intensity of that particular colour in the composite colour. Equal values of all three colours span the grey scale from black to white as they advance from 0 to 1. A yellow colour is produced by equal

values of red and green with the blue component set to 0.

(2) *CIELUV*: the individual components do not represent real colours but are hypothetical primary colours which when added together allow all physically realizable colours to be specified using *positive* values in the range 0 to 1. Standard formulae translate RGB specified colours to CIELUV colours for a specific workstation. The advantage of the CIELUV model is that colours are specified in a device independent way. A device can be tuned to realize the correct colour defined by CIELUV.

(3) *HSV*: a model that is easier for the user to specify colours in terms of hue, saturation and value (darkness). The hue component defines the colour with small values being red, going through yellow to green (around 0.3) through cyan to blue (around 0.7) and back to red with value near 1. The saturation component gives the amount of whiteness. A high saturation value near 1 gives a saturated red while a value around 0.5 gives pink and small values approach white with little redness. The value component close to 0 gives a dark colour which gets lighter as the value goes to 1.

(4) *HLS*: the hue component is similar to HSV. The lightness component defines the brightness going from 0 as the lowest (black) to 1 giving maximum brightness (white). The saturation component again gives the level of saturation.

The required colour model is specified by:

SET COLOUR MODEL(WS, CMODEL)

while the individual representations in the colour table are defined by:

SET COLOUR REPRESENTATION(WS, CI, N, CSPEC)

The array elements CSPEC(1) to CSPEC(N) contain the colour defined for entry CI on workstation WS. An array is used here as some colour models use more or less than 3 parameters to define colours.

If the workstation is monochrome, it is necessary to map the three components into, say, a level of greyness or intensity. PHIGS does not specify how this should be done. However, some implementations use the formulae produced for NTSC TV to map colour pictures to Black and White. The green component contributes most to the intensity (60%) while the red is less (30%) and the blue almost non-existent. Quite a wide range of grey values can be obtained by leaving the red and blue components at some median value and just changing the green component.

4.7 IDENTIFICATION ATTRIBUTES

4.7.1 Name set

Output primitives in PHIGS can have a *name set* attribute associated with them. It is used to identify sets of primitives with similar characteristics. Its principle use is in controlling the overall form of the interaction between the operator and the application. An implementation must allow a minimum of 64 names to be specified and these are mapped to the integers 0 to 63. Some implementations support as many as 1024. For example, if a designer is producing the set of drawings for a house, names might be used to identify those components that belong to a particular room, a particular function (heating say) or made from a particular material (wood say).

Thus, a specific primitive may have names associated with all these classes. Consequently, the name set is a set of data associated with the primitive.

The traversal state list contains an entry which contains the current name set and, on traversal, this set of names is bound to the primitive. Unlike the other attributes, the value of the name set is not specified completely by a SET NAME SET function. Instead, the name set in the traversal state list is initialized to be empty, and the name set entry is changed by the two functions:

ADD NAMES TO SET(N, NMSETA)
REMOVE NAMES FROM SET(N, NMSETA)

On traversal, these functions add or remove the set of names specified from the current set specified in the traversal state list.

4.7.2 Filters

The name set associated with an output primitive is used to control the attributes involved in the interaction with the operator on a specific workstation:

(1) *invisibility* : whether or not the operator is able to see the posted primitive on a specified workstation;

(2) *highlighting* : whether or not a particular primitive is highlighted to bring it to the attention of the operator;

(3) *pickability* : whether or not the primitive is enabled to allow the operator to point at and interact with it.

In each case, the application would like to indicate the names associated with primitives that would cause the required effect to take place (invisibility, highlighting, pickability) and the names associated with primitives that would cause the effect not to take place. An example might be to highlight all the primitives in the drawing that are part of the heating system and are not made of wood.

This leads to the concept in PHIGS of having *filters* specified for a workstation to control these three attributes relevant to the operator.

Each workstation has filters associated with highlighting, invisibility and pickability (for a specific device). A filter consists of a pair of sets of names, called the *inclusion set* and the *exclusion set*. The description of the pick filter is similar to the other two. It is left to Section 9.7.2 for a detailed description. Associated with picking is another identification attribute, the pick identifier, which is also described there.

The functions to set the filters for invisibility and highlighting are:

SET INVISIBILITY FILTER(WS, ISN, ISNA, ESN, ESNA)
SET HIGHLIGHTING FILTER(WS, ISN, ISNA, ESN, ESNA)

Each function defines both the inclusion (IS) and exclusion set (ES) for the attribute. The parameter ISN defines the number of names in the inclusion set. ISNA is an array giving those names. Similarly for the exclusion set.

A primitive on a workstation is highlighted if it has at least one name in its name set that is in the highlighting inclusion set, and *no* names in its name set that appear in the highlighting exclusion set. Invisibility is specified in a similar way.

For example:

OPEN STRUCTURE(HOUSE)

NMSETA(1)=WOOD
NMSETA(2)=HEATING
ADD NAMES TO SET(2, NMSETA)
SHELF

NMA(1)=HEATING
REMOVE NAMES FROM SET(1, NMA)
NMA(1)=FURNITURE
ADD NAMES TO SET(1, NMA)
BOOKCASE

NMA(2)=WOOD
REMOVE NAMES FROM SET(2, NMA)

```
NMSETA(1)=METAL
NMSETA(2)=HEATING
ADD NAMES TO SET(2, NMSETA)
RADIATOR
CLOSE STRUCTURE(HOUSE)
POST STRUCTURE(WS, HOUSE, 0.2)
ISA(1)=HEATING
ESA(1)=WOOD
SET HIGHLIGHTING FILTER(WS, 1, ISA, 1, ESA)
```

The three objects drawn have name sets:

Object	Name set
SHELF	WOOD,HEATING
BOOKCASE	WOOD,FURNITURE
RADIATOR	METAL,HEATING

When the structure is posted, traversal will start and the inclusion and exclusion name sets for the workstation WS will initially be null so all parts of the house (bookcase, radiator and shelf above it) will be drawn normally.

When the highlighting filter is changed, the items to be highlighted are those with the name HEATING in the name set but not those with the name WOOD in the name set.

The two items with the name HEATING in the name set are the SHELF and the RADIATOR. As the SHELF also has the name WOOD which is in the exclusion set, it would not be highlighted. Consequently, the only item highlighted is the radiator.

4.7.3 Rendering

PHIGS does not pretend to be a system defined for high quality rendering or visualization. It is primarily concerned with schematics or simple coloured objects. The extension to PHIGS (PHIGS PLUS) is being standardized and this provides a richer set of output primitives together with the ability to render these in a more impressive way with control of shading and lighting. In its basic form, PHIGS provides some control over the rendering hardware available with modern displays. This allows a minimal amount of control of Hidden Line and Hidden Surface Removal (HLHSR).

PHIGS has another identification attribute called the HLHSR Identifier. The function:

SET HLHSR IDENTIFIER(ID)

sets the entry in the traversal state list for the HLHSR Identifier to ID and the current value of this entry is bound to primitives on traversal.

The HLHSR Identifier can be used to partition the output primitives sent to a workstation for display into sets corresponding to the different values of the HLHSR Identifier. For example, the value might specify whether a wire frame model or solid rendering is required. It might also classify primitives into sets that do not overlap each other. How the HLHSR Identifier is used is implementation specific.

With each workstation is a second identifier called the HLHSR Mode which is set by:

SET HLHSR MODE(WS, MD)

The HLHSR Mode is used in conjunction with the HLHSR Identifier to provide some control of rendering.

For example, the HLHSR Identifier could be used to partition primitives into those to be displayed as wire frames and those to be rendered as solids. The HLHSR Mode could be used to decide whether a particular algorithm such as Z buffering was to be used to render the solid parts of the picture.

PHIGS just provides the two identifiers and does not specify how they are to be used. Consequently, it is essential that the user looks at the details of his specific implementation to see what, if any, facilities are provided.

As PHIGS PLUS, when it is defined, will provide much richer control of rendering, the HLHSR functionality is unlikely be implemented other than in a rudimentary way on those implementations that have included some PHIGS PLUS functionality as the standard develops. Care should be taken when using these extensions until the PHIGS PLUS standardization is complete.

5 NETWORKS

5.1 INTRODUCTION

Chapter 2 gave a description of the main structure creation and editing functions. Chapter 3 gave full details of the structure elements associated with output primitives and their attributes. PHIGS, the Programmer's *Hierarchical* Interactive Graphics System is so named because structures need not be independent but can be related to each other in a hierarchy. This is of particular value when complex pictures are being composed from parts which are themselves defined by lower-level units. If the interaction with such pictures needs to have access to the hierarchy description, the facilities described so far are inadequate.

In this Chapter, the remaining types of structure elements will be described (there are 9 different types and only 4 have been described so far). The main element to be described is the one that defines the hierarchy. However, associated with it are the transformation and clipping facilities that provide a much more extensive descriptive ability than has been suggested so far. Clipping will be described in Section 5.8.

5.2 STRUCTURE HIERARCHY

PHIGS provides a structure element:

EXECUTE STRUCTURE(SI)

which allows one structure to be linked to another. If the above structure element occurs in the traversal of structure ST, the traverser will suspend the traversal of structure ST remembering the current contents of the traversal state list. The structure SI is traversed from its beginning using the current contents of the traversal state list. Consequently, any attribute settings or transformations applying to the structure ST will also apply to the structure SI when its traversal starts. Thus the structure SI inherits the environment created by its parent. The organization of how any modelling transformations of ST are inherited by SI will be described in Section 5.3.

On completing the traversal of SI, the saved PHIGS traversal state list is restored and traversal of SI continues at the element immediately after the EXECUTE STRUCTURE(SI) element. Therefore, nothing that has happened in the traversal of structure SI can effect the traversal of structure ST. This has the advantage that the meaning of structure ST can be deduced without needing to examine in detail the structure SI.

The structure SI can, itself, have EXECUTE STRUCTURE elements in its body. When these are traversed, the same process of saving the current state and traversing the sub-structure applies. There is no limit to the depth of structure nesting that can be specified except for any implementation restrictions on the total storage available.

The structure ST may have several appearances of the EXECUTE STRUCTURE(SI) within it so multiple instances of the same structure can be traversed. If this is done with different settings in the traversal state list when the EXECUTE STRUCTURE element is interpreted, the effect of each traversal of structure SI will be different. For example, the positions of the graphical objects described by structure SI or their appearance may be different for each execution of SI.

The structure posted to a workstation is called the *root* structure. The root structure and all structures linked to it by EXECUTE STRUCTURE elements making up the complete hierarchy is called a structure *network*.

The only constraint placed on a structure network is that it cannot be recursive. For any structure ST that includes, say, an EXECUTE STRUCTURE(SI) element, traversal of SI or any of the structures traversed as part of the traversal of SI cannot result in an execution of structure ST. This applies to all the structures in the network. Effectively, this means that each structure only has to have storage associated with it that can contain one saved traversal state list. In particular, the structure ST cannot contain structure elements of the form EXECUTE STRUCTURE(ST).

If a structure is defined containing an element EXECUTE STRUCTURE(NEW) and NEW does not exist, a null structure NEW is created with no elements.

5.3 MODELLING TRANSFORMATIONS

5.3.1 Introduction

In Section 2.8, a local modelling transformation was described. For single structures, not in a network, it was sufficient to describe modelling transformations in terms of the Current Local Modelling Transformation (CLMT) that could be defined and changed during the execution of a structure. It was stated that the traversal state list had the CLMT set to the identity matrix at the start of structure traversal initiated by the POST

STRUCTURE function.

None of that description is incorrect but it does not describe what happens when a structure traversal occurs as a result of an EXECUTE STRUCTURE function being executed. Clearly, it would be sensible for any modelling transformations already applied to the parent structure to be inherited by the child structure. PHIGS achieves this by defining both local and global modelling transformations.

5.3.2 Global modelling transformation

The PHIGS traversal state list, as shown in Figure 2.3, has entries for both a global and local modelling transformation. Let these matrices have their current values defined as CGMT (Current Global Modelling Transformation) and CLMT (Current Local Modelling Transformation).

When a structure, say STRA, is posted to a workstation, the values of CGMT and CLMT are both set to the identity matrix. The modelling transformation applied to the coordinates of structure elements on traversal is a composition of the two transformations (say COMP) where:

$$COMP = CGMT \times CLMT$$

Effectively, the local modelling transformation is applied to the coordinates followed by the global modelling transformation. For the posted structure, STA, unless the Global Modelling Transformation is changed, the only transformation applied to its elements is the Current Local Modelling Transformation.

When an EXECUTE STRUCTURE element is traversed, the values of CGMT and CLMT are stored. Before executing the sub-structure, the CGMT in the traversal state list is set to COMP, the composition of CGMT and CLMT, and the CLMT is set to identity. Thus the complete set of transformations in force is passed to the sub-structure as its Global Modelling Transformation.

Consider the two structures given below:

	STRA
0	
1	SET LMT (MT1,REPLACE)
2	SET LMT(MT2,POST)
3	EXECUTE STRUCTURE(STRB)
4	PCLYLINE(5,XL,YL)

0	STRB
1	POLYLINE(12,XC,YC)
2	SET LMT(MT3,REPLACE)
3	SET LMT(MT4,PRE)
4	POLYLINE(5,XS,YS)

SET LMT is a shorthand for SET LOCAL TRANSFORMATION in the figure. If the structure, STRA, is posted, on entry the values of CLMT, CGMT and COMP are all identity. The first element in STRA, on traversal, will replace CLMT and COMP by MT1. The second element will replace both CLMT and COMP by MT2 × MT1 (POST implies MT2 is performed after MT1).

On traversal of the third element, EXECUTE STRUCTURE(STRB), the values of CGMT and CLMT will be stored (identity and MT2 × MT1) and the structure STRB will be traversed with CGMT set to MT2 × MT1 and CLMT set to identity. In consequence, the coordinates of the POLY-LINE in the first element of STRB will be transformed by COMP which is MT2 × MT1.

The second element of STRB will, on traversal, set CLMT to MT3, but it will not change CGMT which is still MT2 × MT1, and this will result in COMP being MT2 × MT1 × MT3. The third element on traversal will update the value of CLMT by PRE-multiplying the CLMT. In consequence, CLMT will have value MT3 × MT4 (MT4 applied before MT3). CGMT remains as MT2 × MT1 so that the value of COMP, the composite modelling transformation, becomes MT2 × MT1 × MT3 × MT4 and this is the transformation applied to the POLYLINE element in the fourth position of structure STRB.

On the completion of STRB traversal, the saved values are restored so CGMT will revert to identity and CLMT to MT2 × MT1. The value of COMP is, therefore, MT2 × MT1 and this is applied to the coordinates of the fourth structure element in STRA. As was stated before, this can be deduced just by examining STRA.

5.3.3 Picture composition

The EXECUTE STRUCTURE element provides a powerful facility for composing graphical objects out of parts which may themselves be made from sub-parts. As local transformations can be applied at each level, it is quite feasible for each structure to have its own local coordinate system and the composition of parts into the complete graphical object can include the necessary positioning and scaling as transformations applied to the parts.

In the example in Section 2.7, the parts of the desk were all defined using the same coordinate system and positioned absolutely in the unit square coordinate space. Consequently, the individual parts of the desk are largely hard-wired into their current positions apart from global operations applied to them. In PHIGS, for complex graphical output, it would be more usual for the individual parts to be defined in their own local coordinate system and the picture built up by placing those individual parts relative to each other. This is described in Section 5.4.

The use of PRE and POST concatenation of matrices tends to be a matter of style. If complex objects are defined by a network, the inheritance of transformations effectively gives the local transformation as a PRE multiplication before the global transformation. In consequence, a sequential read of a structure tends to be more natural if the local transformations are defined as PRE multiplications. Most applications can be defined using just PRE multiplication. Mixing PRE and POST multiplications can cause confusion and make the application program less readable.

5.4 A NETWORK EXAMPLE

5.4.1 Introduction

Figure 5.1 shows a typical open plan office layout with a number of desk configurations placed in a room. There are five different desk arrangements with at least two examples of all but one. The desks are made up of standard components both in terms of the parts of the desk and the accessories on the desk. There are two sizes of telephone but the basic design is identical in both cases. This Chapter will show how such an office plan could be derived and the structure network produced.

5.4.2 Strategy

As none of the objects has an absolute coordinate position, the proposed strategy is:

(1) Define the components such as chair, blotter, phone etc in a local coordinate system.

(2) Construct sub-parts from these components. Examples of sub-parts are the large desk with the accessories added.

(3) Construct complete desks from the sub-parts.

(4) Construct a person's work environment including the chair.

(5) Fit the individual work environments into the office plan.

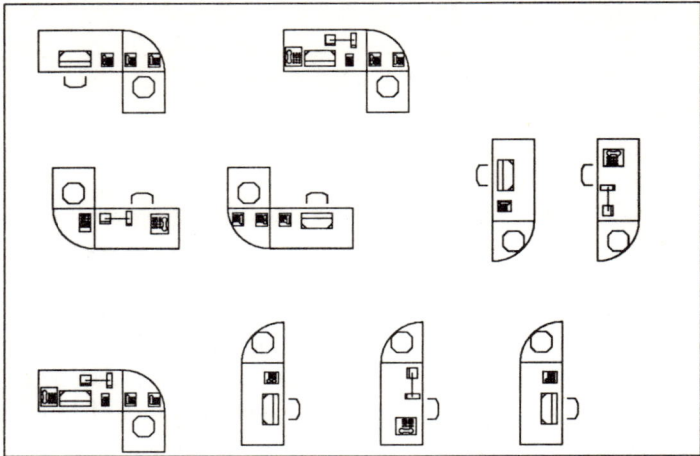

Figure 5.1: *Typical open plan office*

Note that there is some natural structuring to the problem although there are choices to be made. Why define a work environment as a desk plus a chair rather than define the chair as part of the desk? Is the lamp a basic component or a sub-part made up of base, arm and light? To a large extent, these decisions are the ones that require knowledge of the application and the possible modifications allowed. Considerable care should be taken in the overall design of the structure network to make sure it meets the needs of the application.

5.4.3 Components

As stated above, it is sensible to define the components in terms of their own local coordinate system. For example, the large desk defined in Section 2.7 might be defined by:

```
SUBROUTINE DLARGE
REAL XL(5), YL(5)
DATA XL /0.0, 0.0, 0.4, 0.4, 0.0/
DATA YL /0.0, 0.2, 0.2, 0.0, 0.0/
POLYLINE(5, XL, YL)
RETURN
END
```

The large desk is now defined with the origin at the lower left hand corner.

As it appears in many places, this is more sensible than the absolute position defined previously. The polyline defining the large desk could be added to a structure defining the desk and its accessories. Alternatively, the large desk could be defined as a structure:

```
OPEN STRUCTURE(DESK)
DLARGE
CLOSE STRUCTURE
```

There is a danger in proliferating structures unnecessarily as there is quite an overhead in saving and restoring during structure traversal. To simplify the overall structure network in order to make it readable in this book, the desk will be defined as a single polyline as part of a structure defining the large desk and its accessories.

Figure 5.2 shows the accessories that have been defined as separate structures. For simplicity, all have been defined at the required size. To illustrate that this is not necessary, the two instances of the phone in use require the basic components to be scaled for one instance at least. The other components only need to be positioned. The individual components are made up of one or more polylines.

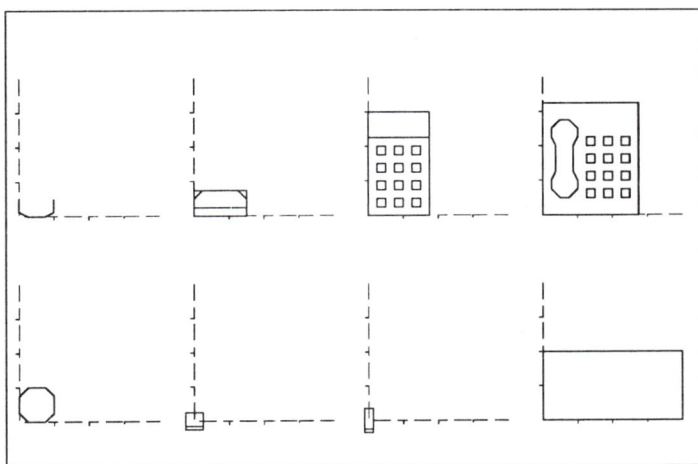

Figure 5.2: *Desk accessories*

The corner and small desks are also positioned at the origin similar to the large desk. The data values in Section 2.7 would be modified by decreasing both X and Y by 0.6 throughout. The origin is, therefore, the bottom left corner of both the small and corner desks. All three desks will appear at the origin by invoking:

```
POLYLINE(5, XL, YL)
POLYLINE(12, XC, YC)
POLYLINE(5, XS, YS)
```

To achieve the desired arrangement, transformations must be applied to the parts.

5.4.4 Transformations

To simplify the description of the transformations, four routines are defined which do specific operations:

```
SUBROUTINE MVRP(DX, DY)
BUILD TRANSFORMATION MATRIX(0, 0, DX, DY, 0, 1, 1, ER, MT)
SET LOCAL TRANSFORMATION(MT, REPLACE)
RETURN
END
```

This routine defines a move of the component relative to the origin. It replaces the current local transformation thus its name of MVRP.

```
SUBROUTINE RTRP(TH)
BUILD TRANSFORMATION MATRIX(0, 0, 0, 0, TH, 1, 1, ER, MT)
SET LOCAL TRANSFORMATION(MT, REPLACE)
RETURN
END
```

This routine defines a rotation of the component about the origin in an anti-clockwise direction. Again, it replaces the current local transformation thus its name, RTRP.

```
SUBROUTINE RTPR(TH)
BUILD TRANSFORMATION MATRIX(0, 0, 0, 0, TH, 1, 1, ER, MT)
SET LOCAL TRANSFORMATION(MT, PRE)
RETURN
END
```

This routine defines a rotation about the origin to occur before any other transformation currently in place, thus its name RTPR (PR for PRE).

```
SUBROUTINE SCPR(S)
BUILD LOCAL TRANSFORMATION MATRIX(0, 0, 0, 0, 0, S, S, ER, MT)
SET LOCAL TRANSFORMATION(MT, PRE)
RETURN
END
```

This routine defines a scaling by S in both X and Y-directions about the origin to occur before any other transformation currently in place, thus its name SCPR.

5.4.5 Define one environment

The aim is to produce the work environment shown in Figure 5.3. This will be done in a set of separate parts.

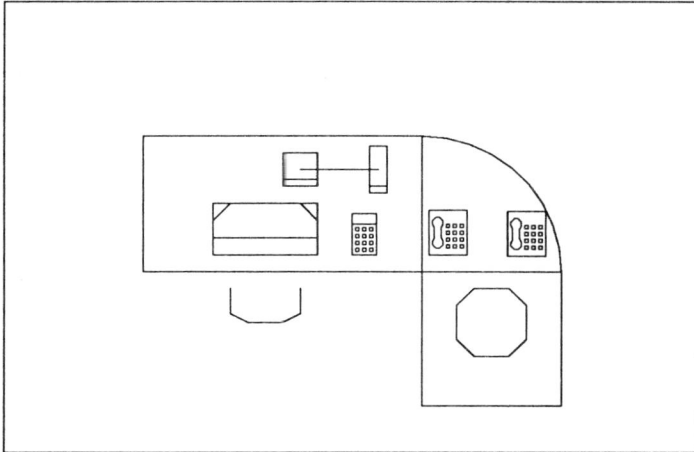

Figure 5.3: *A work environment*

To create the large desk with blotter and calculator requires:

```
OPEN STRUCTURE(LG)

POLYLINE(5, XL, YL)

MVRP(0.1, 0.025)
EXECUTE STRUCTURE(BLOT)

MVRP(0.3, 0.025)
EXECUTE STRUCTURE(CALC)

CLOSE STRUCTURE
```

The structure LG has been defined relative to the coordinates of the large desk. The blotter has been placed on the desk relative to the lower left corner of the desk as has been the calculator. As a result, any global transformation of the desk will also be applied to the blotter and calculator sitting on it.

To define the work environment consisting of the large desk and a chair would require:

```
OPEN STRUCTURE(WKNV)
MVRP(0.2, 0.6)
EXECUTE STRUCTURE(LG)
MVRP(0.325, 0.525)
EXECUTE STRUCTURE(CHAIR)
CLOSE STRUCTURE

POST STRUCTURE(WS, WKNV, PR)
```

To illustrate that the work environment has no obvious origin, the desk and chair have been placed in the unit square coordinate space at the position given before. The structure created is shown in Figure 5.4 and the associated image in Figure 5.5. The abbreviation MVRP denotes the SET LOCAL TRANSFORMATION structure element created by the routine MVRP.

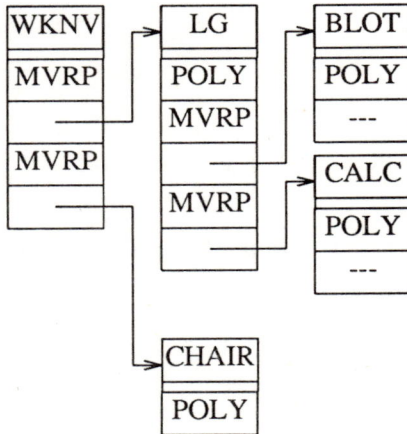

Figure 5.4: *Structure for large desk and chair*

To add the lamp to the desk requires the structure LG to be extended:

```
OPEN STRUCTURE(LG)
MVRP(0.225, 0.15)
EXECUTE STRUCTURE(LMP)
CLOSE STRUCTURE
```

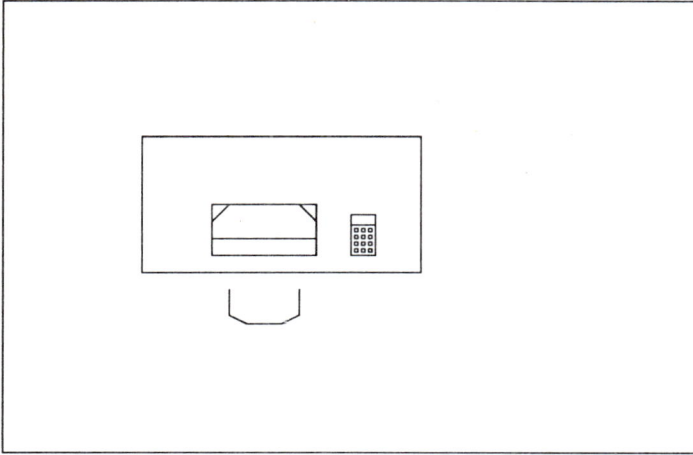

Figure 5.5: *Large desk and chair*

At this stage, the structure LMP has not been defined so a null structure will be created and no change will be made to the display.

The lamp consists of three parts. The base is defined relative to its centre, the arm is defined relative to one end, and the light itself is defined relative to its centre (see Figure 5.2).

To illustrate the concatenation of modelling transformations, the lamp will be defined so that the light itself can rotate about the arm, the arm can rotate about the base, and the base can rotate on the desk:

```
REAL ARMX(2), ARMY(2)

OPEN STRUCTURE(LMP)

RTRP(THBS)
EXECUTE STRUCTURE(LMPB)

RTPR(THAR)
EXECUTE STRUCTURE(ARM)

CLOSE STRUCTURE
ARMX(1)=0
ARMX(2)=LENGTH
ARMY(1)=0
ARMY(2)=0
```

```
OPEN STRUCTURE(ARM)
POLYLINE(2, ARMX, ARMY)
MVRP(ARMX(2), ARMY(2))
RTPR(THLT)
EXECUTE STRUCTURE(LITE)
CLOSE STRUCTURE
```

THBS, THAR and THLT are the rotations to be applied to the base, arm and light respectively. If the structure is traversed, the lamp base is rotated by THBS. The arm is rotated by THAR first and then by THBS so it rotates THAR about the base. The light is rotated by THLT, displaced by the length of the arm, rotated by THAR and then rotated by THBS. Consequently, it rotates around the end of the arm and rotates as the arm and base rotate. The structure network for the environment with the lamp on the desk is illustrated in Figure 5.6.

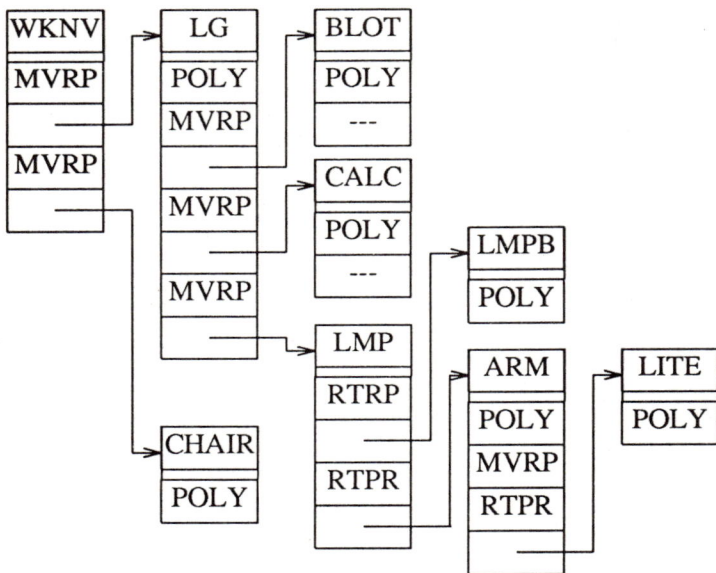

Figure 5.6: *Desk with lamp structure*

To define the complete desk, the number of hierarchy levels defined so far is probably not the best. The environment has been defined as the chair and large desk. It would have been more sensible to define the environment as the chair and complete desk where the complete desk is defined as the large, corner and small desks and so on:

```
OPEN STRUCTURE(WKNV)
MVRP(0.2, 0.6)
EXECUTE STRUCTURE(DESK)
MVRP(0.325, 0.525)
EXECUTE STRUCTURE(CHAIR)
CLOSE STRUCTURE
```

The following defines the structure DESK:

```
OPEN STRUCTURE(DESK)
EXECUTE STRUCTURE(LG)
MVRP(0.4, 0.0)
EXECUTE STRUCTURE(CN)
MVRP(0.4, −0.2)
EXECUTE STRUCTURE(SM)
CLOSE STRUCTURE
```

As neither CN or SM have been defined, the display at the workstation will be as before. Note that the corner and small desks have been defined with a displacement relative to the origin of the large desk. By choosing the contents of the structures carefully, the display can be broken down into manageable parts using local coordinates. The corner and small desks can now be defined with their contents relative to the origin of the particular desk.

```
OPEN STRUCTURE(CN)
POLYLINE(12, XC, YC)
MVRP(0.01, 0.025)
EXECUTE STRUCTURE(PHON)
MVRP(0.123, 0.023)
EXECUTE STRUCTURE(PHON)
CLOSE STRUCTURE
```

```
OPEN STRUCTURE(SM)
POLYLINE(5, XS, YS)
MVRP(0.05, 0.075)
EXECUTE STRUCTURE(INLY)
CLOSE STRUCTURE
```

The complete structure network is shown in Figure 5.7 and the resulting picture in Figure 5.8. The phone has not been scaled to simplify the example. After the MVRP, a SCPR function invocation would have scaled the phone appropriately if it was the wrong size. The example has been constrained to 4 hierarchical levels and one more would have been needed at least for the complete office layout.

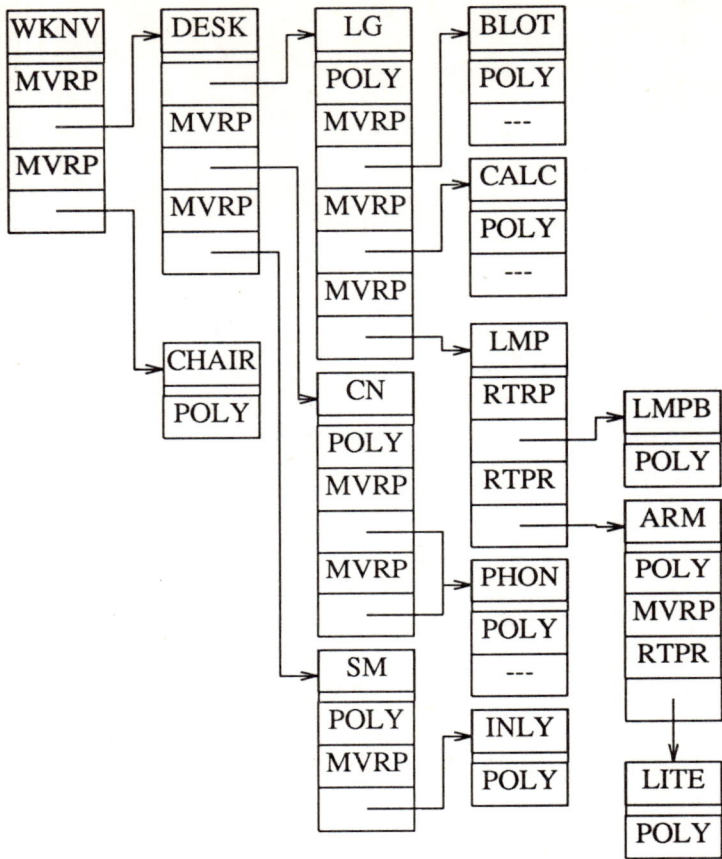

Figure 5.7: *Complete structure network for desk*

The structure has been arranged in levels starting from the complete environment. This is made up of two distinct items, the desk and chair, positioned independently in the environment. The complete desk is made up of three parts defined at the next level down. The next level defines the accessories on the desk. The most complex object, the lamp, has another two levels of hierarchy. As can be seen, quite simple scenes require significant networks. A detailed schematic of a complex object could require between 10 and 20 levels with 2000 structures involved. Care should be taken in ensuring that the inter-relationship of objects and the parts making up them are specified prior to programming the application. A badly defined structure hierarchy will be difficult to debug and difficult to change.

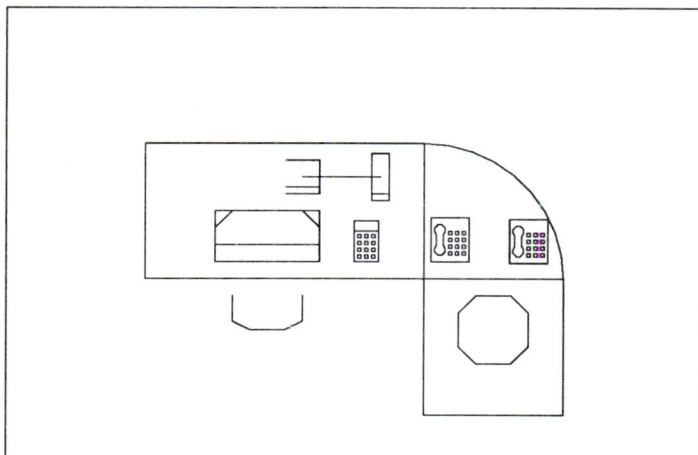

Figure 5.8: *Complete desk*

To reposition the lamp on the desk would require the relevant structures to be modified. The two structures in question are LMP and ARM. The former contains the structure elements that rotate the base and the arm while the latter defines the rotation of the light itself.

The relevant edits to change the orientation of the base, arm and light require the values of THBS, THAR or THLT to be changed. Given the new values, the required edit to change all three is:

```
SET EDIT MODE(REPLACE)
OPEN STRUCTURE(LMP)
SET ELEMENT POINTER(1)
RTRP(THBS)
SET ELEMENT POINTER(3)
RTPR(THAR)
CLOSE STRUCTURE

OPEN STRUCTURE(ARM)
SET ELEMENT POINTER(3)
RTPR(THLT)
CLOSE STRUCTURE
```

It is quite appropriate to use absolute edits in replace mode as the element positions do not change. If this set of commands were repeated in a loop, with different values to the parameters, the lamp could be animated to rotate. Figure 5.9 shows the position of the lamp if THBS was 0.4π, THAR was 0.3π and THLT was 0.5π.

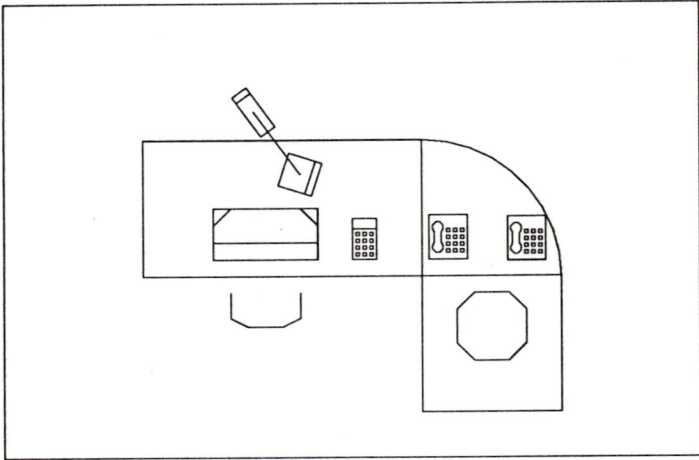

Figure 5.9: *Desk with lamp rotated*

5.5 GLOBAL TRANSFORMATION RESETTING

So far, the global modelling transformation has been defined as the composition of all the modelling transformations defined prior to the execution of the current structure.

In the structure network defined in Figure 5.7, the global modelling transformation applied to the ARM of the light is:

(1) *WKNV*: a move of (0.2, 0.6);

(2) *DESK*: no additional transformation;

(3) *LG*: a move of (0.225, 0.15);

(4) *LMP*: a rotation of THBS with a pre-multiplication of a rotation by THAR.

It is possible that at this stage of the hierarchy, some graphical output is required which has an intrinsic connection to the object being displayed but for which the current global modelling transformation is inappropriate. For example, suppose a dial is required to indicate the amount of rotation to be applied to the light itself. The dial is to be displayed at a fixed position on the display and should only be there if the lamp is part of the accessories on the desk (see Figure 5.10).

PHIGS provides the function:

SET GLOBAL TRANSFORMATION(MT)

This replaces the current global modelling transformation by MT. To place the dial in the top right hand corner, the structure ARM defined in Section

5.4.5 could be extended as shown in the program following.

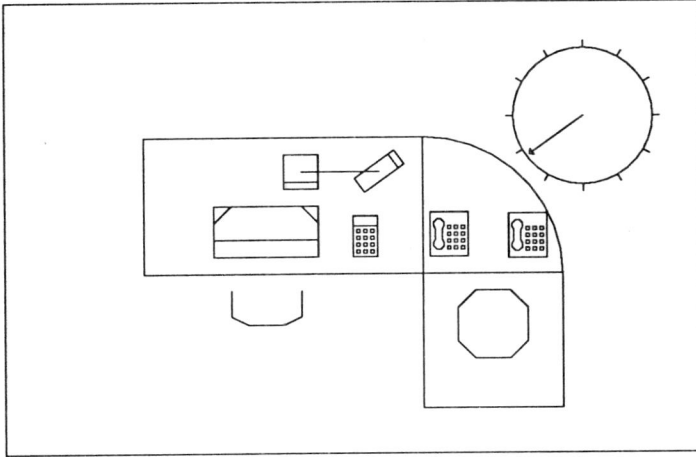

Figure 5.10: *Lamp with associated dial*

```
OPEN STRUCTURE(ARM)
BUILD TRANSFORMATION MATRIX(0, 0, 0.83, 0.83, 0, 1, 1, ER, MT)
SET GLOBAL TRANSFORMATION(MT)
MVRP(0, 0)

DO 10 I=1, 37
DIALX(I)=0.1*COS(PI*(I-1)/18)
DIALY(I)=0.1*SIN(PI*(I-1)/18)
10       CONTINUE

POLYLINE(37, DIALX, DIALY)


DO 20 I=1, 37, 3
TICKX(1)=0.1*COS(PI*(I-1)/18)
TICKY(1)=0.1*SIN(PI*(I-1)/18)
TICKX(2)=0.11*COS(PI*(I-1)/18)
TICKY(2)=0.11*SIN(PI*(I-1)/18)
POLYLINE(2, TICKX, TICKY)
20       CONTINUE
```

RTPR(THLT)
DRAW POINTER
CLOSE STRUCTURE

The global modelling transformation is replaced by a move to the point (0.83, 0.83) which is to be the centre of the dial. The local modelling transformation is reset to the identity matrix by the MVRP function. The dial is then produced centred on the position defined by the global modelling transformation. Finally, the pointer defined by DRAW POINTER is drawn. This is a vertical arrow centred on the origin which will be rotated by THLT, the local modelling transformation defined by RTPR. THLT will be set to the same value that is used to rotate the light. The result is shown in Figure 5.10.

5.6 UTILITY FUNCTIONS

The local and global modelling transformations defined so far have been created using the BUILD TRANSFORMATION MATRIX function. This is an all embracing function. Some simpler functions (MVRP, RTRP, RTPR, SCPR) have been defined in Section 5.4.4 which provide only one of the transformations shift, rotate or scale and create a SET LOCAL TRANSFORMATION structure element. Whether it is replacing the existing matrix is defined by the last two letters. RP for replace and PR for pre-multiply.

PHIGS provides a number of additional utility functions similar to these functions. These are:

TRANSLATE(DX, DY, ER, MT)

This creates a matrix MT that defines a translation by (DX, DY).

SCALE(SX, SY, ER, MT)

This creates a matrix MT that defines a scaling relative to the current origin.

ROTATE(TH, ER, MT)

This creates a matrix MT that defines a rotation of TH radians anti-clockwise about the current origin.

These three functions are similar to the ones defined earlier but the major difference is that they do not create structure elements. In consequence, they can be used for creating both local and global modelling transformations with pre or post-multiplication or replacing the existing local transformation.

Two further functions are provided to create a new matrix from an existing one:

COMPOSE MATRIX(MTA, MTB, ER, MT)

The composition of matrices is needed if several global modelling transformations are required to be concatenated. The SET GLOBAL TRANSFORMATION function only provides a replace capability. Composition is sometimes needed when the application wishes to keep a record of the composite matrix that is being applied to some part of a structure network. As will be seen in Chapter 10, it is sometimes needed when input positions are returned in world coordinates and the application wishes to find the equivalent modelling coordinate position. The resulting matrix MT consists of MTA × MTB.

COMPOSE TRANSFORMATION MATRIX
(MTA, XF, YF, DX, DY, PHI, SX, SY, ER, MT)

This is exactly equivalent to:

BUILD TRANSFORMATION MATRIX
(XF, YF, DX, DY, PHI, SX, SY, ER, MTB)
COMPOSE MATRIX(MTA, MTB, ER, MT)

5.7 STRUCTURE FUNCTIONS

5.7.1 Introduction

PHIGS provides a number of structure handling operations to allow structures to be manipulated in the central structure store. The functions are similar to the set that would be available in a conventional filestore (renaming, copying etc). However, more care is needed as the structures themselves often contain references to other structures.

5.7.2 Changing the name of a structure

The PHIGS function for changing the name of a structure is:

CHANGE STRUCTURE IDENTIFIER(ORIG, RESLT)

The structure with the name ORIG has it changed to RESLT in the central structure store. There are several uses for this function. For example, a structure network may have been defined that shows a view of a car. Two types of wheels may be available for the car and these are defined in structures WH1 and WH2. The structure describing the car has elements EXECUTE STRUCTURE(WH) to define the wheels. To choose a particular type of wheel, say WH1, would require:

CHANGE STRUCTURE IDENTIFIER(WH1, WH)

The problems that can occur are where WH is already defined and where WH1 is being used in some other structure network. If WH is already defined, the function effectively replaces the old contents of WH by the contents of WH1. If WH1 is in use, a new empty WH1 structure is created. This applies whether the use is a reference to it, whether it has been posted to a workstation, or if it is the open structure. This is just done to ensure that PHIGS does not produce an error in this situation. In practice, care should be taken not to change a structure's name while it is being used.

5.7.3 Changing structure references

The same effect could be achieved by changing all the references to WH to either WH1 or WH2 depending on which type of wheel is required. The function is:

CHANGE STRUCTURE REFERENCES(ORIG, RESLT)

All the EXECUTE STRUCTURE elements in the central structure store that refer to ORIG are changed to RESLT. Any references to RESLT remain unchanged. This means that at a subsequent time it will not be easy to change the references to RESLT back to ORIG if only the set changed are to be reversed.

To change the name of the structure and all references to it, the following function is provided:

CHANGE STRUCTURE IDENTIFIER AND REFERENCES
(ORIG, RESLT)

This is equivalent to invoking the CHANGE STRUCTURE IDENTIFIER function followed by CHANGE STRUCTURE REFERENCES.

5.7.4 Adding elements from another structure

It is possible to use the central structure store as a filestore of useful sequences of structure elements. The structures themselves will never be posted or executed as part of a structure network. Instead, they are used to build other structures. The relevant PHIGS function is:

COPY ALL ELEMENTS FROM STRUCTURE(SI)

All the elements of SI are added to the open structure at the element pointer position. By copying templates and editing them, specific structures can be constructed from the parts. Care must be taken if the structure SI contains modelling transformation elements. The effect in this case may be different from executing structure SI even when no changes are made due to the nesting of local transformations. It is even possible to copy the open structure in which case the structure will have its contents copied into itself. For example:

```
        XA(1)=0
        YA(1)=0
        XA(2)=LENGTH
        YA(2)=0
        OPEN STRUCTURE(SI)
        RTPR(0.1*PI)
        POLYLINE(2, XA, YA)

        DO 10 I=1,4
        COPY ALL ELEMENTS FROM STRUCTURE(SI)
10      CONTINUE
        CLOSE STRUCTURE
```

The resulting structure will consist of 16 lines of length LENGTH radiating from the origin and rotated by 0.1π from each other.

5.7.5 Deleting structures

The simplest function available in PHIGS for deleting structures is:

DELETE STRUCTURE(SI)

which deletes the structure SI and all references to it are removed. If it is posted to a workstation, it will be unposted. If it is the open structure, it will remain the open structure but its contents will be removed. This means that the sequence numbers of elements in other structures may change including possibly the open structure. In this latter case, the element pointer is adjusted to point at the same element it was pointing at before the deletion unless it happens to be an EXECUTE STRUCTURE element with the deleted structure as parameter. In this case, the element pointer is moved to point at the element before this one.

To delete a structure network:

DELETE STRUCTURE NETWORK(SI, FLAG)

If FLAG is set to DELETE, the structure SI and all the structures that it EXECUTEs are deleted. For example, the structure network in Figure 5.7 would be completely deleted by:

DELETE STRUCTURE(WKNV, DELETE)

If FLAG is set to KEEP, the same would happen unless the structures in the network were referenced elsewhere. Consequently, if the complete office environment had other references to the items on the desk, deleting WKNV would not delete the structures such as PHON.

To completely clear out the central structure store, PHIGS provides:

DELETE ALL STRUCTURES

This ensures that no structures are inadvertently left in the store. As structures can be archived (see Chapter 14), this may be a sensible function to invoke before starting a separate task in an application.

5.7.6 Emptying structures

The DELETE STRUCTURE function makes changes to any structure that has EXECUTE elements invoking the structure to be deleted. A less severe command which removes the elements in the structure but leaves all the pointers to it intact is:

EMPTY STRUCTURE(SI)

It is as though all the elements in the structure had been deleted by structure editing.

5.8 MODELLING CLIP

5.8.1 Introduction

So far, it has been assumed that the scene created by the traversal of a structure network will be viewed in its entirety. The viewing process may suppress some parts of the scene so that the picture to be displayed is not the complete scene. During structure traversal, it is also possible to remove parts of the output primitives generated so that the scene to be viewed does not contain all of the output primitives generated. This is achieved by a *modelling clip*.

In PHIGS, structure elements can be defined that specify a clip to be performed on all subsequent output primitives once the clip is enabled. The traversal state list contains two entries, the current *modelling clipping volume* and a *modelling clipping indicator*. As output primitives are created on traversal, if the indicator is set to clipping being enabled, the parts of primitives outside the clipping volume will be removed and will not be part of the scene created. During structure traversal, it is possible to change the modelling clipping volume and to set the modelling clipping indicator to clip or not at any time.

5.8.2 The function

The function that defines the extent of a clip is:

SET MODELLING CLIPPING VOLUME(OP, N, HLFSPA)

At the start of structure traversal the modelling clipping volume is infinite, that is no part of the scene will be clipped even if clipping is enabled. The occurrence of this structure element on traversal will change the clipping volume depending on the value of the first parameter OP:

(1) *REPLACE* : if OP is specified as REPLACE, the clipping volume defined by this structure element will replace the current clipping volume.

(2) *INTERSECT* : if OP is set to INTERSECT, the new modelling clipping volume will be the intersection of the current clipping volume with the clipping volume specified by this structure element. The new clipping volume cannot be larger than the previous one. That is anything that would have been clipped by the old clipping volume will continue to be clipped and anything clipped by the new clipping volume just defined will also be clipped.

The modelling clipping volume is specified by a set of half-spaces. The third parameter is an array of N entries where each one defines a half-space. The half-space is defined by a point on its boundary and the *normal* to the half-space in the direction of the clipped part of space. The second parameter, N, defines the number of half-spaces.

The third parameter has entries:

HLFSPA(1,I)=X
HLFSPA(2,I)=Y
HLFSPA(3,I)=DX
HLFSPA(4,I)=DY

where I specifies the definition of the Ith half-space. The point on the boundary is (X, Y) and the normal is the vector from (X,Y) to (X+DX, Y+DY).

The function that enables or stops clipping is:

SET MODELLING CLIPPING INDICATOR(MCLIPI)

When structure traversal starts, the entry in the traversal state list is set to NOCLIP. On traversal, this function will reset the current value of this entry to CLIP or NOCLIP depending on the value of MCLIPI.

When an EXECUTE STRUCTURE element is encountered during structure traversal, the *child* structure to be traversed inherits the current value of the modelling clipping volume and clipping indicator in the same way as other values in the traversal state list are inherited. These values are restored when the traversal of the child structure is complete.

A function is provided to allow the modelling clipping volume inherited by a structure to be restored after it has been changed in the traversal of the child structure. The function is:

RESTORE MODELLING CLIPPING VOLUME

The current value of the modelling clipping volume is replaced by the one in existence when traversal of this child structure started.

5.8.3 A window clip

A simple example of the modelling clip in use would be to define a window (XMIN, XMAX, YMIN, YMAX) within which the scene remains and the outside of which is clipped away.

If the structure in Figure 5.7 is to be modified so that the scene displayed in Figure 5.8 is to be constrained, the WKNV structure would be changed by editing as follows:

```
OPEN STRUCTURE(WKNV)

SET ELEMENT POINTER(0)
SET MODELLING CLIPPING INDICATOR(CLIP)

HLFSPA(1,1)=XMIN
HLFSPA(2,1)=0
HLFSPA(3,1)=0
HLFSPA(4,1)=-1

HLFSPA(1,2)=XMAX
HLFSPA(2,2)=0
HLFSPA(3,2)=0
HLFSPA(4,2)=1

HLFSPA(1,3)=0
HLFSPA(2,3)=YMIN
HLFSPA(3,3)=-1
HLFSPA(4,3)=0
```

```
HLFSPA(1,4)=0
HLFSPA(2,4)=YMAX
HLFSPA(3,4)=1
HLFSPA(4,4)=0
```

```
SET MODELLING CLIPPING VOLUME(REPLACE, 4, HLFSPA)
CLOSE STRUCTURE
```

An example of the result is shown in Figure 5.11.

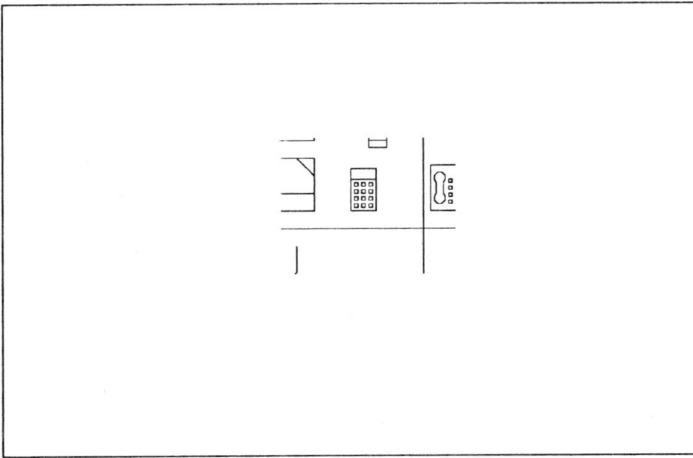

Figure 5.11: *Modelling clip*

5.8.4 Shielding

Currently, it is difficult to do the reverse operation of *shielding* in PHIGS. That is to define a volume within which clipping is to occur and outside of which it is not to occur. Although facilities for doing this were proposed during the standardization of PHIGS, they were not included as part of the standard in its final form.

On a monochrome bit-map display, it can be achieved by:

```
DELETE STRUCTURE(WKNV)
OPEN STRUCTURE(WKNV)
SET MODELLING CLIPPING INDICATOR(CLIP)
```

```
HLFSPA(1, 1)=XMIN
HLFSPA(2, 1)=0
HLFSPA(3,1)=0
HLFSPA(4, 1)=1


SET MODELLING CLIPPING VOLUME(REPLACE, 1, HLFSPA)
MVRP(0.2, 0.6)
EXECUTE STRUCTURE(DESK)


HLFSPA(1, 1)=XMAX
HLFSPA(4, 1)=−1
SET MODELLING CLIPPING VOLUME(REPLACE, 1, HLFSPA)
MVRP(0.2, 0.6)
EXECUTE STRUCTURE(DESK)


HLFSPA(1, 1)=0
HLFSPA(2, 1)=YMIN
HLFSPA(3, 1)=1
HLFSPA(4, 1)=0


SET MODELLING CLIPPING VOLUME(REPLACE, 1, HLFSPA)
MVRP(0.2, 0.6)
EXECUTE STRUCTURE(DESK)


HLFSPA(2, 1)=YMAX
HLFSPA(3, 1)=−1
SET MODELLING CLIPPING VOLUME(REPLACE, 1, HLFSPA)
MVRP(0.2, 0.6)
EXECUTE STRUCTURE(DESK)
CLOSE STRUCTURE
POST STRUCTURE(WS, WKENV, 0.2)
```

This is a cumbersome way of achieving the effect but it does indicate that careful use of the modelling clipping volume can produce a range of effects. The picture is drawn with everything above the bottom boundary of the shield clipped followed by drawing the picture again with everything below the top boundary clipped. This gives the top part and bottom part of the picture. The picture is drawn a third time with everything drawn to the right of the left hand shield boundary clipped and finally it is drawn a fourth time with everything to the left of the right hand boundary clipped. This generates the picture shown in Figure 5.12. The four corners have been drawn twice but as it is a monochrome display with a single bit per pixel, this will not be noticeable!

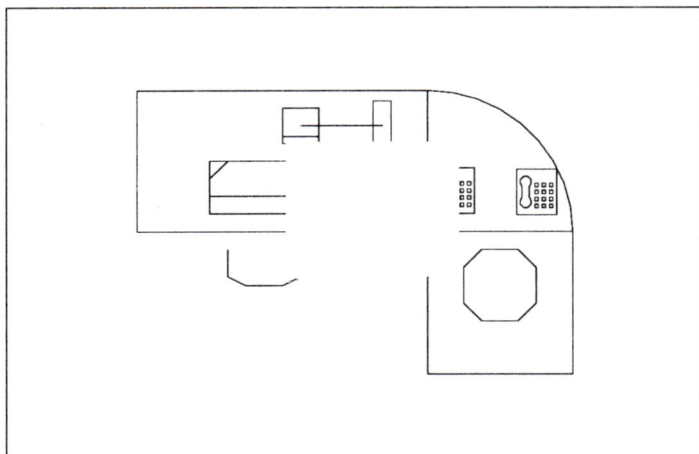

Figure 5.12: *Four modelling clips producing a shield*

5.9 APPLICATION DATA

The following function is provided in PHIGS to relate the PHIGS structure store to any application database associated with the application:

APPLICATION DATA(LDR, DATREC)

On traversal, this structure element has no effect (just like label elements). Its use is mainly to provide additional information relevant to the application. Section 10.2.4 gives the format of the data record. A frequent use is to store pointers in the central structure store that point to the equivalent parts of the application database.

5.10 GENERALIZED STRUCTURE ELEMENT

Just as the generalized drawing primitive extends the output primitive structure elements in an unspecified way, the function:

GENERALIZED STRUCTURE ELEMENT(GSEID, LDR, DATREC)

defines an element of type GSEID. Its usage is undefined. It provides a mechanism for implementations to define non-standard activities. The local implementation manual needs to be consulted to see what, if any, values of the function have been defined.

6 VIEWING IN 2D

6.1 INTRODUCTION

In Chapter 5, the desk and its accessories were defined in modelling coordinates which, on traversal, generated a display with coordinates in the range 0 to 1 in the X and Y-directions. PHIGS guarantees that the defaults set by the system will ensure that this unit square will be visible on the display. In this Chapter, the viewing facilities in PHIGS will be described which allow the application to choose an appropriate coordinate system and orientation for the description of the scene to be viewed. PHIGS allows the application to control how the scene is mapped down to the unit square so that it can be displayed.

PHIGS is primarily a 3D system with a 2D subset. The form of viewing in PHIGS is defined with the functionality required for 3D. The 2D viewing is kept as similar to the 3D as possible. Consequently, the 2D viewing is not as elegant as it might be but it includes additional functionality not normally present in a straightforward 2D system.

The 2D functionality will be described first as it provides a good introduction to the concepts used in the more complex 3D viewing and completes the description of the 2D functionality before tackling the 3D.

6.2 VIEWING

Viewing in PHIGS can be split into two separate sections. The first takes a PHIGS structure that is to be traversed and describes how it is to be mapped onto a device independent coordinate space called *Normalized Projection Coordinates (NPC)*. PHIGS guarantees that it is possible to display on a device the part of NPC space in the range 0 to 1 in the X and Y-directions. The second section of viewing is to take the *picture* defined in NPC space and describe where it is to be positioned on the display of the device or on the sheet of paper.

In this Chapter, the first section of viewing will be described which produces the NPC picture. The term *scene* is used to describe the graphics produced by the structure traversal and *picture* to describe the parts of the scene, converted to NPC coordinates, that are available for display.

The viewing process which maps the scene to the picture has 4 main components:

(1) *Partition by view index*: the scene to be displayed may consist of a number of separate parts some of which may be magnified or have different viewing characteristics from the rest. PHIGS allows an attribute called the *view index* to be associated with the graphics primitives generated on structure traversal. This is used to differentiate the parts of a scene.

(2) *Orientate the view*: for each part of the scene differentiated by a view index, the application may redefine the origin and orientation of the world coordinate system. This new coordinate system is called the *View Reference Coordinate* (VRC) system. It should be defined such that it is the most appropriate for the view mapping.

(3) *Map to NPC*: define the window to viewport mapping that maps part of a scene defined by a specific view index from its description in VRC coordinates to one in NPC.

(4) *Clip*: decide whether the resulting NPC picture part should be clipped against a specified boundary defined in NPC coordinates. This can be distinct from the viewport used in the window to viewport mapping.

View Indices in PHIGS play a similar role to Normalization Transformations in GKS. They give the application the ability to compose a picture in the NPC space out of a set of distinct parts. Similar to GKS, PHIGS has a default setting of view index which is 0 and the view associated with view index 0 cannot be changed. For view index 0, both orientation and mapping are identity matrices with clipping set at the boundary of the unit square. This is why the examples so far have all worked as long as the output has been constrained to the unit square in world coordinates. Effectively, WC, VRC and NPC are the same coordinate system. That is, the position (X,Y) in each coordinate system represents the same point in the graphics to be displayed. A major difference between the viewing function in GKS and PHIGS is that in PHIGS the mapping from world to NPC coordinates can be defined differently for each workstation.

6.3 VIEW INDEX

The view index attribute is defined by a structure element:

    SET VIEW INDEX(I)

On traversal, all subsequent output primitives generated have view index I associated with them until the view index attribute is changed by another SET VIEW INDEX element. The current value of view index is stored in the traversal state list. The initial default value is 0. For example:

```
OPEN STRUCTURE(ENV)
POLYLINE(5, XA, YA)
SET VIEW INDEX(1)
EXECUTE STRUCTURE(DESK)
SET VIEW INDEX(2)
EXECUTE STRUCTURE(DESK)
CLOSE STRUCTURE
```

will, on traversal, define a polyline to be viewed using the default view 0 and two views of the same desk. How they will appear in the NPC picture will depend on the definition of the views set up for view index 1 and 2.

6.4 METRIC DESK

The desk defined previously could be redefined using a more realistic coordinate system, say metres:

```
SUBROUTINE DLARGE
REAL XL(5), YL(5)
DATA XL / 0, 0, 2, 2, 0 /
DATA YL / 0, 1, 1, 0, 0 /
POLYLINE(5, XL, YL)
RETURN
END
```

This defines a desk 2 metres long and 1 metre across with the origin at the bottom left corner.

The corner desk defined previously could also be redefined as:

```
SUBROUTINE DCORNR
REAL XC(12), YC(12)
REAL PI
INTEGER I
XC(1)=0
YC(1)=0
XC(2)=0
YC(2)=1
PI=4*ATAN(1.0)
DO 50 I=3,10
XC(I)=COS((11-I)*PI/18)
YC(I)=SIN((11-I)*PI/18)
50    CONTINUE
```

```
XC(11)=1
YC(11)=0
XC(12)=0
YC(12)=0
POLYLINE(12, XC, YC)
RETURN
END
```

This is a desk with 1 metre radius. The complete desk could be defined by:

```
OPEN STRUCTURE(DESK)
DLARGE
MVRP(2, 0)
DCORNR
MVRP(2, −1)
BUILD LOCAL TRANSFORMATION(0, 0, 0, 0, 0, 0.5, 1, ER, MT)
SET LOCAL TRANSFORMATION(MT, PRE)
DLARGE
CLOSE STRUCTURE
```

The small desk has been defined as an asymmetrically scaled version of the large desk where the X-dimension has been halved giving a metre square desk.

The individual pieces of the desk have been defined in their own coordinate systems (modelling coordinates). On traversal, the complete desk produced is defined in World Coordinates (WC) which extends from 0 to 3 metres in the X-direction and −1 to 1 metres in the Y-direction as the origin is at the bottom left corner of the large desk. The various desk accessories could also be defined and scaled to fit on the desk as before.

6.5 VIEW ORIENTATION

View Orientation is specified in PHIGS by a 3×3 homogeneous matrix similar to the modelling transformations specified using BUILD TRANSFORMATION MATRIX. A special utility function is provided specifically to define the View Orientation Matrix:

EVALUATE VIEW ORIENTATION MATRIX
(VRPX, VRPY, VUPDX, VUPDY, ER, VOM)

The aim of view orientation is to change the origin and orientation of the world coordinate scene to be viewed to one more appropriate for the mapping to NPC coordinates. The point (VRPX,VRPY) defines the new origin to be used and (VUPDX,VUPDY) is a vector from (VRPX,VRPY) that specifies the new Y-direction of the axes. The function builds the matrix

VOM that performs this change of origin and orientation. The parameter ER is set to 0 if a matrix has been built successfully or to a non-zero error value otherwise.

In the example above, it may be desired to view the desk, which extends from 0 to 3 metres in the X-direction and −1 to 1 metres in the Y-direction, at an angle of rotation about the centre point. To do this conveniently would require the origin to be moved to the point (1.5,0). By specifying the Y-axis as a vector from this point of dimension (1,1), this would define the Y-axis as being in the direction from (1.5,0) to (2.5,1). Effectively the desk is rotated by 45° anti-clockwise to the initial origin. Note that the up direction could equally well have been defined by the vector (2,2), the direction remains the same.

To produce the desired change of orientation requires:

EVALUATE VIEW ORIENTATION MATRIX(1.5, 0, 1, 1, ER, VOM)

A mistake often made is to take (VUPDX,VUPDY) to mean an absolute position rather than a vector direction.

Although changing the orientation angle is provided mainly to allow the viewing of 3D objects from different angles, it can be equally effective in the 2D area.

6.6 VIEW MAPPING

Once the view reference coordinates have been established, the mapping to NPC space needs to be defined. Again, a specific utility function is provided to construct the 3×3 homogeneous view mapping matrix:

EVALUATE VIEW MAPPING MATRIX(WL, PVL, ER, VMM)

WL defines the X and Y-limits of an area in view reference coordinates (called the window) to be mapped onto the area defined by the X and Y-limits specified in PVL (called the viewport) in NPC coordinates. The limits are specified in the order XMIN, XMAX, YMIN, YMAX.

If the desk defined above has its origin moved to the middle, it will extend by 1.5 metres in the X or Y-direction depending on the orientation given. To map this onto the centre part of the NPC unit square would require:

WL(1)=−1.6
WL(2)=1.6
WL(3)=−1.6
WL(4)=1.6

PVL(1)=0.25
PVL(2)=0.75
PVL(3)=0.25
PVL(4)=0.75
EVALUATE VIEW MAPPING MATRIX(WL, PVL, ER, VMM)

As before, the required view mapping matrix is returned in VMM with ER set to 0 if successful otherwise a non-zero error value is returned.

6.7 VIEW DEFINITION AND CLIPPING

So far, the production of the two matrices that define view orientation and view mapping have been described. The definition of the view itself is given by:

SET VIEW REPRESENTATION(WS, VI, VOM, VMM, VC, XYC)

The workstation WS has the view transformation for view index VI defined by the two matrices VOM and VMM generated by the utility functions described above. The view representation is defined by this single function invocation to ensure that intermediate definitions cannot be produced with illegal transformations. As the view representation can be redefined while a structure is posted, the effect occurs as soon as is possible. All that remains is to describe the final two parameters which decide whether clipping should be applied and where.

The parameter VC defines that part of NPC space to clip against. Frequently, the values of the clipping limits VC and the viewport specified by PVL in the function EVALUATE VIEW MAPPING MATRIX are identical. However, this is not essential and in some applications it is necessary to separate the definition of the window/viewport mapping which defines the coordinate transformation from the clipping limits themselves. Although the parameter VC defines the clipping region, it does not specify that it is operative. The final parameter XYC can be set to CLIP or NOCLIP and specifies whether the clipping limits VC have any effect.

To clip the desk defined above so that only the part between 0.4 and 0.6 were visible would require:

VC(1)=0.4
VC(2)=0.6
VC(3)=0.4
VC(4)=0.6
XYC=CLIP
SET VIEW REPRESENTATION(WS, VI, VOM, VMM, VC, XYC)

6.8 A COMPLETE EXAMPLE

Let us assume that the desk with its 3 parts has been defined in metres with all the accessories placed on it. Suppose a view of the complete desk is required at some angle of rotation and, at the same time, a detail of a part of the desk is required. To delineate the two views a boundary round each view is drawn. An example of the overall picture is shown in Figure 6.1. The desk has been displayed without rotation and the detail is of the phone on the left side of the corner desk.

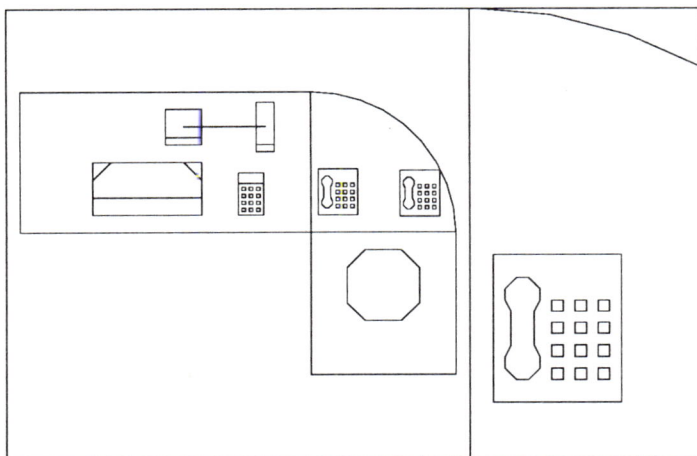

Figure 6.1: *Two views of desk*

View index 0, the default view, could be used to specify the boundary around the two separate views of the desk:

```
REAL AX(8), AY(8)
DATA AX / 0.666, 0, 0, 0.666, 0.666, 1, 1, 0.666 /
DATA AY / 1, 1, 0.333, 0.333, 1, 1, 0.333, 0.333 /
OPEN STRUCTURE(ENV)
POLYLINE(8, XA, YA)
SET VIEW INDEX(1)
EXECUTE STRUCTURE(DESK)
SET VIEW INDEX(2)
EXECUTE STRUCTURE(DESK)
CLOSE STRUCTURE
```

The polyline defines the two areas in NPC space as the square from (0,0.333) to (0.666,1) and the rectangle from (0.666,0.333) to (1,1). Before

posting the structure ENV, the two views 1 and 2 need to be defined otherwise the default view which is the same as view 0 will be used:

```
EVALUATE VIEW ORIENTATION MATRIX(1.5, 0, VUPDX, VUPDY, ER, VOM1)
WL1(1)=-1.6
WL1(2)=1.6
WL1(3)=-1.6
WL1(4)=1.6
PVL1(1)=0
PVL1(2)=0.666
PVL1(3)=0.333
PVL1(4)=1
EVALUATE VIEW MAPPING MATRIX(WL1, PVL1, ER, VMM1)

VC1(1)=0
VC1(2)=0.666
VC1(3)=0.333
VC1(4)=1
XYC1=CLIP
SET VIEW REPRESENTATION(WS, 1, VOM1, VMM1, VC1, XYC1)
```

This defines the first view in the left top square of the NPC space. The
orientation of the desk will depend on the values of VUPDX and VUPDY.
If VUPDX=0 and VUPDY=1, the desk will not be rotated. The clipping
rectangle is initially defined so that the clipping boundary coincides with
the limits of the viewport. As the window is defined greater than the boundary of the desk, all the desk should be visible in this viewport.

In the rectangular area to the right, a detail of the desk at normal orientation is to be displayed. The main item to be focussed on initially is the
left telephone on the corner desk so the origin is placed at the bottom left of
the corner desk and the orientation is with the Y-axis vertical:

```
EVALUATE VIEW ORIENTATION MATRIX(2, 0, 0, 1, ER, VOM2)
WL2(1)=0
WL2(2)=0.5
WL2(3)=0
WL2(4)=H
PVL2(1)=0.666
PVL2(2)=1
PVL2(3)=0.333
PVL2(4)=1
EVALUATE VIEW MAPPING MATRIX(WL2, PVL2, ER, VMM2)
```

VC2(1)=0.666
VC2(2)=1
VC2(3)=0.333
VC2(4)=1
XYC2=CLIP
SET VIEW REPRESENTATION(WS, 2, VOM2, VMM2, VC2, XYC2)

POST STRUCTURE(WS, ENV, 0.2)

With the value of H set to 1, the aspect ratio in the right area (1:2) is the same for both the window in view reference coordinates and the viewport in normalized projection coordinates giving a picture as in Figure 6.1.

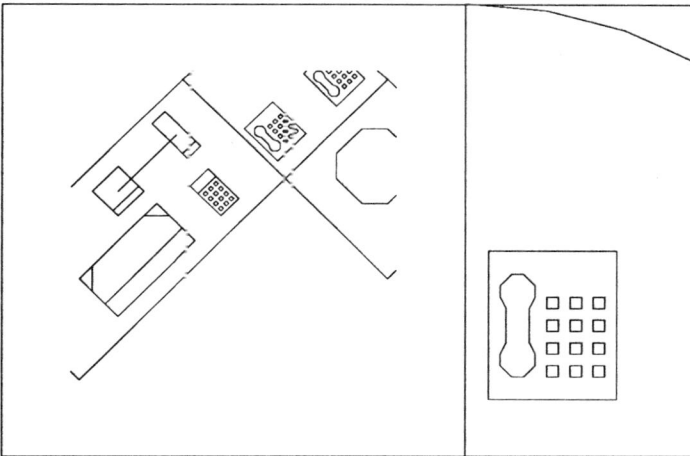

Figure 6.2: *Changed orientation in first view*

If the values of (VUPDX,VUPDY) are set to (1,1), the orientation of the desk in view 1 would be rotated by 45° anti-clockwise. If the clipping limits for view 1 were reset to (0.1,0.566,0.433,0.9), the result would be as in Figure 6.2. If H is changed to 0.5, the aspect ratio is changed in the viewing transformation giving the picture in Figure 6.3.

This type of display is often used in computer aided design when the operator requires to manipulate the complete scene while still having a detailed view of the particular part currently being defined. As will be seen in Chapter 10, it is possible for the application to allow the operator to interact with the display in either of the two regions

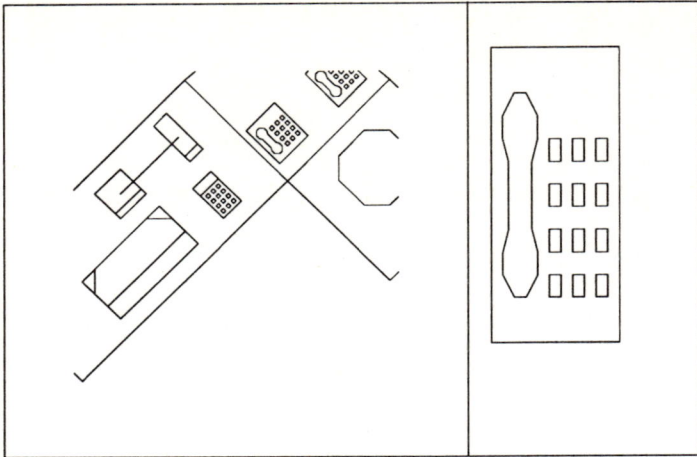

Figure 6.3: *Changing aspect ratio*

This emphasizes the point that the viewing transformation can change the aspect ratio in the transformation from world coordinates to NPC coordinates and this can be set differently for each view.

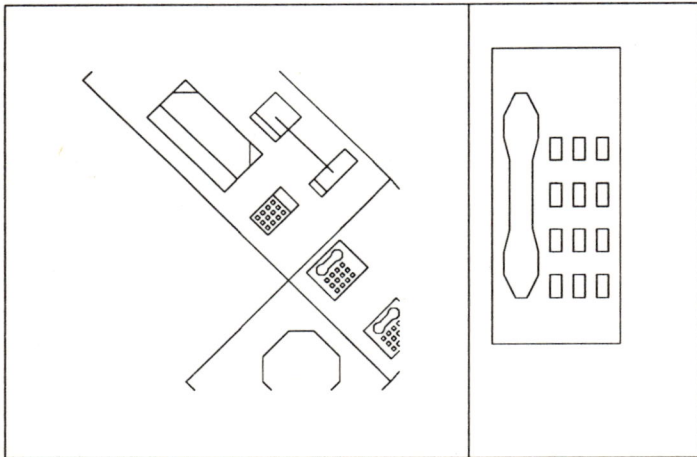

Figure 6.4: *Change rotation in first view*

By changing (VUPDX,VUPDY) to (−1,1), the desk rotation is in the opposite direction in view 1 while retaining the same view in the right area (see Figure 6.4).

This shows the flexibility possible using multiple views in 2 dimensions. The potential uses in 3 dimensions are much greater as it is often only through multiple views that an impression of the scene can be obtained.

7 3D PHIGS

7.1 INTRODUCTION

7.1.1 Relationship to 2D

It is now time to look at the 3D side of PHIGS. The emphasis so far has been on the 2D side partly because some of the features (for example, structures) can equally well be explained in 2D and 3D (with 2D being simpler) but also because PHIGS is an effective standard or system for structured 2D graphics and for applications where the control of output to the workstation is greater than is possible in, say, GKS.

PHIGS is a 3D system. While structure elements can be defined in the 2D form and will be stored as such, traversal in PHIGS only generates 3D primitives. The output primitives described so far are really shorthand notations for the equivalent 3D primitive. Thus, traversing the structure element:

POLYLINE(5, XA, YA)

creates the same output primitive as:

POLYLINE 3(5, XA, YA, ZA)

if ZA(1) to ZA(5) are all equal to 0. In this Chapter, the more complex viewing model for 3D graphics is described. Hopefully, the introduction to viewing via the 2D description in Chapter 6 should make it easier to understand.

7.1.2 Coordinate systems

For 2D graphics, most systems use a coordinate system where the positive X-direction is to the right, and the positive Y-direction is upwards. This convention is generally accepted apart from one or two exceptions mainly related to hardware systems where the image is generated from the top downwards and it is consequently more convenient to have the positive Y-direction being downwards.

In 3 dimensions, the situation is less clear. If positive X increases to the right and positive Y increases upwards, does positive Z increase as you come out of the paper or go into it? Figure 7.1 illustrates the situation where positive Z increases as you come out of the paper. This is called a *right-handed coordinate system.* Holding up the right hand with the thumb as the X-direction, the first finger as the Y-direction, then the second finger defines the positive Z-direction and this has to point towards you. The opposite is the case for the left-handed coordinate system.

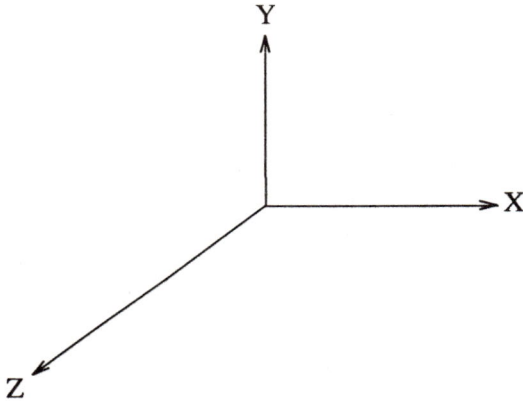

Figure 7.1: *Right-handed coordinate system*

All coordinate systems used by PHIGS are right-handed coordinate systems. This is different from some current practice where a mixture of left and right-handed coordinate systems are used. Consequently, care should be taken when looking at some standard texts. A drawback with right-handed coordinate systems is that the Z=0 plane of the NPC unit cube is the back face. Thus the 2D functions all generate output on the back rather than front face which may be less intuitive in some cases.

Coordinates used by PHIGS in 3 dimensions are normally expressed in a homogeneous form as (X,Y,Z,1). Consequently, transformations in 3D are 4×4 homogeneous matrices. For example, on traversal, the coordinates of a point in modelling coordinates (MCX,MCY,MCZ) are transformed by the current modelling transformation C to give a point in world coordinates (WX,WY,WZ) as follows:

$$
\begin{bmatrix} WCX \\ WCY \\ WCZ \\ WCW \end{bmatrix} = \begin{bmatrix} C_{11} & C_{12} & C_{13} & C_{14} \\ C_{21} & C_{22} & C_{23} & C_{24} \\ C_{31} & C_{32} & C_{33} & C_{34} \\ C_{41} & C_{42} & C_{43} & C_{44} \end{bmatrix} \begin{bmatrix} MCX \\ MCY \\ MCZ \\ 1 \end{bmatrix}
$$

where WX=WCX/WCW, WY=WCY/WCW and WZ=WCZ/WCW.

7.1.3 3D functions

Most of the 3D functions are a simple extension of the equivalent 2D functions. The rule is to add the number 3 to the name of the function, add an additional parameter for the Z-component where a position has been defined by X and Y parameters, extend arrays of 4 elements representing limits of an area to 6 elements representing the limits of a volume, and replace 3 × 3 matrices by 4 × 4. Some examples of the pairs of functions are shown below:

```
POLYLINE(N, XA, YA)
POLYLINE 3(N, XA, YA, ZA)

SET LOCAL TRANSFORMATION(MT2, TYPE)
SET LOCAL TRANSFORMATION 3(MT3, TYPE)

SET GLOBAL TRANSFORMATION(MT2)
SET GLOBAL TRANSFORMATION 3(MT3)

SET MODELLING CLIPPING VOLUME(OP, N, HLFSPA)
SET MODELLING CLIPPING VOLUME 3(OP, N, HLFSPA)
```

MT2 is a 3 × 3 matrix while MT3 is a 4 × 4 matrix. MT2 is a shorthand for MT3. The relationship is:

$$\begin{bmatrix} a & b & c \\ d & e & f \\ g & h & j \end{bmatrix} \rightarrow \begin{bmatrix} a & b & 0 & c \\ d & e & 0 & f \\ 0 & 0 & 1 & 0 \\ g & h & 0 & j \end{bmatrix}$$

In 3D, the modelling clipping volume requires a parameter HLFSPA(6) which has values:

```
HLFSPA(1,I)=X
HLFSPA(2,I)=Y
HLFSPA(3,I)=Z
HLFSPA(4,I)=DX
HLFSPA(5,I)=DY
HLFSPA(6,I)=DZ
```

The point on the boundary is (X,Y,Z) and the normal is from this point to (X+DX, Y+DY, Z+DZ).

7.1.4 Building transformation matrices

The 2D version of BUILD TRANSFORMATION MATRIX (see Section 2.8) is quite simple defining a fixed point and the scale, rotate and shift to apply. In 3D, the situation is more complex as the rotation can be about three axes:

BUILD TRANSFORMATION MATRIX 3
  (XF, YF, ZF, DX, DY, DZ, PHX, PHY, PHZ, SX, SY, SZ, ER, MT3)

The function builds the 4×4 homogeneous matrix, MT3, to be returned to the application. The parameter ER is set to 0 if a matrix has been built successfully, or to a non-zero value otherwise. The transformation built is a mixture of scaling, rotation and shifting. The parameters (XF, YF, ZF) define a fixed point to be used as an origin for scaling and rotation. The parameters (DX, DY, DZ) define the translation to be applied. PHX defines the anti-clockwise rotation in radians to be applied about the X-axis through the fixed point. Similarly, PHY and PHZ define rotations about the Y and Z-axes. The parameters (SX, SY, SZ) scale the coordinates about the fixed point. If all transformations are defined with non-identity transformations, the operations are performed in the order scale, rotate, and shift. The rotations are performed in the order rotate X, rotate Y and rotate Z. The utility functions defined in Section 5.6 in 2D have 3D equivalents:

TRANSLATE 3(DX, DY, DZ, ER, MT3)
SCALE 3(SX, SY, SZ, ER, MT3)
ROTATE X(TH, ER, MT3)
ROTATE Y(TH, ER, MT3)
ROTATE Z(TH, ER, MT3)
COMPOSE MATRIX 3(MTA3, MTB3, ER, MT3)
COMPOSE TRANSFORMATION MATRIX 3(MTA3, XF, YF, ZF,
  DX, DY, DZ, PHX, PHY, PHZ, SX, SY, SZ, ER, MT3)

The meanings of these functions are, in general, obvious assuming the 2D function is known. The three ROTATE functions specify an anti-clockwise rotation about the specified axis.

7.2 VIEWING

7.2.1 Viewing pipeline

The viewing pipeline is shown in Figure 7.2. On structure traversal, output primitives are defined with their coordinates defined in world coordinates. This is the WC Scene. As for 2D, an intermediate coordinate system is defined called View Reference Coordinates (VRC). This coordinate system is a reorientation of the World Coordinate system to one more appropriate for viewing. View mapping is then applied to produce a picture in Normalized Projection Coordinates (NPC).

It is the view mapping operation that is quite different from the 2D case. The scene is effectively projected onto a 2D plane. The device independent picture in NPC coordinates has to be placed on the display of the workstation at the appropriate position possibly with local workstation clipping. That final stage is also shown in Figure 7.2.

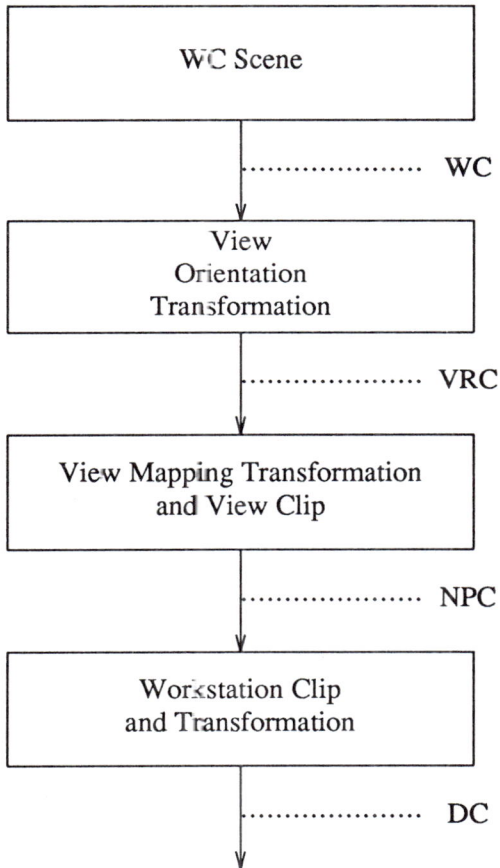

Figure 7.2: *Coordinate transformations in PHIGS*

In this Chapter, the description will concentrate on the view orientation and mapping. View orientation and mapping are the same for both PHIGS and GKS-3D. The model is sufficiently comprehensive to meet most requirements.

7.2.2 View example

To illustrate viewing in 3D, the 2D desk as the standard example will be replaced by the four letters L, E, F and T.

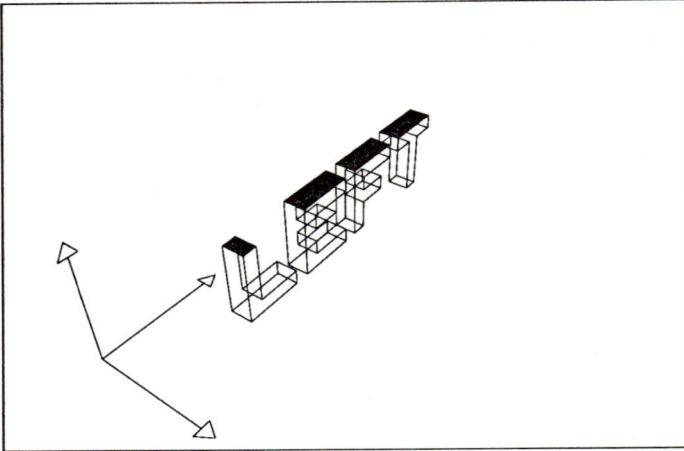

Figure 7.3: *Position of LEFT relative to WC axes*

The world coordinate space in which they sit is centred around the point (50,50,50). The letters are 20 units high, 16 units across and 6 units deep. They are spaced 20 units apart. Consequently, they extend from 10 units to 90 units in the X-direction, 40 to 60 units in the Y-direction and 47 to 53 units in the Z-direction. The data values defining the front faces are:

```
DATA XL / 10, 10, 14, 14, 26, 26, 10 /
DATA YL / 40, 60, 60, 44, 44, 40, 40 /
DATA ZL / 53, 53, 53, 53, 53, 53, 53 /

DATA XE / 30, 30, 46, 46, 34, 34, 42, 42, 34, 34, 46, 46, 30 /
DATA YE / 40, 60, 60, 56, 56, 52, 52, 48, 48, 44, 44, 40, 40 /
DATA ZE / 53, 53, 53, 53, 53, 53, 53, 53, 53, 53, 53, 53, 53 /

DATA XF / 50, 50, 66, 66, 54, 54, 62, 62, 54, 54, 50 /
DATA YF / 40, 60, 60, 56, 56, 52, 52, 48, 48, 40, 40 /
DATA ZF / 53, 53, 53, 53, 53, 53, 53, 53, 53, 53, 53 /

DATA XT / 76, 76, 70, 70, 86, 86, 80, 80, 76 /
DATA YT / 40, 56, 56, 60, 60, 56, 56, 40, 40 /
DATA ZT / 53, 53, 53, 53, 53, 53, 53, 53, 53 /
```

A view of the world coordinate scene with the faces of the letters defined as
fill areas is shown in Figure 7.3. The top face is made solid to improve the
comprehension. At some angles of projection, the wire frame image can be
ambiguous without this.

7.2.3 Viewing model

As the 3D scene has to be represented on a 2D display, the mapping from
3D to 2D has to be chosen to either give a general overall impression of the
scene or to ensure that certain aspects of the scene are retained in the 2D
picture, maybe at the loss of information in other areas.

To produce the 2D picture from the 3D scene, each point of an object
in the scene must be mapped onto a plane. The way this mapping is
accomplished differentiates the type of projection chosen. The projections
used in PHIGS are the standard planar geometric projections. Such a projection of an object is generated by passing lines called *projectors* through
each point of the object and finding where these projectors intersect with a
plane called the *view plane*.

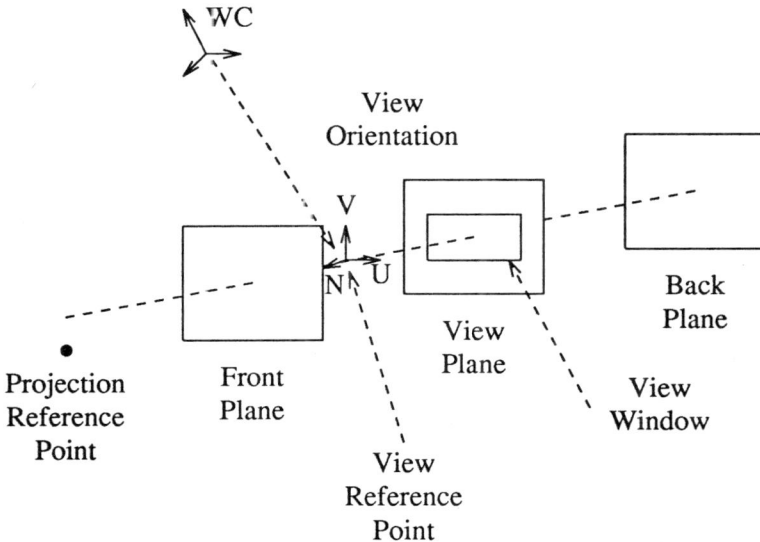

Figure 7.4: *PHIGS viewing model*

The two main types of projection are *perspective* and *parallel*. A perspective projection has all the projectors starting from a single point called the
Projection Reference Point. A parallel projection has all the projectors
parallel, effectively they all start from a point at infinity.

The PHIGS viewing model is shown in Figure 7.4. The basic operations are the same as the 2D operations described in Section 6.2. First, the view is orientated by choosing an appropriate coordinate system from which to do the view mapping. As for 2D, this means defining a new origin called the *View Reference Point* and a new orientation for the axes to establish the view reference coordinates. In 3D, the three axes are labelled U,V and N for historical reasons rather than X, Y and Z. As in 2D, the scene described in view reference coordinates is mapped onto normalized projection coordinates. Whereas in 2D, this is primarily a window to viewport mapping that transforms the VRC scene to a picture in NPC space, in 3D a projective mapping takes place that effectively maps the 3D object into a 2D picture. (This is not completely accurate as the Z-values are retained to allow depth cueing and hidden line or hidden surface elimination to be performed if required. The object is mapped onto the plane but the Z-value is retained.)

The mapping can either be a parallel or a perspective mapping. In either case, a view plane is defined in an X-Y plane of the VRC coordinate system and the scene is projected onto that plane. As for 2D viewing, the definition of the coordinates of the View Window establishes the X,Y-coordinates of the mapping to NPC space. Front and back planes are defined parallel to the view plane which define the Z-coordinates of NPC space. They are also used to limit the part of the scene that can be viewed. Only the unit cube of NPC space can be displayed on a workstation.

Similar to 2D viewing, setting the view representation can also define clipping limits which restrict the part of the NPC space that can appear at the workstation. The X-Y clipping limits are independent of the view window that establishes the NPC coordinates. In the Z-direction, the front and back planes both establish the coordinates in the Z-direction and act as clipping planes.

A projection reference point is defined which orientates the projectors defining the view volume. For perspective projections, all projectors pass through the projection reference point. For parallel projections, all projectors are parallel to the vector joining the projection reference point to the centre of the view window.

7.3 VIEW ORIENTATION

The utility function that defines the view orientation matrix is:

EVALUATE VIEW ORIENTATION MATRIX 3
(VRX, VRY, VRZ, VNX, VNY, VNZ, VUX, VUY, VUZ,
ER, VMM3)

(VRX,VRY,VRZ) defines the origin of the view reference coordinate system called the view reference point. It is usual to define the view reference point as having some connection with the object or scene to be viewed. For example, the centre of the scene or a point on the surface of the main object in the scene. The view plane is defined on the N-axis (remember coordinates in the view reference coordinate system are defined as UVN rather than XYZ). Placing the view reference point in the scene to be viewed gives a much better chance of seeing the object to be viewed! It is all too easy in 3D to define a projection which does not project the object to be viewed onto the view plane! The N or Z-axis of the VRC coordinate system is defined by (VNX,VNY,VNZ) which defines a vector from the view reference point. Similarly, (VUX,VUY,VUZ) is a vector from the view reference point which defines the UP direction, the V or Y-axis. With the V and N-axes defined and, knowing that it is a right-handed coordinate system, this effectively defines the U or X-axis also. If the view orientation is well defined, the function returns a 4 × 4 matrix, VMM3, and the parameter ER is set to 0. A non-zero value returned in ER indicates that the matrix could not be generated. This would occur, for example, if the V and N-axes specified were defined as being the same.

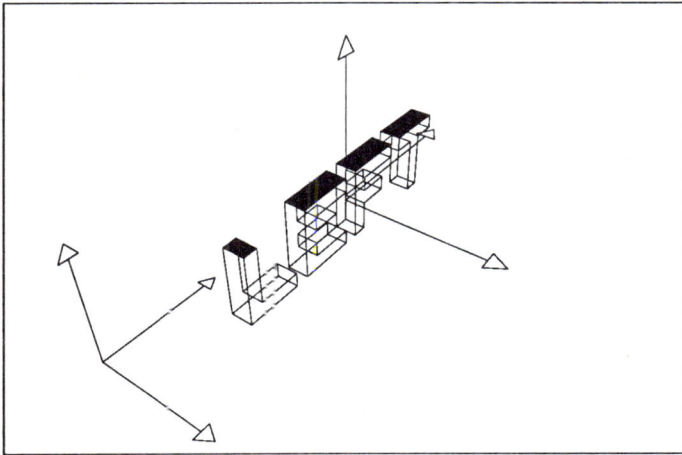

Figure 7.5: *VRC Coordinate system displaced from WC system*

In the example in Section 7.2.2, the origin of the world coordinate system is at a distance from the object LEFT. The origin could be set at the centre of the scene by

EVALUATE VIEW ORIENTATION MATRIX3
(50, 50, 50, 0, 0, 1, 0, 1, 0, ER, VMM3)

This is shown in Figure 7.5. The new origin is at the left-hand side of the letter F and half way up it.

In this case, the N-axis is parallel to the Z-axis of the world coordinate system. To view the LEFT scene from above or rotated would require the UVN axis system to be rotated. This is relatively easy to do in 2D as only one vector has to be defined to give the Y-axis. In 3D, two orthogonal axes need to be defined.

To aid the definition of such vectors, PHIGS provides the following utility function:

TRANSFORM POINT 3(X, Y, Z, MAT3, ER, XT, YT, ZT)

Given a point (X,Y,Z) and a transformation matrix MAT3, the function returns the point (XT,YT,ZT) which is the point (X,Y,Z) transformed by MAT3. As usual, ER is set non-zero if the transformation could not be performed and zero if it was.

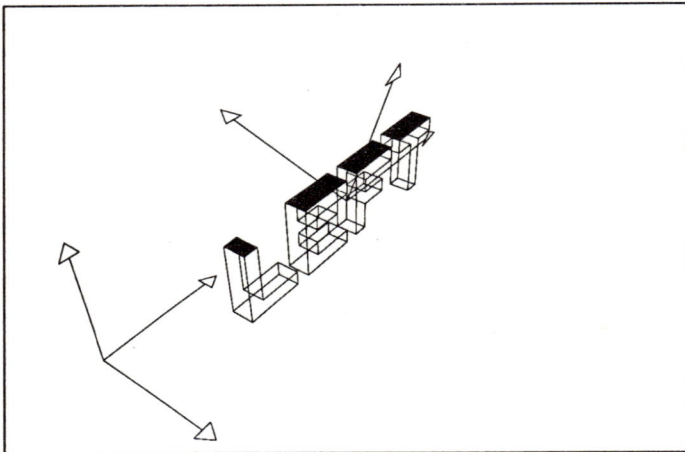

Figure 7.6: *Rotated VRC coordinates relative to WC*

Using BUILD TRANSFORMATION MATRIX 3 to define the transformation, known orthogonal vectors can be rotated to the desired position using TRANSFORM POINT 3. For example:

```
BUILD TRANSFORMATION MATRIX 3
(0, 0, 0, 0, 0, 0, PX, PY, PZ, 1, 1, 1, ER, MAT3)
TRANSFORM POINT 3(0, 0, 1, MAT3, ER, VNX, VNY, VNZ)
TRANSFORM POINT 3(0, 1, 0, MAT3, ER, VUX, VUY, VUZ)
EVALUATE VIEW ORIENTATION MATRIX 3
(50, 50, 50, VNX, VNY, VNZ, VUX, VUY, VUZ, ER, VMM3)
```

This would define a UVN coordinate system which is rotated by PX, PY and PZ radians anti-clockwise with respect to the world coordinate X,Y,Z-axes. If PX is set to $0.4*\pi$, and PY,PZ set to 0, the axes would be positioned as shown in Figure 7.6.

7.4 VIEW MAPPING

The utility function that defines the view mapping matrix is:

EVALUATE VIEW MAPPING MATRIX 3
(WL, PVL, TYPE, FRPU, PRPV, PRPN, VPD, BPD, FPD,
ER, VMM3)

The position (PRPU,PRPV,PRPN) defines the projection reference point (see Figure 7.4) for the view mapping. VPD defines the position of the view plane by giving its distance along the N-axis from the view reference point. Most frequently, the value of VPD is negative so that the view plane is behind the scene to be viewed. The view plane is parallel to the U,V-axes of the view reference coordinate system. Note that it is not necessary for the projection reference point to be on the N-axis.

BPD and FPD define the back and front plane positions by giving their distances from the origin. If all the scene is to be viewed, these should be placed sufficiently behind and in front of the scene so that they do not remove parts of the scene. Their effect will be described later.

WL(1) to WL(4) define the limits of the part of the view plane (in the order UMIN, UMAX, VMIN, VMAX) that is to be made available to the workstation for display. It is important to remember that for parallel projections, the projectors are parallel to the line from the projection reference point to the centre of the view window. So, for example, if the projection reference point is on the N-axis and the projectors are required perpendicular to the view plane, the centre of the view window must be (0,0,VPD).

The mapping from view reference coordinates to normalized projection coordinates is defined by specifying the projection viewport limits PVL(1) to PVL(4) in NPC coordinates that correspond to the window limits, effectively the window to viewport mapping. A difference from the 2D case is that the NPC coordinates are still three dimensional. The N-coordinates of points in the scene are retained and used to define the equivalent Z-value in NPC coordinates. The NPC Z-value of the backplane is defined as PVL(5) and the Z-value of the front plane is defined as PVL(6). The Z-value of the point (U,V,N) is (N–BPD)/(FPD–BPD). The U,V-values are defined by the projection of (U,V,N) onto the view plane and then the transformation of the U,V-coordinates to the NPC X,Y-coordinates using the window to viewport mapping. The Z-value is retained as it may be of use in any hidden line or hidden surface calculations. Finally, the parameter TYPE is set to PARALLEL or PERSPECTIVE to define the type of projection used in the view mapping.

An example of view mapping using the view reference coordinates defined before is:

EVALUATE VIEW ORIENTATION MATRIX 3
(50, 50, 50, 0, 0, 1, 0, 1, 0, ER, VOM3)
WL(1)=−60
WL(2)=60
WL(3)=−60
WL(4)=60
PVL(1)=0
PVL(2)=1
PVL(3)=0
PVL(4)=1
PVL(5)=0
PVL(6)=1
EVALUATE VIEW MAPPING MATRIX 3
(WL, PVL, PARALLEL, 0, 0, 1000, −300, −900, 300, ER, VMM3)

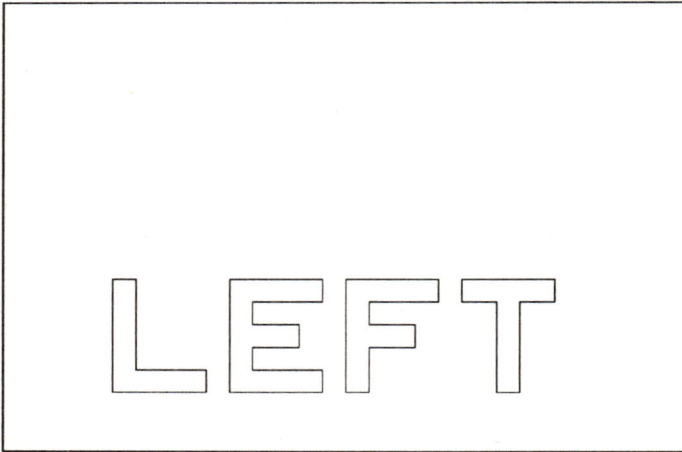

Figure 7.7: *Head-on view of LEFT*

The change of origin in the view orientation means that the scene LEFT extends from −40 to +40 in the U-direction, −10 to +10 in the V-direction and −3 to +3 in the N-direction. The parallel projection with the projection reference point on the axis and the window limits defining the centre of the window on the N-axis and extending further than the extent of LEFT ensures that all the scene will be projected onto the window and will be mapped into the NPC unit square. This front-on view will produce the picture in Figure 7.7.

7.5 DEFINING A VIEW

The function that defines a view cf a scene on a workstation is:

SET VIEW REPRESENTATICN 3
 (WS, VI, VOM3, VMM3, VCL, XYC, BC, FC)

The view with view incex VI on workstation WS is defined by the view orientation matrix VOM3 and the view mapping matrix VMM3. As for the 2D case, view clipping limits for the X, Y and Z-directions of NPC space can be defined by VCL(1) to VCL(6). Whether clipping is applied in the X, Y-directions depencs on whether XYC is set to CLIP or NOCLIP. Whether clipping is applied against the VCL(5) lowest Z-value depends on whether BC is set to CLIP or NOCLIP and similarly clipping against the largest Z-value, VCL(6), depends on whether FC is set to CLIP or NOCLIP. For example:

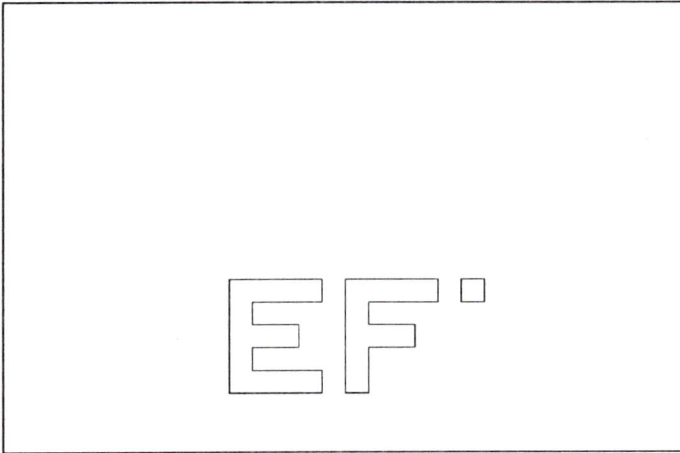

Figure 7.8: *Clipping set to CLIP*

VCL(1)=0.3
VCL(2)=0.7
VCL(3)=0.3
VCL(4)=0.7
VCL(5)=0
VCL(6)=1
SET VIEW REPRESENTATION 3
(WS, 1, VOM3, VMM3, VCL, CLIP, CLIP, CLIP)

if used with the matrices defined in the example in Section 7.4 will clip the projected picture of LEFT so that only the centre part is presented to the workstation for display (see Figure 7.8).

The part of the T still visible has the right edge drawn creating a square. This is because the individual faces are being drawn as fill areas and the outline of a HOLLOW fill area is drawn including the edges created by clipping.

8 EXAMPLES

8.1 PARALLEL PROJECTION EXAMPLES

8.1.1 Introduction

In this section, the facilities available to vary a view of an object are described. Parallel projections will be used in the examples. For most, the examples are equally applicable for perspective projections as well.

8.1.2 View orientation

In the simplest parallel projection, the projectors are perpendicular to the view plane and, therefore, parallel to the N-axis. This is obtained by having the projection reference point on the N-axis and the view window with its centre at the origin. For example:

```
EVALUATE VIEW ORIENTATION MATRIX 3
(50, 50, 50, 0, 0, 1, 0, 1, 0, ER, VOM3)
WL(1)=-60
WL(2)=60
WL(3)=-40
WL(4)=40
PVL(1)=0
PVL(2)=1
PVL(3)=0.333
PVL(4)=1
PVL(5)=0
PVL(6)=1
EVALUATE VIEW MAPPING MATRIX 3
(WL, PVL, PARALLEL, 0, 0, 1000, -300, -900, 300, ER, VMM3)
```

The view orientation defines the view reference point in the centre of the object LEFT leaving the orientation of the axes the same. The view mapping keeps the projection reference point and planes well away from the object. The window is larger than the object and maps to the top of the

NPC space keeping the aspect ratio the same.

    VCL(1)=0
    VCL(2)=1
    VCL(3)=0.333
    VCL(4)=1
    VCL(5)=0
    VCL(6)=1
    SET VIEW REPRESENTATION 3
     (WS, 1, VOM3, VMM3, VCL, CLIP, CLIP, CLIP)

This will generate the picture in Figure 8.1, a head-on view.

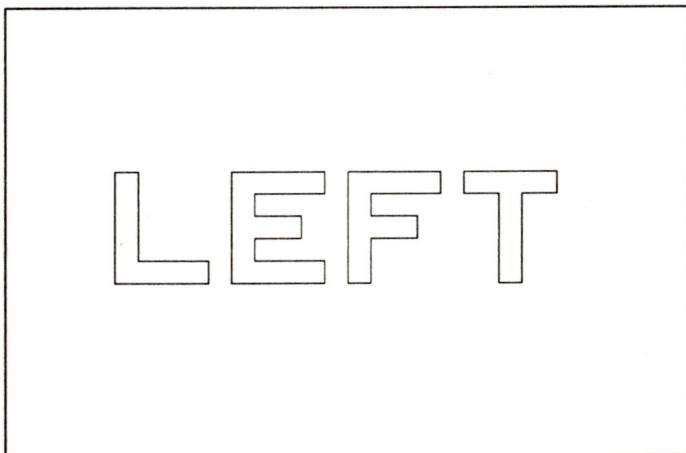

Figure 8.1: *Head-on view of LEFT*

As shown in Section 7.3, by changing the view orientation, an axis system for the VRC coordinates can be set up which is rotated relative to the directions of the world coordinate axes. By setting the view orientation to each of the principle axes of the object, three distinct views can be obtained. This technique is frequently used in CAD and architecture to view complex man-made objects such as buildings or mechanical parts.

The axes set up in Figure 7.6 would result in the picture shown in Figure 8.2. To get a good impression of a complex object, presentation of the object in real time with a continually changing orientation is a technique frequently used. A good example is drug design where it is necessary to examine the structure of complex molecules. The molecule is rotated in real time bringing the static picture to life. The way the orientation is changed will often be controlled by the operator. The best sequence of orientations to display will depend on the structure and shape of the object being viewed.

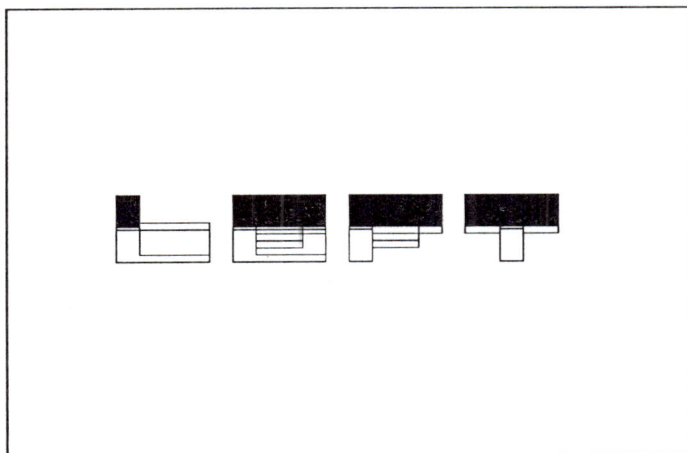

Figure 8.2: *LEFT viewed from above*

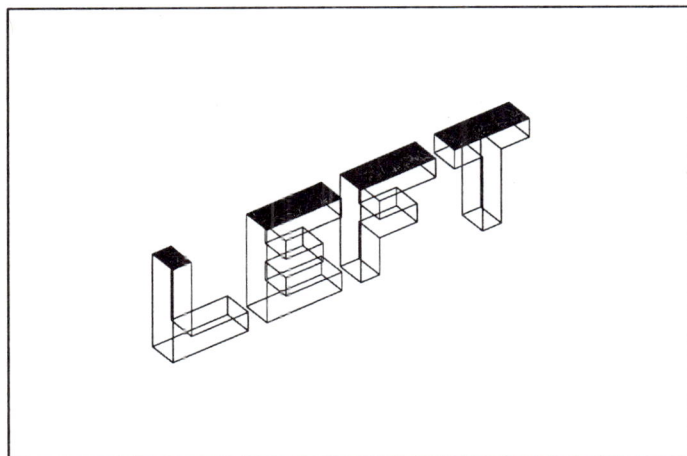

Figure 8.3: *Rotated 0.2 π about X and Y-axes*

Rotating the UVN axes clockwise relative to the world axes by 0.2π about both the X and Y-axes would give the picture in Figure 8.3. Note that rotating about the two axes ensures that all the faces of the letters are visible. Rotating by 0.2π in the X and 0.4π in the Y would give the picture in Figure 8.4. Rotating by 0.2π in the X and 0.7π in the Y would give the picture in Figure 8.5.

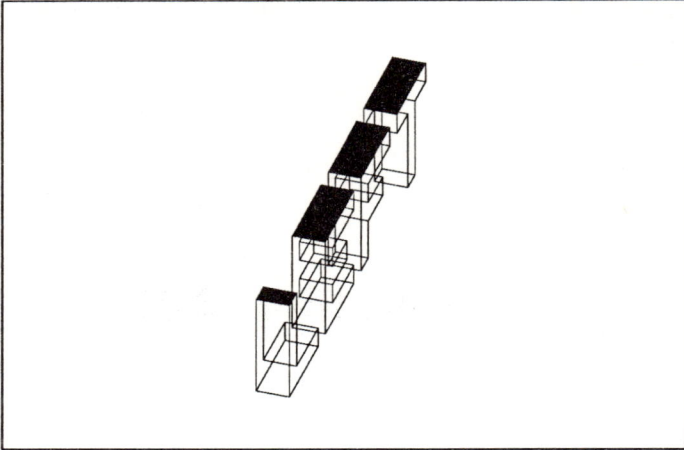

Figure 8.4: *Rotating by 0.2π in X and 0.4π in Y*

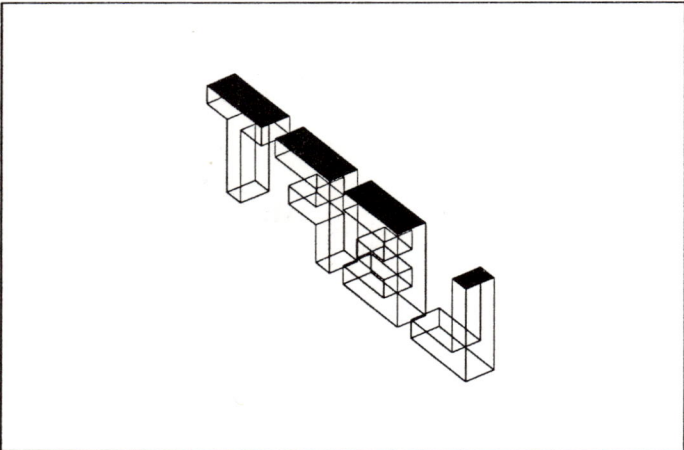

Figure 8.5: *Rotating by 0.2π in X and 0.7π in Y*

Orientating the view of an object from a variety of directions can give a much better idea of its overall form. It is possible in simple cases to achieve the same effect by a modelling transformation applied to the object on traversal. However, for complex objects made up of several posted structures this may not always be easy. Changing the view orientation is the natural way to obtain different views of an object.

8.1.3 Changing the window to viewport mapping

In Section 7.4, the definition of the window on the view plane and its mapping to the projection viewport were described. The example in the previous section mapped the window from −60 to 60 in the U-direction and −40 to 40 in the V-direction of VRC coordinate space on the view plane to the viewport from 0 to 1 in the X-direction and 0.333 to 1 in the Y-direction of NPC space. By preserving the aspect ratio in the mapping from window to viewport, the appearance in the two coordinate systems will be similar.

Making the window larger while retaining the same size of viewport will decrease the size of the object in the NPC picture. For example, changing the window to −90 to 90 in the U-direction and −60 to 60 in the V-direction will produce the picture in Figure 8.6 which is much smaller than the object in Figure 8.3.

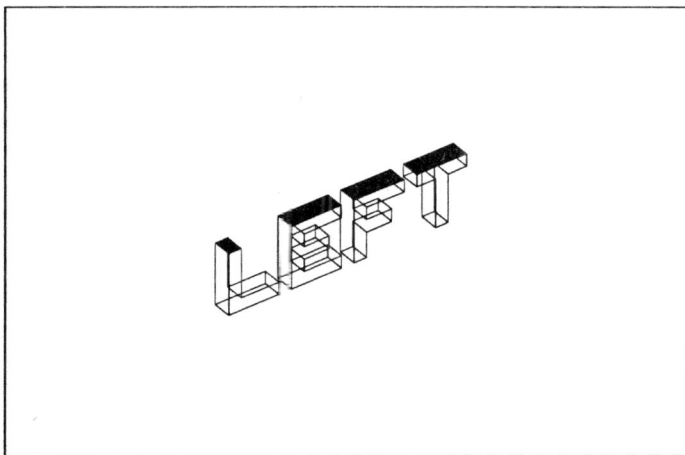

Figure 8.6: *Increasing window size makes picture smaller*

The position of the object in NPC space can be changed by redefining the viewport. For example, changing the viewport to 0 to 1 in the X-direction and 0.233 to 0.9 in the Y-direction would give the picture in Figure 8.7. If the aspect ratio of the window and viewport are different, a non-uniform mapping will result. For example, if −90 to 90 in the U-direction and −40 to 40 in the V-direction is mapped onto 0 to 1 in the X-direction and 0.333 to 1 in the Y-direction, the resulting picture will be as in Figure 8.8. This can be a useful facility if the major requirement is to fill the space available and there is no obvious metric relation between the X and Y-directions.

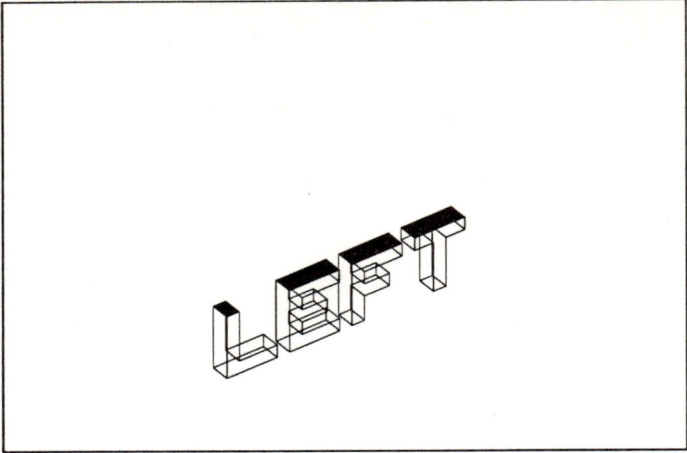

Figure 8.7: *Changing viewport can change position*

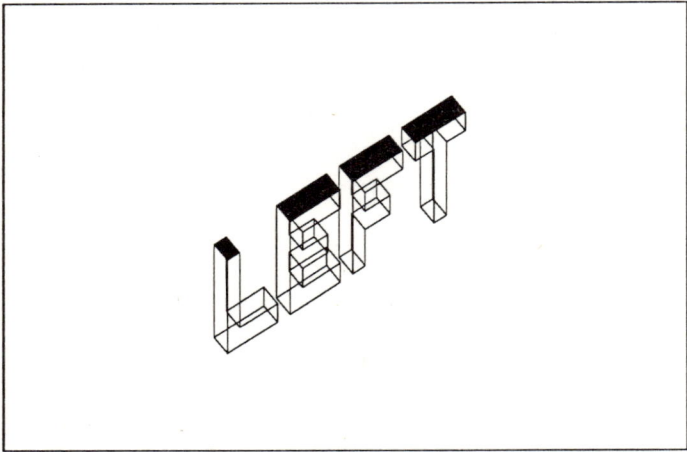

Figure 8.8: *Changing aspect ratio*

Changing the window limits to −60 to 60 in the U-direction and −60 to 60 in the V-direction and mapping onto the same viewport will produce the picture in Figure 8.9.

As can be seen, changing the window to viewport mapping is useful for positioning the picture in the NPC space and defining its overall shape and size. Changing position can clearly be done by changing either the window or the viewport. It should be remembered that the window limits also define the direction of the projectors in a parallel projection. Consequently it is usual to make the positional changes by changing the viewport.

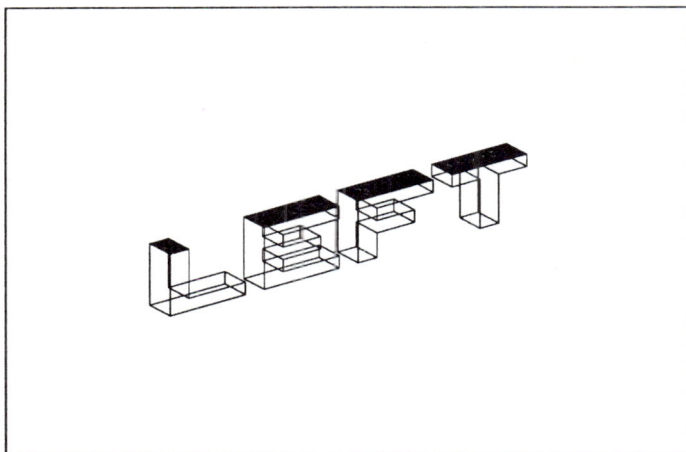

Figure 8.9: *Changing aspect ratio*

8.2 PARALLEL PROJECTION CATEGORIES

8.2.1 Introduction

Parallel projections can be sub-divided into a set of categories depending on the orientation of the viewing axis compared with the principal axes of the object and the position of the projection reference point relative to the N-axis. If the projection reference point is not on the N-axis, it is called an *oblique* projection, otherwise it is called an *orthographic* projection.

8.2.2 Orthographic projections

Attempting to represent a 3D object in a 2D drawing is a compromise between showing the general shape of the object and showing more precise information about some aspect of the object. Figure 8.1 is an example of an orthographic projection which has the N-axis coinciding with one of the major axes of the object. To get a good impression of an object, it is necessary to take 3 separate views with the N-axis coinciding with each of the 3 major axes of the object. Such projections give an exact view of one face of the object and little information of the other two.

The alternative type of orthographic projection is one where the N-axis is chosen so that 3 adjacent faces of an object are visible. Figure 8.3 is an example of such a projection called *axonometric*. Such a projection has parallel lines in the object equally foreshortened.

8.2.3 Oblique projections

Oblique projections are where the projection reference point is not on the N-axis. For example, if the program defining Figure 8.1 in Section 8.1.2 was changed as follows:

EVALUATE VIEW MAPPING MATRIX 3
(WL, PVL, PARALLEL, 700, 500, 500, −300, −900, 100, ER, VMM3)

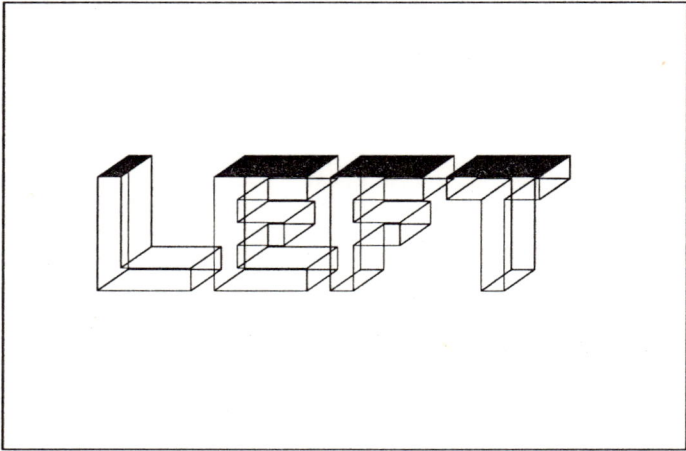

Figure 8.10: *Oblique view*

This would produce the view in Figure 8.10. This is a distorted view of the object. The front face of the object which is parallel to the view plane is not distorted while the planes in the other two principal directions are.

8.3 PERSPECTIVE PROJECTIONS

Perspective projections are typified by all projectors passing through the projection reference point (PRP). Five values determine the form of the perspective projection. These need to be chosen carefully to ensure the required emphasis is established in the resulting view:

(1) *Orientation of object*: the orientation of the object relative to the view plane;

(2) *PRP height*: the height of the PRP relative to the view reference point;

(3) *Distance*: the distance of the PRP from the view reference point;

(4) *View plane position*: the distance of the view plane from the view reference point;

(5) *Displacement*: the horizontal displacement of the PRP from the N-axis.

8.3.1 Orientation

Keeping the projection reference point on the N-axis, the view of the object is significantly different depending on whether the view plane is parallel to a face of the object (one-point perspective), parallel to an axis of the object but not a face (two-point perspective), or not parallel to any axis (three-point perspective).

To emphasize the perspective in the examples, the object to be viewed has been reduced to just the E and F and the Z-dimension increased from 47 to 53 to now being from 41 to 59. For example, the following program will produce the picture in Figure 8.11.

```
EVALUATE VIEW ORIENTATION MATRIX 3
(50, 50, 50, 0, 0, 1, 0, 1, 0, ER, VOM3)
WL(1)=-80.
WL(2)=130.
WL(3)=-90.
WL(4)=50.

PVL(1)=0
PVL(2)=1
PVL(3)=0.333
PVL(4)=1
PVL(5)=0
PVL(6)=1
EVALUATE VIEW MAPPING MATRIX 3
(WL, PVL, PERSPECTIVE, 0, 0, 70, -70, -900, 50, ER, VMM3)

VCL(1)=0
VCL(2)=1
VCL(3)=0.3333
VCL(4)=1
VCL(5)=0
VCL(6)=1
SET VIEW REPRESENTATION 3
(WS, 1, VOM3, VNN3, VCL, CLIP, CLIP, CLIP)
```

Figure 8.11: *Perspective projection*

Note that the lines of the EF object in the Z-direction all meet in a single point while the lines of the object parallel to the X and Y-axes remain parallel (thus the name one-point perspective).

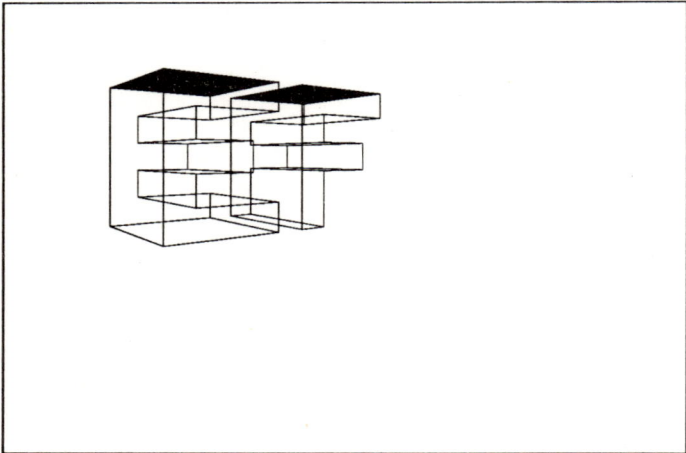

Figure 8.12: *Two-point perspective*

If the projection reference point and view plane are orientated by 0.2π about the Y-axis of EF, the picture produced would be as in Figure 8.12. Here, lines of the object parallel to the Y-axis remain parallel while the lines parallel to the X and Z-axes meet in separate points (thus the name two-point perspective).

If the projection reference point and view plane are rotated from the original position by 0.1π about the X-axis and 0.3π about the Y-axis of the object, the picture produced is as in Figure 8.13.

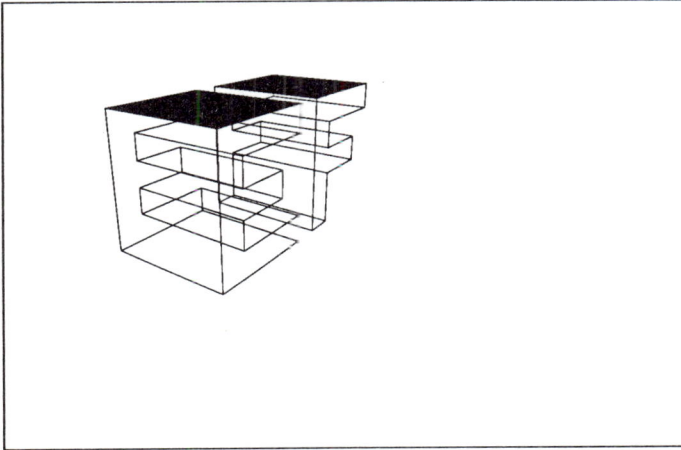

Figure 8.13: *Three-point perspective*

Here, each set of lines parallel to an axis of the object meets at a different point (thus the name three-point perspective). In general, this gives the most visual impression of 3-dimensions but sacrifices the ability to make measurements in any of the directions. All are foreshortened by the perspective view mapping.

8.3.2 Changing the projection reference point

By moving the projection reference point off the N-axis, a distorted view of the object can be obtained. For example, if the projection reference point is changed to $(-40, 20, 70)$ so that it no longer lies on the N-axis, and the object is rotated by 0.1π about the X and Y-axes, the picture generated is as in Figure 8.14.

One problem with perspective projections when the projection reference point is moved off the N-axis is that the projection of the object onto the view plane moves. Consequently, there is a continuing need to adjust the position of the window on the view plane. The application may need to build some tools on top of PHIGS if the aim is to keep the object being viewed in the centre of the display.

Figure 8.14: *Projection reference point off N-axis*

If the projection reference point is moved nearer to the object, the view of the object distorts, accentuating the perspective. Moving the projection reference point to (−20, 15, 50) produces the view in Figure 8.15.

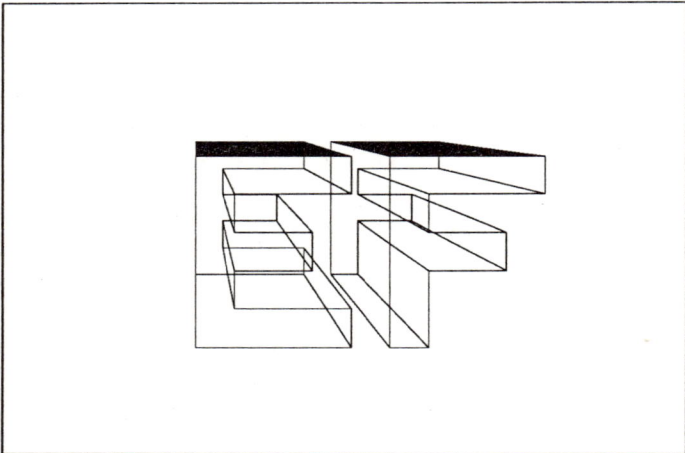

Figure 8.15: *Near projection reference point*

The size of the object itself on the view plane depends on the position of the view plane. Bringing the view plane nearer the object decreases the size of the picture of the object. Moving the projection reference point away from the object also decreases the size of the picture of the object but the two effects are different.

8.4 MULTIPLE VIEWS

The PHIGS viewing system is sufficiently general to produce all the parallel and perspective projections in common use. The ability to define multiple views of an object and position them independently in the view plane by defining different projection viewports allows a composite image to be generated showing several different views of the same object. This type of display is frequently used in Computer-Aided Design to give a good overall view of the detail of an object.

For example, if the object LEFT is defined as a structure in four different orientations with different view indices set for each, by defining the projection viewport to be (0.1,0.4,0.35,0.65) for the first, (0.1,0.4,0.65,1.0) for the second and so on, four different positions on the view plane can be established for the views as shown in Figure 8.16.

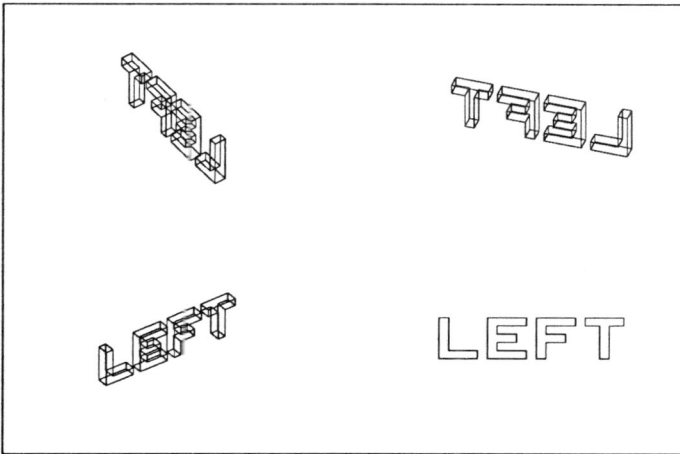

Figure 8.16: *Multiple views*

The clipping rectangle for each of these views can be distinct from the projection viewport. The viewport is defined by the view mapping while the clipping is specified as part of the definition of the view itself.

For example, all four could have the clipping set to the volume with limits (0.2, 0.8, 0.4, 0.9, 0.0, 1.0) in which case the picture generated would be as in Figure 8.17.

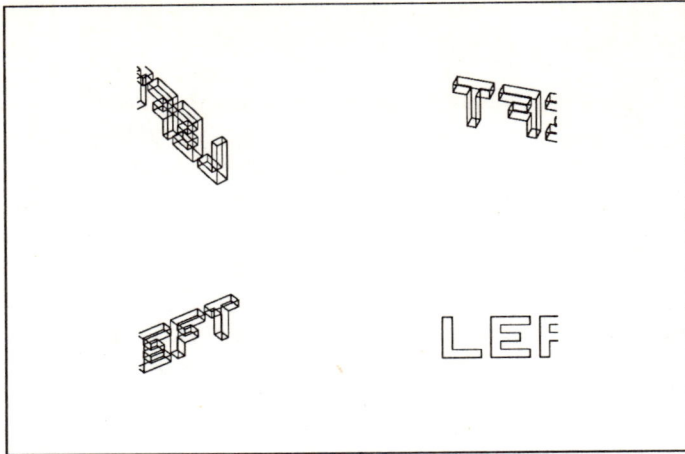

Figure 8.17: *Multiple views with the same clip volume*

By defining the limits as (0.0,1.0,0.0,1.0,0.48,0.52), clipping can be achieved in the Z-direction (see Figure 8.18). The values 0.48 and 0.52 depend on where the front and back plane are, as these map to 1.0 and 0.0 respectively. In the example, they were set to 300.0 and −300.0.

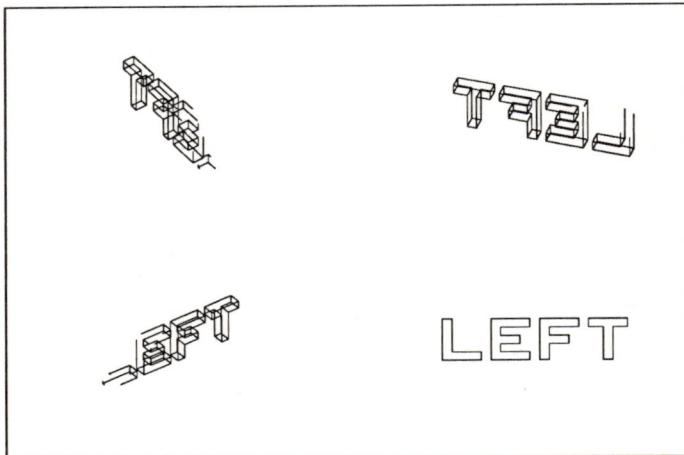

Figure 8.18: *Clipping in the Z-direction*

8.5 VIEW CULLING

So far, the complete object to be viewed has had the bounds of the VRC coordinate volume to be mapped to NPC coordinates sufficiently large that it includes the complete object. To remove part of the complete scene, clipping has been applied to the projected picture.

To limit the part of the scene that is projected, it is possible to define the front and back planes such that some part of the object is not in between them. In this case, only that part of the scene between the front and back planes is projected.

For example, if the object LEFT is enhanced by an additional letter F placed at the position 15 in the N-direction, and another letter L placed at position −30 in the N-direction, the overall scene would be as in Figure 8.19 assuming the front plane was at N=30, the view plane at N=10 and the back plane at N=−90 and the projection is parallel. Both additional letters are well within the area between the front and back planes.

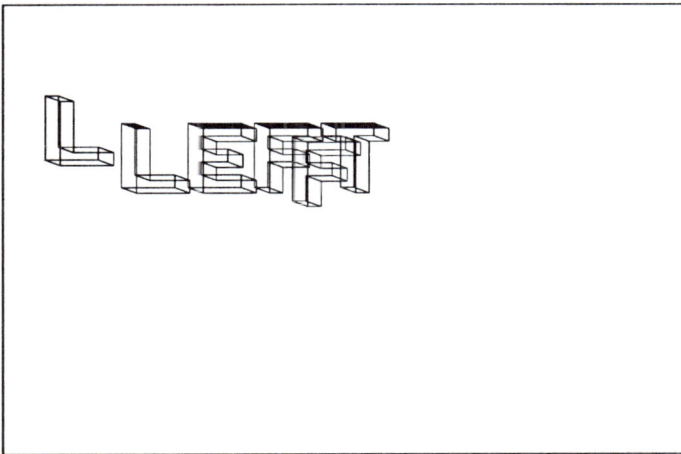

Figure 8.19: *Scene with letters at front and back*

Now, if the front plane is moved to N=10, the front F will not be part of the scene projected as it is now in front of the front plane. This results in the picture in Figure 8.20.

This allows the computation of complex scenes to be limited to the current points of interest and removes from the computation irrelevant detail. How this is handled by the implementation will vary. The aim is to give the implementation the ability to optimize the viewing function while giving the application the ability to localize the computation to the areas of interest. It can also be used to ensure that parts of the scene of particular importance are not obscured.

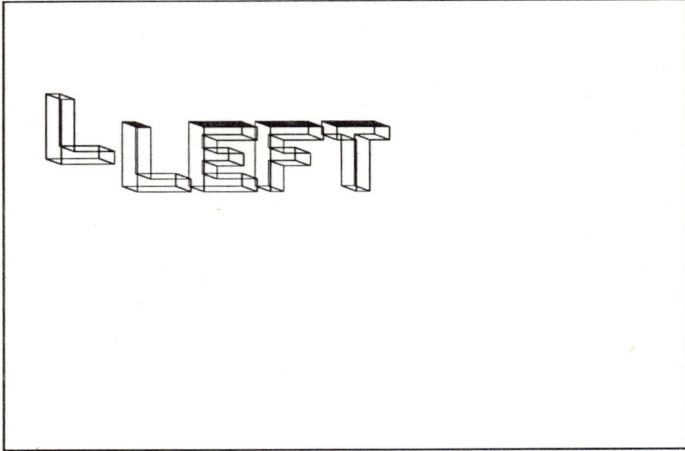

Figure 8.20: *Moving front plane nearer view plane*

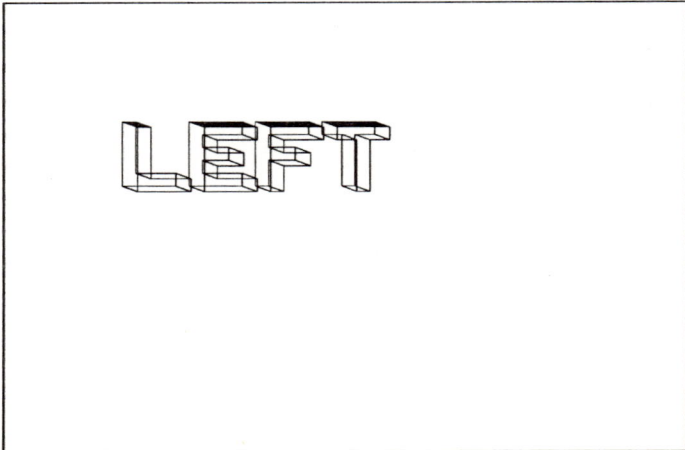

Figure 8.21: *Moving back plane nearer view plane*

By moving the back plane to N=−15, the picture produced would be as in Figure 8.21. Both the front F and back L have been culled.

9 INPUT CLASSES

9.1 INTRODUCTION

The previous Chapters in this book have described the facilities for graphical output in PHIGS and for controlling the appearance of graphical output, both in terms of geometric and non-geometric content. PHIGS, as the name indicates, is a graphical system that provides support for interaction, and in this Chapter and the next the functionality in PHIGS which supports graphical input is described, together with the mechanisms which relate graphical input to the central structure store.

PHIGS shares the same model of input as GKS, and readers familiar with GKS will note that the differences lie in the choice of measure values for the input device classes.

Input in PHIGS is accomplished through *logical input devices*. The idea behind logical input devices is that they provide an abstraction from specific hardware input devices, for example, mouse, tablet, keyboard, lightpen, and enable applications to be written in such a way that they are portable across a wide range of input device hardware. The application is only concerned with the values delivered by logical input devices, for example a position in world coordinates and view index, not with the specific details of how the value is derived from the values generated by the physical input devices.

PHIGS provides six classes of logical input devices. The types of values returned by each class are:

(1) *LOCATOR*: a position in world coordinates and a view index;

(2) *STROKE*: a sequence of positions in world coordinates and a view index;

(3) *VALUATOR*: a real number;

(4) *CHOICE*: a CHOICE status and an integer representing selection from a set of choices;

(5) *PICK*: a PICK status and pick path;

(6) *STRING*: a character string.

As in GKS, there are three *operating modes* for logical input devices. They differ in whether the operator or the application has the initiative to generate logical input values. The three operating modes are:

(1) *REQUEST*: input is produced by the operator in direct response to the application;

(2) *SAMPLE*: input is acquired directly by the application;

(3) *EVENT*: input is generated asynchronously by the operator and is collected in a queue for the application.

PHIGS allows the application to control some characteristics of logical input devices, for example the forms of prompting to be used to indicate to the operator that input is required. The logical input device classes and operating modes are explained in detail in the following sections.

9.2 REQUEST MODE

Before describing the logical input device classes, the default operating mode, REQUEST, is outlined. The logical input device classes are then described for REQUEST mode input. The functions which support the other operating modes are described in Chapter 10.

In REQUEST mode, input is produced by the operator in direct response to a request by the application program. This corresponds very closely to the forms of input provided by programming languages such as Fortran, Pascal and C. In Fortran, when a READ statement is executed, the program is suspended and waits for the values requested to be provided by the input sub-system. Execution of the Fortran program continues when the values have been provided. This is exactly the effect of REQUEST mode input in PHIGS. The application requests input from a particular logical input device. The application is then suspended until the logical input device has obtained the input from the operator. In this mode, either the application is active or the logical input device is active, but never both. A consequence of this is that never more than one logical input device can be active at a time in REQUEST mode.

The form of the function for REQUEST input is:

REQUEST XXX(WS, DV, ST, ...)

XXX identifies the class of logical input device (VALUATOR, CHOICE, etc), WS and DV identify the particular device of that class from which input is requested and ST is an output parameter which is a status indicator providing information on the completion of the request. WS identifies the workstation with which the logical input device is associated and DV identifies the particular device of the class on that particular workstation. It is possible for a workstation to provide more than one logical input device in a class, thus a workstation might provide three LOCATOR devices.

The form of the remaining parameters to the REQUEST function varies between the different logical input device classes, and is described in the following sections.

9.3 LOCATOR

The LOCATOR input device returns a single position to the application program together with information that relates the point on the display with the view associated with this point. Two functions are provided in PHIGS to request input from a LOCATOR device:

REQUEST LOCATOR 3(WS, DV, ST, VI, XPOS, YPOS, ZPOS)
REQUEST LOCATOR(WS, DV, ST, VI, XPOS, YPOS)

REQUEST LOCATOR 3 returns a position (XPOS,YPOS,ZPOS) in world coordinates and a view index VI. REQUEST LOCATOR returns a 2D position in world coordinates (XPOS,YPOS) and a view index VI. The 2D position is obtained by discarding the Z-coordinate of the 3D position which is the intrinsic value of the LOCATOR logical input device irrespective of how it is invoked.

It is worth stressing that all LOCATOR devices in PHIGS are 3D devices. The REQUEST LOCATOR 3 and REQUEST LOCATOR functions can be used to access *any* LOCATOR device.

Referring to the viewing pipeline depicted in Figure 7.2, it will be seen that to generate an input value in world coordinates from a value in the workstation dependent device coordinate system, it is necessary to apply the inverse of the workstation and viewing transformations. Each workstation has a single workstation transformation (see Section 11.3), but may have multiple viewing transformations. The parameter VI identifies which of the viewing transformations was used to transform the logical input value. This transformation will be one whose view clipping limits contain the position. The mechanism for selecting the viewing transformation is discussed shortly, after an example has been described.

For illustration of LOCATOR input, a simple 2D example will be given, based on a part of the structure network defining a work environment given in Figure 5.6 (Section 5.4.5). A work environment consisting of the large desk, blotter, calculator and chair is defined by:

```
OPEN STRUCTURE(WKNV)
MVRP(0.2, 0.6)
EXECUTE STRUCTURE(LG)
MVRP(0.325, 0.525)
EXECUTE STRUCTURE(CHAIR)
CLOSE STRUCTURE

POST STRUCTURE(WS, WKNV, PR)
```

The MVRP function defines a single SET LOCAL TRANSFORMATION structure element which is a translation that replaces any local transformation currently in force. It can be thought of as a shorthand form of the SET LOCAL TRANSFORMATION structure element.

The structure created is shown in Figure 9.1.

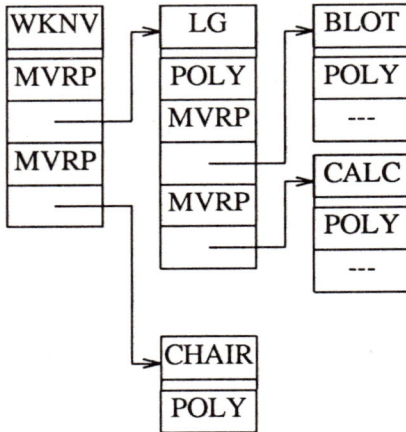

Figure 9.1: *Structure for large desk*

The large desk and its contents are positioned at the point (0.2,0.6) in the modelling coordinate system of the work environment. As this is the only transformation applied to the structure, this is also the point (0.2,0.6) in world coordinates.

The example is to use a LOCATOR device to reposition the desk in the unit square coordinate system. The operator selects the position in world coordinate space at which the bottom left hand corner of the desk is to be positioned, using a LOCATOR device. Assuming the structure WKNV above has already been created and posted, the following program would accomplish this. This is the first example of editing using REPLACE mode which is particularly appropriate in this case.

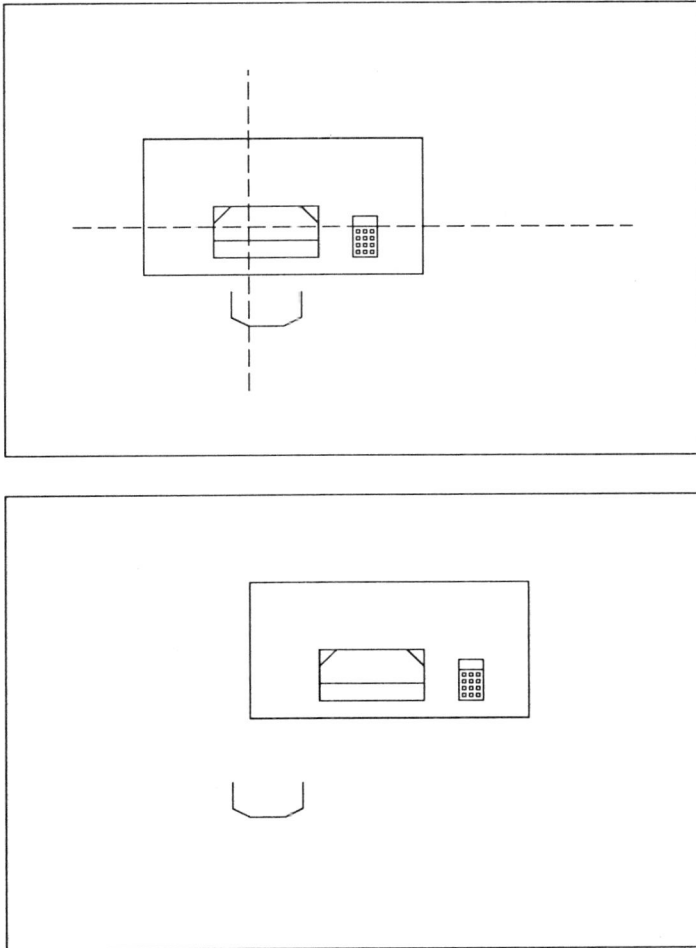

Figure 9.2: *Example of LOCATOR input*

```
      OPEN STRUCTURE(WKNV)
      SET EDIT MODE(REPLACE)
      SET ELEMENT PCINTER(1)

100   CONTINUE
      REQUEST LOCATOR(WS, DV, ST, VI, X, Y)
      MVRP(X, Y)
      GOTO 100
```

The key idea is to use the position input by the LOCATOR device to construct a transformation matrix which will position the bottom left-hand corner of the desk at the position input. The structure editing facilities in PHIGS are then used to replace the local modelling transformation defined by MVRP (at element position 1 in the structure) with the new one. This program then loops forever requesting new positions for the desk.

The structure WKNV is posted after creation. Subsequent edits to the structure result in the modified structure being displayed on the workstation, and so the effect of editing the structure will be immediately visible. A typical movement is shown in Figure 9.2. The intersection of the cross hairs define the point to which the desk is to be moved.

The major difficulty with this style of programming is to relate LOCATOR input in world coordinates to the modelling coordinate systems in which the components of a scene are specified. In the worst case this can involve the application in considerable work maintaining details of the coordinate systems used and the transformations between them.

9.3.1 Multiple viewing transformations

Typically, several views will be in use on a workstation, for example in Figure 9.3 the desk is drawn with view index 1, and the word STOP with view index 2.

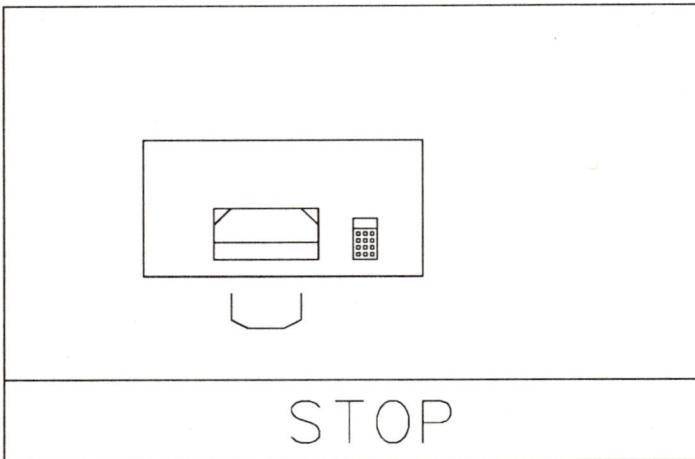

Figure 9.3: *Multiple views*

The operator needs to be able to input LOCATOR positions in either view and the application program needs to be able to differentiate between the views in use. This is the purpose of the view index parameter of the REQUEST LOCATOR function.

For this example, a program which will move the desk to a new position if a LOCATOR input is received in view 1, and will terminate if a position is received in view 2 is the following:

```
OPEN STRUCTURE(WKNV)
SET VIEW INDEX(1)
MVRP(0.2, 0.6)
EXECUTE STRUCTURE(LG)
MVRP(0.325, 0.525)
EXECUTE STRUCTURE(CHAIR)
CLOSE STRUCTURE
POST STRUCTURE(WS, WKNV, PR)

OPEN STRUCTURE(STOP)
SET VIEW INDEX(2)
DRAW STOP
CLOSE STRUCTURE
POST STRUCTURE(WS, STOP, PR1)

OPEN STRUCTURE(WKNV)
SET EDIT MODE(REPLACE)
SET ELEMENT POINTER(2)

100   CONTINUE
REQUEST LOCATOR(WS, DV, ST, VI, X, Y)
IF(VI .NE. 1) GOTO 110
MVRP(X, Y)
GOTO 100

110   CONTINUE
CLOSE STRUCTURE
SET EDIT MODE(INSERT)
STOP
```

The view transformation selected to transform the LOCATOR position from NPC to world coordinates is that whose view clipping limits contain the position in NPC coordinates.

9.3.2 Overlapping views

In the example in the previous section, view representation 1 and view representation 2 were defined so that the areas defined by the view clipping limits of the two views do not overlap. In general the areas may overlap with the result that an NPC position may fall within the view clipping limits of more than one view transformation. The view transformation associated with view index 0 maps the unit cube in world coordinates into the unit cube in NPC, and the associated view clipping limits define a unit cube. For 2D working, the view clipping limits of view index 0 are the unit square, and since the representation of this view index cannot be changed, any position in NPC space will always fall into the view clipping limits of view index 0, and possibly the representations of other view indices also.

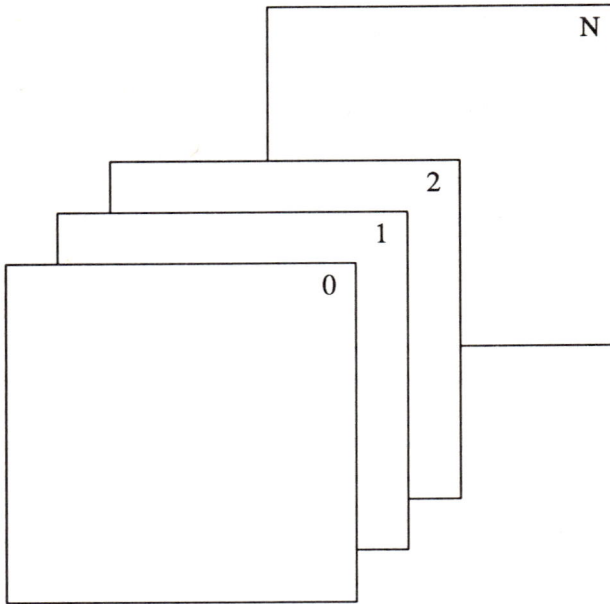

Figure 9.4: *Default view representation ordering*

To resolve conflicts between view representations, PHIGS has a *view transformation input priority* mechanism which is very similar to the viewport input priority mechanism in GKS used to resolve conflicts between normalization transformations in the GKS LOCATOR input mechanisms. A view transformation input priority is associated with every view representation defined on a workstation. If a LOCATOR position falls within the view clipping limits of more than one view representation, the view by which the position is transformed is that with the highest view transformation input priority.

The view representations are ordered by view transformation input priority. Workstations are initialized so that view representation 0 has the highest view transformation input priority, and view representation N (where N denotes the maximum view index) has the lowest. This is illustrated in Figure 9.4.

All input is returned with view index 0 until the default view representation ordering is changed. Thus the examples given so far were not strictly correct. View transformation input priority is changed by the function:

SET VIEW TRANSFORMATION INPUT PRIORITY
(WS, VI, RVI, RP)

The effect is to set the view transformation input priority of view index VI on workstation WS, either immediately higher (if RP has the value HIGHER) or immediately lower (if RP has the value LOWER) than that of the reference view index (RVI).

For the example in Section 9.3.1 to work correctly, the priority of view transformation 0 needs to be lower than those of view transformation 1 and 2. Since the view clipping limits of view transformations 1 and 2 do not overlap, the relative priorities of these two transformations is not important. A satisfactory ordering can be achieved by the function invocation:

SET VIEW TRANSFORMATION INPUT PRIORITY(WS, 0, 2, LOWER)

This produces the priority ordering:

1>2>0>3>.....>N

The position of view transformation 0 is moved to immediately below that of view transformation 2. This method of setting priorities ensures that no two view transformations have the same priority.

A more complex example is shown in Figure 9.5. Here view 0 overlaps views 1 to 5. Views 1, 2 and 3 do not overlap, but views 4 and 5 overlap view 3. To obtain LOCATOR input positions in view transformations 1 to 5 can be achieved by the view transformation input priority ordering:

4>5>1>2>3>0

This can be achieved by the following invocations of SET VIEW TRANSFORMATION INPUT PRIORITY:

SET VIEW TRANSFORMATION INPUT PRIORITY(WS, 0, 3, LOWER)
SET VIEW TRANSFORMATION INPUT PRIORITY(WS, 4, 1, HIGHER)
SET VIEW TRANSFORMATION INPUT PRIORITY(WS, 5, 4, LOWER)

The first invocation produces the ordering:

1>2>3>0>4>5>...

The second produces:

4>1>2>3>0>5>...

and the final invocation produces the desired ordering.

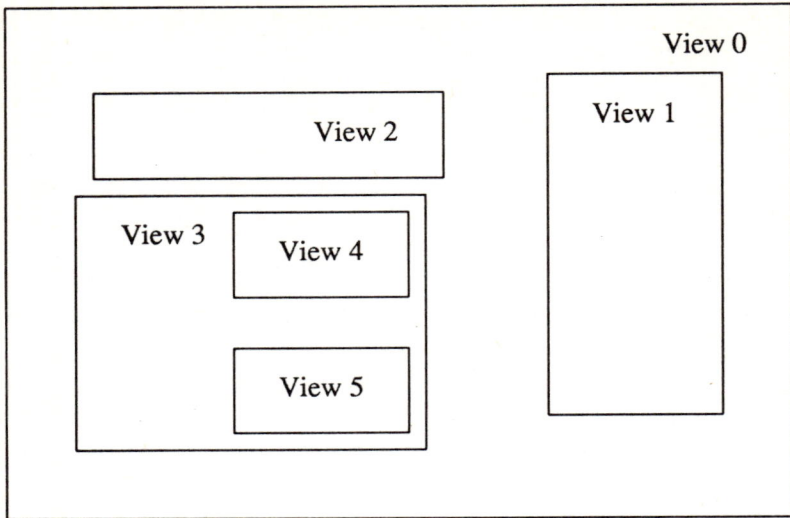

Figure 9.5: *Overlapping view clipping regions*

9.4 STROKE

Whereas the LOCATOR logical input device returns a single position in world coordinates and a view index, to the application program, the STROKE logical input device returns a sequence of positions and a view index. Two PHIGS functions are provided to request input from a STROKE device:

REQUEST STROKE 3
  (WS, DV, N, ST, VI, NPTS, XPOSA, YPOSA, ZPOSA)
REQUEST STROKE
  (WS, DV, N, ST, VI, NPTS, XPOSA, YPOSA)

The parameters WS, DV, ST and VI have the same meanings as the corresponding parameters in REQUEST LOCATOR 3 and REQUEST LOCATOR. The parameter N is the dimension of the arrays XPOSA, YPOSA (and ZPOSA). The output parameter NPTS returns the number of points in the STROKE value input, and the remaining parameters are arrays of coordinate values which contain the coordinates of the points in the STROKE. The provision of STROKE input as well as LOCATOR input is to allow a sequence of positions to be input without placing too much load on the PHIGS system and, in consequence, producing a faster response to the operator's input of positions.

All the points in the STROKE are transformed by the inverse of the view transformation corresponding to view index VI. The view transformation selected is that with highest view transformation input priority whose view clipping limits contain *all* of the points in the STROKE. This is illustrated in Figure 9.6. The view transformation input priorities are the same as in Figure 9.5.

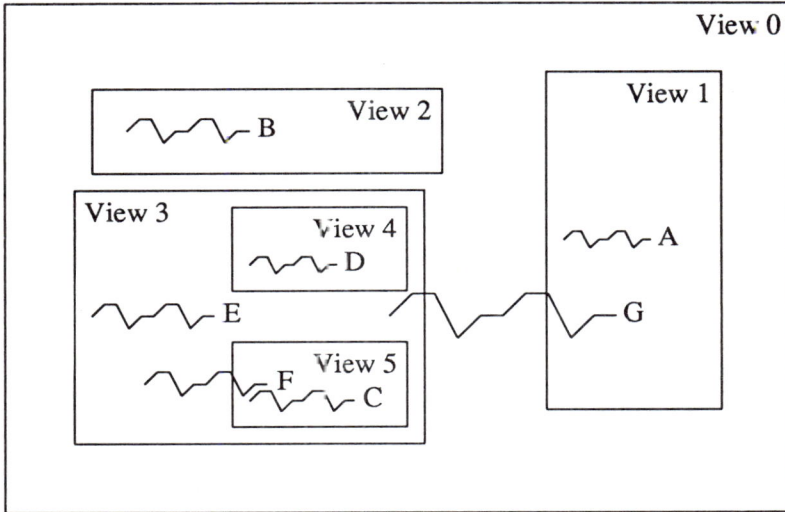

Figure 9.6: *Examples of STROKE input*

The view index associated with each STROKE is shown in the table below.

STROKE	View Index
A	1
B	2
C	5
D	4
E	3
F	3
G	0

The points in STROKEs A, B, C, D, and E all lie within the clipping limits of a single view transformation. STROKE F overlaps the clipping limits of transformations 3 and 5, but all the points falling in the clipping limits of transformation 5 also fall within the clipping limits of transformation 3. The points also all fall within the clipping limits of the view transformation 0. The priority of transformation 3 is greater than that of transformation 0 and so view index 3 is associated with the STROKE.

STROKE G overlaps the view clipping limits of transformations 1 and 3, but only the view clipping limits of transformation 0 contain all the points, and hence the view index associated with STROKE G is view index 0.

9.5 2D INPUT DEVICES

LOCATOR and STROKE input are conceptually 3D in PHIGS. If the physical input device generating LOCATOR and STROKE values is a 2D device, a third coordinate value is appended either internally from the PHIGS state tables, or externally, for example by requesting the operator to type the Z-value from a keyboard device.

9.6 LOCATOR AND STROKE IN 3D

Section 9.3 and Section 9.4 have described LOCATOR and STROKE input concentrating on the 2D form of the REQUEST functions. The same principles apply to the 3D form of the functions, with some additional complications. LOCATOR 3 and STROKE 3 logical input values are obtained by applying the inverse of the workstation transformation and the inverse of the selected view transformation.

In 3D, it is possible that these transformations do not have inverses. These situations are handled as follows. If the workstation transformation does not have an inverse, the Z-component of the LOCATOR position, and the Z-components of all the STROKE positions are set to the minimum Z-value of the workstation window.

In the case of the view transformation, the only view transformations considered are those which are invertible. Any view transformation, which does not have an inverse, is rejected. View transformation 0 is invertible, so it is guaranteed that a view transformation can always be found which can back transform LOCATOR and STROKE positions from NPC to world coordinates.

9.7 PICK

The PICK logical input device provides a link between the image displayed on a workstation and the central structure store. The operator can pick a portion of the display. The value returned by the pick logical input device identifies the structure element in the central structure store which generated the picked primitive. The PHIGS function to request input from a PICK device is:

REQUEST PICK(WS, DV, DEPTH, ST, PPD, PP)

DEPTH is an input parameter which specifies the maximum depth of pick path to return. PPD is the depth of the actual pick path returned and PP is the pick path which identifies the primitive picked. This will be explained in the example below.

A pick path defines the traversal path through the central structure store, which generated the output primitive picked. A pick path is a list of items, each item consisting of:

structure identifier
pick identifier
element position

Pick identifiers will be described shortly.

The following example illustrates the idea of a pick path. Figure 9.7 illustrates a work environment and Figure 9.8 the structure network from which it is generated.

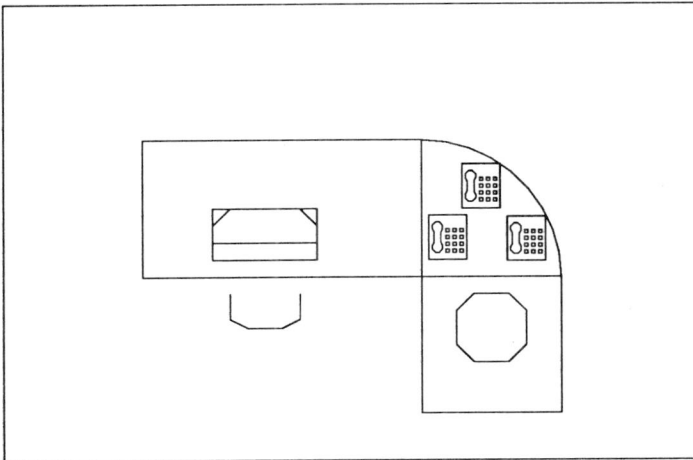

Figure 9.7: *A work environment*

Suppose the operator wishes to indicate items on the desk on which some action is to be performed. In the case of the telephones, the information required may be which phone it is, which desk it is sitting on and so on. The operator input will normally result in the need to edit the relevant part of the picture. The information returned is aimed at giving the application all that is required to edit the structure at a required level of detail.

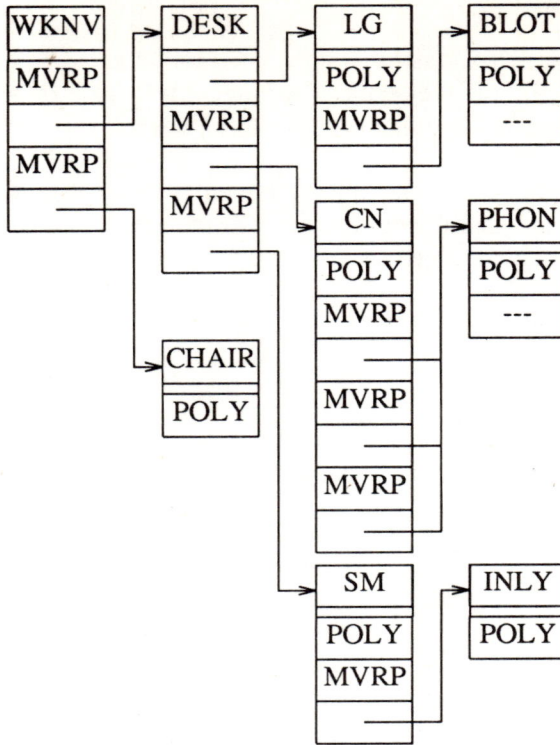

Figure 9.8: *Structure network for work environment*

The border of the blotter is generated by the structure element at position 1 in the structure BLOT. If the operator indicates the border in response to a REQUEST PICK, the pick path returned by the application program will be a list of items as follows:

Structure	Pick Identifier	Element Position
WKNV	0	2
DESK	0	1
LG	0	3
BLOT	0	1

The last entry in the list identifies the structure element which generated the primitive picked; in this case, it is the element at position 1 in structure BLOT. The remaining items describe the path taken by the traverser through the central structure store to that element. In this case, traversal starts in the posted structure WKNV, then through structures DESK and LG to BLOT. The element position in each of the first three items is the position of the execute structure element which invokes the next structure in the list. In this case there is only one path through the central structure store to the structure element generating the primitive picked. However, for the output primitives generated by the structure PHON, there are three alternative paths, corresponding to the three instances of the phone in the scene.

In Fortran, PP is an INTEGER array of dimension (3, DEPTH). The (1,*) components contain the structure identifiers, the (2,*) components the pick identifiers and the (3,*) components the element positions.

If the border of the left-most phone in Figure 9.7 is picked, the pick path returned is:

Structure	Pick Identifier	Element Position
WKNV	0	2
DESK	0	3
CN	0	3
PHON	0	1

In this instance, the structure PHON is invoked by the structure element at position 3 in structure CN. If the border of the centre phone is picked, the pick path returned is:

Structure	Pick Identifier	Element Position
WKNV	0	2
DESK	0	3
CN	0	5
PHON	0	1

This example illustrates how pick paths are used to differentiate between different instances of an output primitive generated by different traversal paths through the central structure store.

9.7.1 Pick identifier

Another method for differentiating between several instances of a primitive is to give the instances different pick identifiers. A pick identifier is a primitive attribute which provides an additional level of naming of primitives for the application program to use. The pick identifier attribute is bound to a primitive on creation. The function:

SET PICK IDENTIFIER(ID)

creates a structure element in the currently open structure, which, on traversal, results in the value ID being bound to subsequently created output primitives until a further set pick identifier structure element is traversed.

The following program:

```
OPEN STRUCTURE(BLOT)
SET PICK IDENTIFIER(1)
POLYLINE(4, XBRD, YBRD)
. . . .
```

will associate pick identifier 1 with the output primitives in the blotter. If the border of the blotter is now picked by the operator, the last item in the pick path will be:

Structure	Pick Identifier	Element Position
BLOT	1	2

The pick identifier has the value 1 and the element position is now 2, because of the insertion of the extra item into the BLOT structure.

When a structure is traversed, the pick identifier is inherited from its parent structure as other attributes are inherited. Thus different pick identifiers can be associated with the three instances of PHON, in the following way:

```
OPEN STRUCTURE(CN)
. . . . .
SET PICK IDENTIFIER(1)
EXECUTE STRUCTURE(PHON)
. . . . .
SET PICK IDENTIFIER(2)
EXECUTE STRUCTURE(PHON)
. . . . .
SET PICK IDENTIFIER(3)
EXECUTE STRUCTURE(PHON)
. . . . .
```

If the border of the left-most phone in Figure 9.7 is picked, the last item in the pick path returned is now:

Structure	Pick Identifier	Element Position
PHON	1	1

If the centre phone is picked, the item is:

Structure	Pick Identifier	Element Position
PHON	2	1

and for the right-most phone, it is:

Structure	Pick Identifier	Element Position
PHON	3	1

Thus the object picked can be uniquely identified by examining the name of the structure in the last item in the pick path and the pick identifier.

9.7.2 Pick filters

For many applications it is not desirable that all primitives in a scene are able to be picked by a PICK logical input device. Using the work environment as an example, an application for constructing work environments might want to allow the operator to select a desk by picking. It should therefore be possible to pick the border of the desk, but not the accessories on it. Namesets and pick filters in PHIGS allow the application program to control which primitives can be picked by a particular PICK logical input device.

Each PICK logical input device has an associated pick filter, consisting of a pair of sets of names, called the *inclusion* set and the *exclusion* set. By default, the inclusion set and the exclusion set are empty and as a consequence, primitives are by default not pickable. Pick filters operate in the same way as the invisibility and highlighting filters described in Section 4.7.2. The examples of PICK input given above require namesets and pick filters to be set up before the primitive can actually be picked.

All primitives in the work environment can be made pickable in the following way. A nameset consisting of the single name NWKNV is associated with every output primitive in the scene. This may be accomplished by the program:

```
OPEN STRUCTURE(WKNV)

NMSETA(1)=NWKNV
ADD NAMES TO SET(1,NMSETA)
...
EXECUTE STRUCTURE(DESK)
...
```

The effect of the ADD NAMES TO SET function is to insert an *add names to set* structure element at the head of structure WKNV. On traversal, the name NWKNV is added to the current nameset which is bound to primitives created subsequently. The current nameset is inherited by a child structure from the parent, and in this example will result in the nameset containing the single name NWKNV being bound to each primitive.

To make all primitives pickable by a particular pick device requires the pick inclusion set for that device to be set to a nameset which contains the single name NWKNV, and the exclusion set to the empty set. Pick filters are set by the functions:

SET PICK FILTER(WS, PDEV, NIS, IS, NES, ES)

WS and PDEV identify the PICK logical input device, NIS and NES are the number of names in the inclusion and exclusion sets respectively, and IS and ES are arrays of names. For the example here, the pick filter is set to the required value by:

INS(1)=NWKNV
SET PICK FILTER(WS, PDEV, 1, INS, 0, ENS)

A more complex example which illustrates the power of the nameset and filter mechanism is to make only the phones pickable, and then to make all but one of the phones pickable. The name PHONES will be included in the nameset of the primitives of each phone. The names PHONEL, PHONEC and PHONER respectively will be included in the namesets of the individual phones (the names denote the left, centre and right phones respectively). This enables the three phones to be manipulated individually. These manipulations to the namesets can be accomplished with the following structure:

```
OPEN STRUCTURE(CN)
POLYLINE(12,XC,YC)
NMSETA(1)=PHONES
ADD NAMES TO SET(1,NMSETA)
NMSETA(1)=PHONEL
ADD NAMES TO SET(1, NMSETA)
MVRP(0.01,0.025)
EXECUTE STRUCTURE(PHON)
REMOVE NAMES FROM SET(1,NMSETA)
NMSETA(1)=PHONEC
ADD NAMES TO SET(1,NMSETA)
MVRP(0.058,0.0998)
EXECUTE STRUCTURE(PHON)
REMOVE NAMES FROM SET(1,NMSETA)
NMSETA(1)=PHONER
ADD NAMES TO SET(1,NMSETA)
MVRP(0.123,0.023)
EXECUTE STRUCTURE(PHON)
CLOSE STRUCTURE
```

The function invocation:

```
INS(1)=PHONES
SET PICK FILTER(WS, PDEV, 1, INS, 0, ENS)
```

sets the inclusive set for the PICK logical input device PDEV to the single name PHONES, and the exclusion set to the empty set. All primitives which contain the name PHONES in their namesets will be pickable by the device.

Suppose the left and right-most phones are to be pickable and the phone in the centre is not to be pickable. One way to achieve this is to set the inclusion name set to contain the names PHONEL and PHONER and the exclusion set to be empty:

```
INS(1)=PHONEL
INS(2)=PHONER
SET PICK FILTER(WS, PDEV, 2, INS, 0, ENS)
```

The namesets of the primitives representing the left-most phone contain the names PHONES and PHONEL. These primitives will be eligible for picking because their namesets have at least one element in common with the inclusion set of the pick filter (in this case the single name PHONEL), and no names in common with the exclusion set. Similarly the primitives representing the right-most phone will be pickable because their namesets have the name PHONER in common with the inclusion set and no names in common with the exclusion set. The primitives representing the centre phone contain the names PHONEC and PHONES in their nameset. None of these primitives will be eligible for picking because they have no names in common with the inclusion set.

An alternative way to achieve the same effect is to set the pick filter as follows:

```
INS(1)=PHONES
ENS(1)=PHONEC
SET PICK FILTER(WS, PDEV, 1, INS, 1, ENS)
```

The inclusion set contains the name PHONES and the exclusion set contains the name PHONEC. The primitives representing the left-most phone have the names PHONES and PHONEL in their nameset. The name PHONES is common with the inclusion set and no names are in common with the exclusion set and so the primitives representing the phone are pickable. The primitives representing the right-most phone have the names PHONES and PHONER in their namesets and similarly these primitives are pickable also. The primitives representing the centre phone have the names PHONES and PHONEC in their namesets. The name PHONES is in common with the inclusion set, but the name PHONEC is in common with the exclusion set, and so these primitives are not eligible for picking.

An earlier section (Section 4.7.2) has described the filter mechanisms for controlling visibility and highlighting of primitives. If an application wishes to indicate to the operator which primitives are eligible for picking by a particular PICK logical input device, this may be achieved by setting the highlighting filter to the same value as the PICK device pick filter. Any nameset accepted by the pick filter will also be accepted by the highlighting filter and so the primitive will be highlighted; any nameset which does not satisfy the pick filter will also fail to satisfy the highlighting filter and so the primitive will not be highlighted.

In the last example above, the primitives representing the left-most and right-most phones which are eligible for picking can be highlighted as follows:

```
INS(1)=PHONES
ENS(1)=PHONEC
SET HIGHLIGHTING FILTER(WS, 1, INS, 1, ENS)
```

The inclusion filter would allow all the phones to be highlighted but the exclusion filter stops the highlighting of the central phone.

9.8 VALUATOR

The VALUATOR logical input device returns a real value to the application. The function to request input from a VALUATOR logical input device is:

REQUEST VALUATOR(WS, DV, ST, VAL)

The application can specify the range within which the value may be; the mechanism for achieving this is described in a later section (Section 10.2.4).

The most natural physical input device to map onto the VALUATOR logical input device would be a potentiometer, but in common with the other logical input devices, the logical device can be supported by a wide range of physical input devices. PHIGS input devices are most likely to support input of values from a mouse at the very least. Many workstations provide a set of dials which will normally be mapped into a set of VALUATORs. At the other extreme, inputting the value from a keyboard may be provided.

An example of the use of a VALUATOR logical input device is to control the orientation of the lamp base in the example of Figure 5.8 (see Section 5.4.5). A program that allows the operator to input a new orientation of the base is:

```
OPEN STRUCTURE(LMP)
SET EDIT MODE(REPLACE)
SET ELEMENT POINTER(1)
```

```
100   CONTINUE
      REQUEST VALUATOR(WS, DV, ST, V)
      RTRP(V*(2*PI)/360)
      GOTO 100
```

It is assumed that the VALUATOR logical input device returns values in the range $0 \leq V \leq 360$, Thus the angle of rotation provided to RTRP will be in the range 0 to 2π. The input value provided by the operator is used to construct a transformation matrix which replaces the local modelling transformation at the head of the structure LMP.

A typical interaction is shown in the sequence from Figure 9.9 to Figure 9.12. Figure 9.9 shows the work environment with the lamp in a standard orientation.

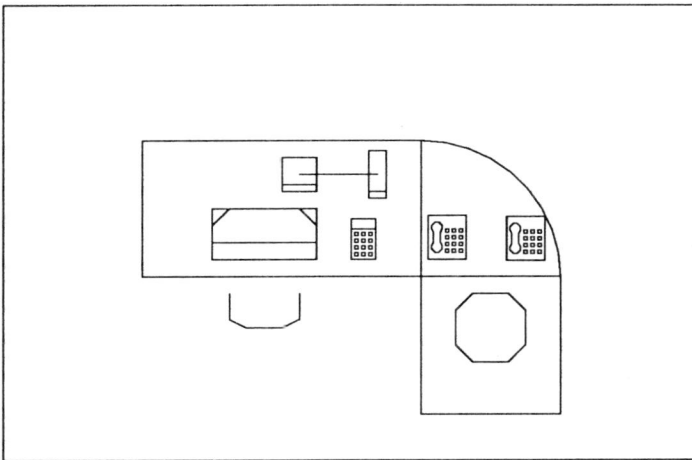

Figure 9.9: *Start of interaction*

In Figure 9.10, input has been requested from the operator; the state of the VALUATOR is echoed by the position of the pointer on the dial. Initially the value is 0. The logical input device could be presented to the operator as a dial. Alternatively, the operator might be required to point with a mouse at the tick mark on the dial or have the pointer follow the mouse as it moves around the circumference of the dial.

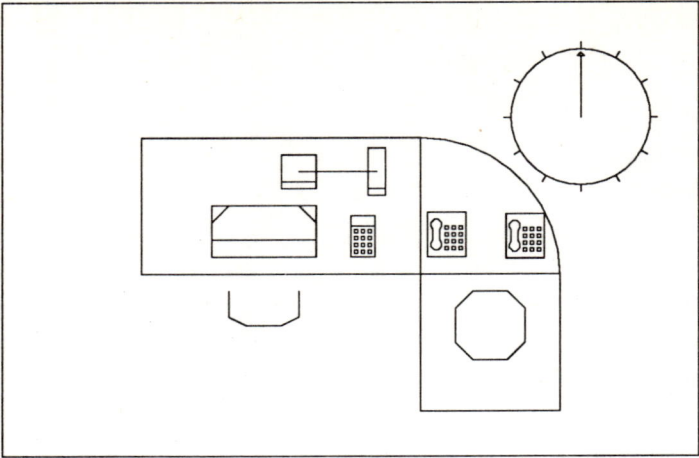

Figure 9.10: *Valuator initialized to 0*

Figure 9.11 shows the state just before the operator terminates the interaction. The value of the logical input device echoed by the dial is 108° anticlockwise.

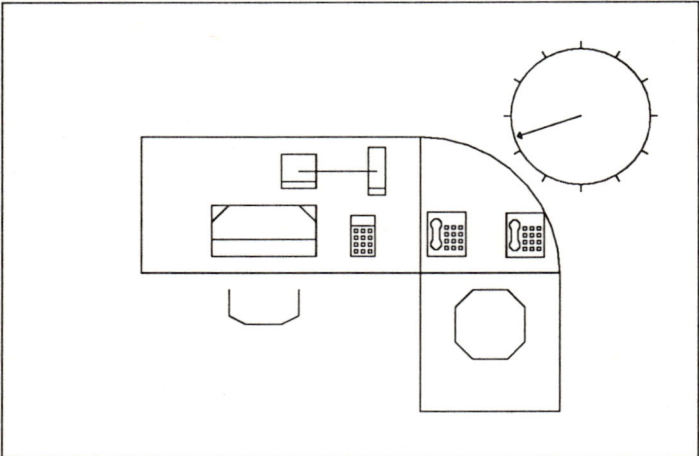

Figure 9.11: *VALUATOR set to 108°*

In Figure 9.12, the interaction has terminated and the lamp is redrawn in the new orientation. The application has regained control and the dial echoing the logical input device has disappeared.

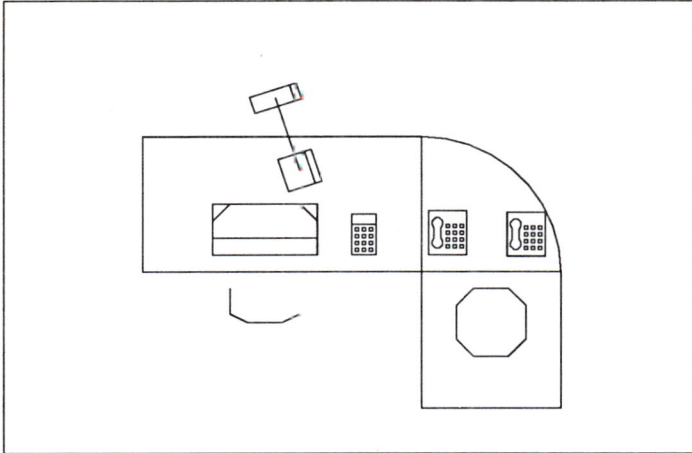

Figure 9.12: *Interaction complete with base rotated*

The only feedback given to the operator during the interaction is the position of the pointer on the dial indicating the current value of the logical input device. The operator does not see the effect of a particular logical input value on the lamp until the interaction has terminated. A later section (Section 10.1.5) will show how the lamp can be made to move under direct operator control using SAMPLE mode input.

9.9 CHOICE

The CHOICE logical input device returns an integer (greater than 0) which indicates which of a number of possibilities has been chosen by the operator. The PHIGS function to invoke a CHOICE logical input device in REQUEST mode is:

REQUEST CHOICE(WS, DV, ST, CH)

where CH returns the integer representing the selection made.

The example in the previous section showed how a VALUATOR logical input device could be used to allow the operator to define the orientation of an object, in this case the lamp base in the work environment. The structure network which models the lamp also allows the arm and light to be rotated (see Section 5.4.5).

A program which allows the operator to select the lamp, arm or light and then define the orientation of the component selected, could use a CHOICE logical input device to select the component, and a VALUATOR logical input device, as in the previous section, to define the orientation. A program to do this is:

```
    SET EDIT MODE(REPLACE)


50    CONTINUE
      REQUEST CHOICE(WS, CH1, ST, CH)
      IF(CH .GT. 3) GOTO 400
      REQUEST VALUATOR(WS, LOC1, ST, ROT)
      ROT=ROT*(2*PI)/360
      GOTO(100, 200, 300), CH



100   CONTINUE
C  LAMP
      OPEN STRUCTURE(LMP)
      SET ELEMENT POINTER(1)
      RTRP(ROT)
      CLOSE STRUCTURE
      GOTO 50


200   CONTINUE
C  ARM
      OPEN STRUCTURE(LMP)
      SET ELEMENT POINTER(3)
      RTPR(ROT)
      CLOSE STRUCTURE
      GOTO 50


300   CONTINUE
C  LIGHT
      OPEN STRUCTURE(ARM)
      SET ELEMENT POINTER(3)
      RTPR(ROT)
      CLOSE STRUCTURE
      GOTO 50


400   CONTINUE
      SET EDIT MODE(INSERT)
      STOP
```

Choice number 1 corresponds to changing the orientation of the base and, therefore, the whole lamp, choice number 2 to the arm (and light) and choice number 3 to the light. Changing the orientation of a component is achieved by replacing the structure element which controls the orientation.

CHOICE logical input devices can be realized by many different physical input devices. One obvious way to implement a CHOICE device is as a menu of items selectable by a mouse. The application program needs to be able to associate menu items with choice numbers; the mechanism for doing this is described when the logical input device initialization is discussed (see Section 10.2).

9.10 STRING

The STRING logical input device returns a character string to the application program. The PHIGS function for requesting input from a STRING logical input device is:

REQUEST STRING(WS, DV, ST, NCHARS, STR)

STR returns the character string that was input and NCHARS returns the number of characters it contains. STRING input is useful for inputting items such as filenames and labels.

STRING logical input devices would normally be mapped to a physical keyboard but hand-drawn characters or clicking with a mouse on a displayed pseudo-keyboard would be equally valid. As with the STROKE device, it is necessary to define the completion of the input by specifying an event which terminates the input.

10 INTERACTION

10.1 MODES OF INTERACTION

10.1.1 The PHIGS input model

In Chapter 9, the six logical input device classes of PHIGS have been described using REQUEST mode for illustration. In this section, the other input modes, SAMPLE and EVENT, are described.

The discussion in Chapter 9 has concentrated on the application's view of a logical input device rather than the operator's view. In part this has been done because PHIGS standardizes much more about the application program interface than about the operator interface. However, there are some aspects of the operator interface which are standardized by PHIGS and can be controlled by the application program. The control provided over logical input devices in PHIGS is very similar to that provided in GKS. PHIGS and GKS in fact share the same input model. To explain the three modes of interaction and the control provided over the operator interface, it is convenient first to describe the input model.

When a logical input device is activated in REQUEST mode, the operator will be given some visual or other signal that the device is active and input is required from it. This is called the *prompt* of the device. The operator will then be able to manipulate the value of the logical input device, for example, if the physical device is a mouse which is mapped onto a LOCATOR logical input device, the operator can move the mouse around and thus change the value of the LOCATOR. PHIGS gives the operator visual feedback of the LOCATOR position through the *echo* of the logical input device. For a LOCATOR, one possible echo is a cursor displayed at the current LOCATOR position on the display. To convert input values from the physical input device, for example raw relative movements from a mouse, into values of the logical input device requires some processing to be performed. This processing is called the *measure process*. The measure of a logical input device is a conceptual process which converts the input value of the logical input device. As the operator manipulates the device, for example moves the mouse, the measure process maintains the current measure value of the logical input device, that is the logical input value corresponding to the current state of the physical input device into which it is mapped. The current measure value is echoed to the operator by the device's echo. This also can be thought of as a process which is concurrent with the measure process.

In REQUEST mode input, the operator manipulates the measure of the logical input device, and at some point has to indicate that a particular input value is the one that satisfies the request, so that the interaction can terminate and the application program resume. In the input model, the action performed to indicate that a particular value is to satisfy a request, is called the *trigger*. The trigger of a logical input device can be thought of as a process which runs concurrently with the measure and echo processes. In the most general form, a trigger is a condition, for example a button press, or a timer click. When the condition is satisfied, the trigger process is said to fire. In REQUEST mode, when a device's trigger fires, the current value of the measure is returned to the application and the interaction with the device terminates.

When an interaction with a logical input device is complete, an *acknowledgement* is provided to the operator. The disappearance of the cursor when interaction with a LOCATOR logical input device is complete is a form of acknowledgement.

There are three other components of the input model which need to be described. The application program can provide an *initial value* for the device's measure. This is the value to which the device's measure will be initialized when an interaction commences.

The application can control the region of the display space in which the echo of the device will be displayed. In 3D this is called the *echo volume* and in 2D the *echo area*.

Finally, a *data record* may be passed to a logical input device upon initialization. This provides a way of passing additional control information, usually of a device specific or implementation specific kind, to the device upon initialization.

The three operating modes are now described in terms of this input model. A more detailed discussion of the device initialization functions is postponed until Section 10.2.

10.1.2 Mode setting

Each device can be in only one mode of operation at a time. By default, the operating mode for all devices is REQUEST mode.

The mode of operation is selected by calling a function of the type:

SET XXX MODE(WS, DV, MODE, EC)

where XXX denotes a device class (LOCATOR, STROKE, VALUATOR,

CHOICE, PICK, STRING). The first two parameters identify the specific device whose operating mode is to be set. The third parameter defines the mode of operation and can take one of three values REQUEST, SAMPLE, and EVENT.

The last parameter, EC, can have one of two values, ECHO and NOE-CHO. If ECHO is specified, the operator will be given some indication of the current value of the device, for example by displaying a cursor on the display space. If NOECHO is specified, echoing is turned off. The default setting is ECHO.

10.1.3 REQUEST mode

A typical REQUEST mode function is:

REQUEST CHOICE(WS, DV, ST, CH)

When REQUEST CHOICE is called, a new interaction with the logical input device commences. The measure process (initialized to the device's initial value) and trigger process for the device are started, and if echoing is enabled, the initial value will be echoed in the echo volume or area. The operator then moves the physical device (moves a mouse, rotates a tracker ball etc); the screen echo is updated accordingly. When the operator is satisfied with the current measure value, the operator can activate a trigger to indicate the input is complete. The physical trigger may be, for example, a mouse button click or a button press on a tracker ball.

A typical interaction with a CHOICE logical input device is shown in Figure 10.1 to Figure 10.4. The example is based on the lamp example from Section 9.9 in which the operator uses a CHOICE logical input device to indicate whether a rotation of the base, arm or light is to be specified next. For simplicity, only the large desk is shown with one accessory, the lamp. Figure 10.1 shows the state of the display before the interaction commences.

When REQUEST CHOICE is invoked, the echo appears on the screen, displaying the initial value of the logical input device. In this case the echo is a pop-up menu, and the initial value is CHOICE number 1 which corresponds to the 'BASE' of the lamp being selected. This is shown in Figure 10.2.

The form of the menu is primarily defined by the PHIGS implementation although the application will usually have the ability to tailor it to its own requirements, at the very least to define the text to go within the boxes. Which mouse button is used to signal the choice will be implementation dependent and may even depend on the window manager upon which the PHIGS implementation sits.

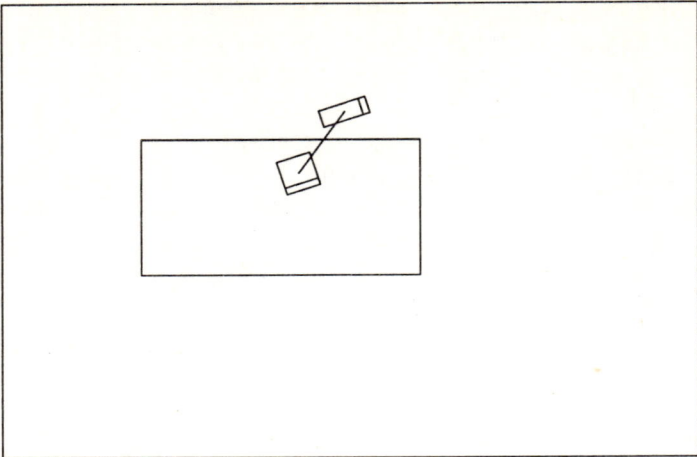

Figure 10.1: *Start of interaction*

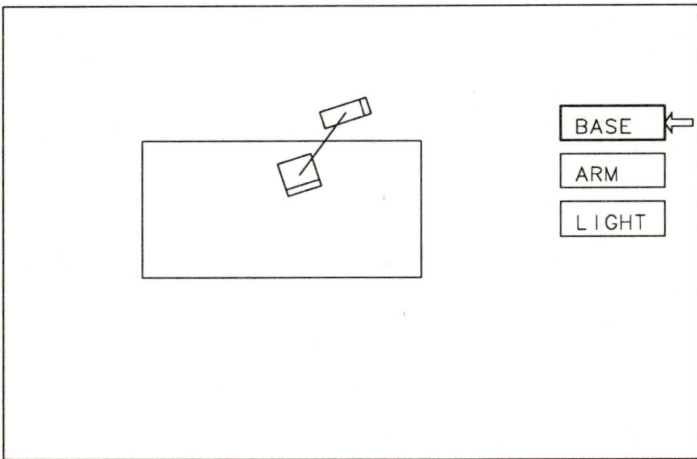

Figure 10.2: *CHOICE device starts with first initialized*

The current value of the device's measure is indicated by displaying the corresponding string in bold and emboldening the outline of the corresponding menu box; the position of the mouse device which controls the selection of menu items is shown by the cursor to the right of the menu. As the mouse is moved down, the second and then the third item of the menu is highlighted. This is shown in Figure 10.3.

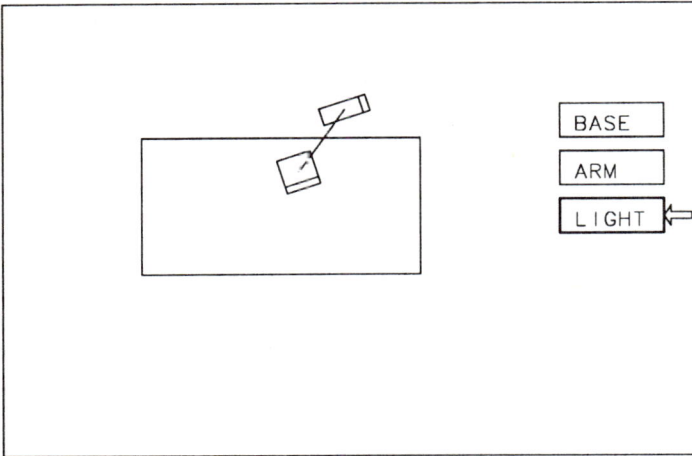

Figure 10.3: *A different choice is selected*

As the operator moves the mouse, the selected choice is highlighted until the decision is made as to what should be rotated next.

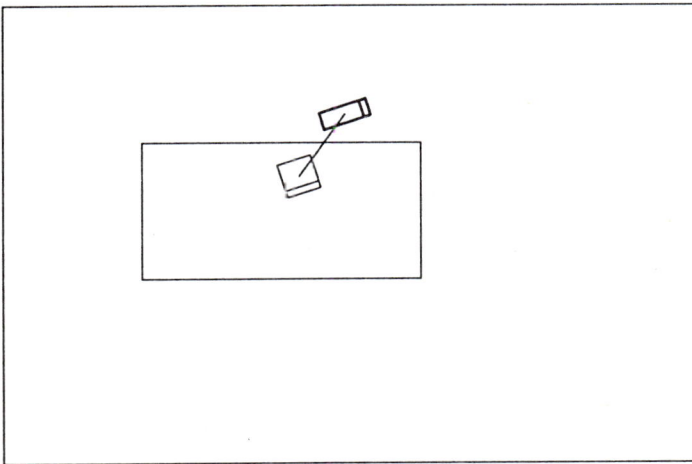

Figure 10.4: *Light is selected for rotation*

For example, the operator selects the third choice and fires the trigger (mouse button) to indicate that it is the LIGHT that is to be rotated. At this stage the CHOICE device is completed and the light is highlighted to indicate this is the selected part for rotation. This is shown in Figure 10.4.

10.1.4 Status

The REQUEST mode input functions each return a status parameter to indicate whether the request succeeded or not. For all device classes, the values OK and NONE are possible. If a REQUEST function returns the status value OK, this indicates that the operator completed the input normally and the remaining data specify a valid logical input value.

If the status value returns with the value NONE, the remaining data will not represent a valid logical input value, because the operator has terminated the REQUEST abnormally by indicating a *break*.

How the operator indicates a break depends on the input device. For a LOCATOR logical input device, an invalid LOCATOR position might be taken to indicate a break; alternatively the device might have two trigger conditions, one to indicate normal termination, the second to indicate a break. The left and right-hand buttons of a three button mouse might be used for this purpose.

The first LOCATOR example in Section 9.3 contained an infinite loop from which there was no exit. The device status could be used to provide an exit condition as shown below.

```
100   CONTINUE
      REQUEST LOCATOR(WS, DV, ST, VI, X, Y)
      IF(ST .EQ. NONE) GOTO 200
      MVRP(X, Y)
      GOTO 100


200   CONTINUE
```

The function REQUEST PICK and REQUEST CHOICE can return additional status values. For PICK input, the status value NOPICK can be returned. This differs from status value NONE in that the operator can terminate a REQUEST PICK with the normal trigger, but the device may not be pointing at any pickable output primitive.

Similarly, the CHOICE logical input device can return a status value NOCHOICE when the measure of the device does not correspond to any of the possible choices.

10.1.5 SAMPLE mode

In REQUEST mode input, either the logical input device is active or the application is active, at any time. The application is suspended while the device is active, and the entire interaction with the device is contained within the invocation of the REQUEST function.

SAMPLE mode input on the other hand allows the logical input device and the application to be active simultaneously. The operator can manipulate the device, and independently, the application can sample the current value of the device. Control returns immediately to the application, without waiting for the operator to perform any action.

An interaction with a device in SAMPLE mode is started by setting the device mode to SAMPLE. The VALUATOR device will be used for illustration. A device is set into SAMPLE mode by calling the function:

SET VALUATOR MODE(WS, DV, SAMPLE, EC)

The effect of setting the mode to SAMPLE is to start the measure process for the device, initialized to the initial value for the device, and to echo the measure of that device if echoing is turned on. The operator can then change the value of the device's measure by manipulating the physical input device.

The application can ascertain the current value of the device's measure by calling the function:

SAMPLE VALUATOR(WS, DV, VAL)

The SAMPLE functions for VALUATOR, LOCATOR, STRING and STROKE do not have a status parameter, but SAMPLE CHOICE and SAMPLE PICK do have status parameters:

SAMPLE CHOICE(WS, DV, ST, CH)

The SAMPLE PICK function has an additional input parameter, DEPTH, which indicates the depth of pick path to be returned and has output parameters PPD indicating the depth of pick path actually returned in the array PP:

SAMPLE PICK(WS, DV, DEPTH, ST, PPD, PP)

For SAMPLE CHOICE and SAMPLE PICK, the status value NONE cannot be returned by the functions. For SAMPLE CHOICE, the possible status values are OK and NOCHOICE and for SAMPLE PICK, OK and NOPICK.

In Section 9.8, a VALUATOR logical input device was used in REQUEST mode to control the orientation of the lamp on the desk in the work environment. The use of REQUEST mode input in such a context provides a rather unsatisfactory style of interaction. It would be more natural for the operator to be given immediate feedback, with the lamp rotating as the operator manipulates the VALUATOR device. This can be achieved by operating the device in SAMPLE mode as shown in the example below.

```
      OPEN STRUCTURE(LMP)

      SET EDIT MODE(REPLACE)
      SET ELEMENT POINTER(1)
      SET VALUATOR MODE(WS, DV, SAMPLE, ECHO)

100   CONTINUE

      SAMPLE VALUATOR(WS, DV, V)
      RTRP(V*2*PI/360)

      GOTO 100
```

There is no apparent way to terminate the loop in this program. The operator cannot, for example, use a break facility to indicate that the loop is to be terminated; as would be possible for REQUEST mode input. It is most natural to terminate the interaction using a second logical input device. One way of doing this, using a CHOICE logical input device in EVENT mode, is shown in Section 10.1.7.

The above example can be extended to use three VALUATOR logical input devices, each operating in SAMPLE mode, to control the orientation of the lamp base, arm and light, as follows:

```
      SET VALUATOR MODE(WS, DV1, SAMPLE, ECHO)
      SET VALUATOR MODE(WS, DV2, SAMPLE, ECHO)
      SET VALUATOR MODE(WS, DV3, SAMPLE, ECHO)
      SET EDIT MODE(REPLACE)

100   CONTINUE

C
C  lamp orientation controlled by DV1
C
      OPEN STRUCTURE(LMP)
      SET ELEMENT POINTER(1)
      SAMPLE VALUATOR(WS, DV1, ROT)
      RTRP(ROT*PI/180)


C
C  arm orientation controlled by DV2
C
      SET ELEMENT POINTER(3)
      SAMPLE VALUATOR(WS, DV2, ROT)
      RTPR(ROT*PI/180)
      CLOSE STRUCTURE
```

```
C
C  light orientation controlled by DV3
C
        OPEN STRUCTURE(ARM)
        SET ELEMENT POINTER(3)
        SAMPLE VALUATOR(WS, DV3, ROT)
        RTPR(ROT*PI/180)
        CLOSE STRUCTURE


        GOTO 100
```

The program samples the three devices in turn, updating the structure element controlling the orientation of lamp, arm and light so that the display reflects the status of the three devices. The effectiveness of this style of interaction in practice is dependent upon the ability of the implementation to display the structure network sufficiently rapidly to keep pace with the changes to the VALUATOR devices made by the operator.

As in REQUEST mode input, pairs of functions are provided for LOCATOR and STROKE logical input devices:

```
SAMPLE LOCATOR 3(WS, DV, VI, XPS, YPS, ZPS)
SAMPLE LOCATOR(WS, DV, VI, XPS, YPS)
SAMPLE STROKE 3(WS, DV, N, VI, NPTS, XPSA, YPSA, ZPSA)
SAMPLE STROKE(WS, DV, N, VI, NPTS, XPSA, YPSA)
```

The first of each pair returns positions in 3D world coordinate space; the second returns positions in 2D world coordinate space, obtained by dropping the Z-coordinate of the 3D positions returned through the input pipeline.

An interaction with a device in SAMPLE mode is terminated by resetting the operating mode of the device by calling the appropriate SET XXX MODE function. If the SET XXX MODE function is invoked to set a device to SAMPLE mode and it is already in SAMPLE mode, the current interaction with the device will be terminated and a new interaction initiated. Setting the operating mode to REQUEST returns the device to the inactive state and is the usual way of terminating an interaction with a device which is not to be used immediately in a new interaction.

10.1.6 EVENT mode

EVENT mode input is generated by the operator and entered into a central input queue. The application can asynchronously remove input events from the queue.

An input device is set into EVENT mode by calling the appropriate SET XXX MODE function with parameter EVENT. If there is an interaction with the device underway, the interaction is terminated. The device's measure process is started and initialized to the initial value; an echo process starts if echoing is enabled. The trigger process is also started unlike in SAMPLE mode.

As in REQUEST mode, the operator can change the value of the device's measure by manipulating the physical input device. When the operator has set the measure to the required value, the trigger is activated. In REQUEST mode at this point, the current measure value would be returned to the application program and the interaction with the device would terminate. In EVENT mode, an event report consisting of the identification of the logical input device (workstation identifier, device class, device identifier, logical input value, and control information) is added to the central input queue. The interaction with the device continues and a further event report is added to the queue from the device each time the trigger is activated.

There is one central input queue to which event reports from all logical input devices in EVENT mode are added.

The function AWAIT EVENT enables the application program to remove events from the event queue:

AWAIT EVENT(TIMEOUT, WS, DVCLASS, DV)

The queue is examined to see if it is empty. If it is, the application program is suspended until either an event report is added to the queue, or a maximum of TIMEOUT seconds have elapsed. If the latter condition is satisfied, DVCLASS returns the value NONE. TIMEOUT can be zero in which case the application program is not suspended and control passes back to the application immediately.

If the input queue is not empty, either when AWAIT EVENT is called or before TIMEOUT expires, the identification of the first event in the queue is returned to the application. DVCLASS specifies the input class of the event (LOCATOR, STROKE etc); WS and DV specify the device itself. The event input data are removed from the queue and transferred to the *current event report*.

The logical input value can be read from the current event report by the GET function corresponding to the input class of the event:

GET VALUATOR(VAL)
GET CHOICE(ST, CH)
GET STRING(NCHARS, STR)
GET PICK(DEPTH, ST, PPD, PP)

The GET CHOICE function returns either the status value OK, in which case the parameter CH contains a valid choice number, or the status NOCHOICE. The GET PICK function returns a status value (OK or NOPICK) and if the status is OK, a pick path is returned in the parameters PPD and PP. The first parameter is an input parameter which specifies the depth of pick path to return.

For the LOCATOR input class, two GET functions are provided:

GET LOCATOR 3(VI, XPOS, YPOS, ZPOS)
GET LOCATOR(VI, XPOS, YPOS)

Each function returns a view index and a position in world coordinates. The difference is that GET LOCATOR 3 returns a 3D position and GET LOCATOR a 2D position. As has been noted already, the LOCATOR logical input device is a 3D device and a 3D position is entered into the event report in the input queue. GET LOCATOR returns the X and Y-coordinates of the position only and ignores the Z-coordinate. Thus if the same event report were to be retrieved with GET LOCATOR 3 and GET LOCATOR, the view index and both X and Y-coordinates of the position would be returned with the same values by each function.

Similarly for the STROKE input class, two GET functions are provided:

GET STROKE 3(N, VI, NPTS, XPA, YPA, ZPA)
GET STROKE(N, VI, NPTS, XPA, YPA, ZPA)

The second discards the Z-coordinates of each of the points in the STROKE event report.

The power of EVENT mode input really stems from the asynchronous nature of this mode, in other words the operator can generate input events independently of the application's processing of them. This is most useful when more than one device is operating in EVENT mode at the same time (the operator can generate events from the devices in any order and the application can readily process the events in the order in which they were generated). It is also useful in conjunction with SAMPLE mode input; this will be illustrated in Section 10.1.7.

The first example of EVENT mode input is a simple application which enables the operator to input a sequence of points. Although it is somewhat contrived, it illustrates a number of important considerations which apply equally to more complex examples.

The operator can input a sequence of points one at a time, and can define the symbol with which the points are to be marked. The marker symbol can be changed at any time, with the result that all points input so far and points input subsequently will be marked with the new symbol until such time as the marker size is changed again. At this point, all the symbols will take the new form.

The example uses two logical input devices, both operating in EVENT mode. A LOCATOR device allows the operator to define points and a CHOICE device enables the operator to define the symbol with which the points are to be marked and to terminate the program. A typical screen layout is shown in Figure 10.5.

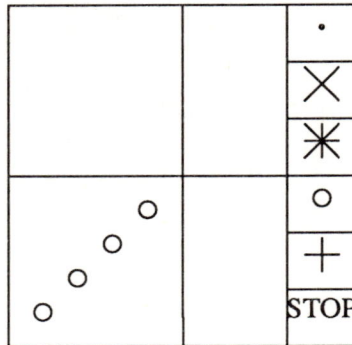

Figure 10.5 Example EVENT interaction

The marker symbol is selected by the CHOICE device from the menu displayed on the right of the screen. Positions are input by the LOCATOR device; in the screen layout shown, the LOCATOR echo is the pair of cross hairs.

The two devices might be implemented using a mouse with the pressing of one button signalling a LOCATOR event and another giving the CHOICE event. As the echo is a pair of cross hairs extending across the menu, the horizontal cross hair could be used to define the CHOICE position irrespective of where the vertical cross hair is. Consequently, there would be no need to physically move to the right to activate the CHOICE device, it could be done from the current X-position of the mouse, the Y-position controlling the measure of the CHOICE logical input device.

One solution to the problem is the program:

```
SET EDIT MODE(INSERT)

OPEN STRUCTURE(SPMEG)
POST STRUCTURE(WS, SPMEG, 0.2)

SET MARKER TYPE(2)
SET LOCATOR MODE(WS, DV1, EVENT, ECHO)
SET CHOICE MODE(WS, DV2, EVENT, ECHO)
```

```
100   CONTINUE
      AWAIT EVENT(60, WST, CLASS, DV)
      IF(CLASS .EQ. NONE) GOTO 100
      IF(CLASS .EQ. LOCATOR) GOTO 200

      GET CHOICE(ST, OCHOIC)
      IF(ST .EQ. NOCHOICE) GOTO 100
      IF(OCHOIC .EQ. 6) GOTO 300
      SET EDIT MODE(REPLACE)
      SET ELEMENT POINTER(1)
      SET MARKER TYPE(OCHOIC)
      GOTO 100

200   CONTINUE
      CLOSE STRUCTURE
      OPEN STRUCTURE(SPMEG)
      SET EDIT MODE(INSERT)
      GET LOCATOR(VI, XA(1), YA(1))
      POLYMARKER(1, XA, YA)
      GOTO 100

300   CONTINUE
      CLOSE STRUCTURE
      SET EDIT MODE(INSERT)
      STOP
C     STOP option selected, terminates program
```

This approach uses a single structure. The first element in the structure is a set marker type element. Subsequent elements are polymarker elements, each of which marks one of the positions input. The structure is:

0	SPMEG
1	SET MARKER TYPE
2	POLYMARKER (1, XA, YA)
3	
4	

The program structure consists of an initialization section to set up the initial structure (consisting of a single structure element to set the marker type to 2, the plus symbol, which is the default marker symbol) and initialize the logical input devices.

The main body of the program is a loop which removes events from the queue one at a time and performs the appropriate action depending on whether the event is a CHOICE or LOCATOR event. If no input arrives before the timeout expires on AWAIT EVENT, the variable CLASS will be returned with the value NONE, and the program will loop waiting for input to arrive.

For CHOICE input, choice number 6 corresponds to the menu item STOP. If this item is selected, the program terminates. Other choice numbers correspond to the selection of a new marker symbol. The choice numbers correspond to the marker type used by SET MARKER TYPE. The action of the program in processing a choice number in the range 1 to 5 is to replace the set marker type structure element at position 1 in the structure. An alternative way to position the element pointer will be shown in Section 12.4 when INQUIRY functions are described.

Although this solution works, it lacks elegance in certain respects. One structure is always open, but the position of the element pointer and the edit mode at the start of the central loop (label 100) depends on whether the previous event was a CHOICE or a LOCATOR event. This style of programming can lead to programs which are difficult to understand and consequently, to maintain.

An alternative solution is given below. This uses two structures, the first of which (SPMEG1) holds the set marker type element and executes a second structure (SPMEG2) which holds the polymarker elements.

As the second structure is undefined when SPMEG1 is posted initially, an empty structure will be created. Each time a new polymarker position is entered, the appropriate polymarker structure element is added to the end of the structure SPMEG2.

```
        SET EDIT MODE(INSERT)
        OPEN SRUCTURE(SPMEG1)
        SET MARKER TYPE(2)
        EXECUTE STRUCTURE(SPMEG2)
        CLOSE STRUCTURE

        SET LOCATOR MODE(WS, DV1, EVENT, ECHO)
        SET CHOICE MODE(WS, DV2, EVENT, ECHO)
        POST STRUCTURE(WS, SPMEG1, 0.2)

100     CONTINUE
        AWAIT EVENT(60, WST, CLASS, DV)
        IF(CLASS .EQ. NONE) GOTO 100
        IF(CLASS .EQ. LOCATOR) GOTO 200
```

```
        GET CHOICE(ST, CCHOIC)
        IF(ST .EQ. NOCHOICE) GOTO 100
        IF(OCHOIC .EQ. 6) GOTO 300

        OPEN STRUCTURE(SPMEG1)
        SET EDIT MODE(REPLACE)
        SET ELEMENT POINTER(1)
        SET MARKER TYPE(OCHOIC)
        CLOSE STRUCTURE
        SET EDIT MODE(INSERT)
        GOTO 100

200     CONTINUE
        GET LOCATOR(VI, XA(1), YA(1))
        OPEN STRUCTURE(SPMEG2)
        POLYMARKER(1, XA, YA)
        CLOSE STRUCTURE
        GOTO 100

300     CONTINUE
C       STOP option selected, terminates program
```

The appropriate structure is opened when each event is processed and then closed before the next event is processed. Edit mode has the value INSERT at the end of processing each event. In general it is important to consider the operations that will be performed upon a structure network when it is designed. Careful design of the structure network can lead to a tidier, easier to understand and more maintainable program structure.

PHIGS provides a useful housekeeping function to manipulate the input queue. It is possible for the operator to input more than one value from an input device when in a particular context the application program only requires one. The function:

FLUSH DEVICE EVENTS(WS, DVCLASS, DV)

removes all events from the specified logical input device from the input queue.

10.1.7 Mixed input modes

Section 10.1.3 showed the use of a CHOICE logical input device in REQUEST mode to select the component of an object to which a rotation, specified by a VALUATOR logical input device in REQUEST mode was to be applied. Section 10.1.5 showed the use of SAMPLE mode to achieve a smoother interaction with the VALUATOR device, and the use of multiple VALUATOR devices to control independent rotations in an object. The example in this section is the same lamp example as used earlier in this Chapter in which the orientation of the base, arm and light can be controlled by the operator. However this time a single VALUATOR device is used in SAMPLE mode to control the orientation, and a CHOICE device is used in EVENT mode to determine which rotation the VALUATOR should be coupled to. The program is as follows:

```
        SET VALUATOR MODE(WS, DV1, SAMPLE, NOECHO)
        SET CHOICE MODE(WS, DV2, EVENT, ECHO)
        SET EDIT MODE(REPLACE)
        OCH=1

100     CONTINUE
        SAMPLE VALUATOR(WS, DV1, ROT)
        GOTO(200, 300, 400), OCH

200     CONTINUE
C  lamp orientation
        OPEN STRUCTURE(LMP)
        SET ELEMENT POINTER(1)
        RTRP(ROT*PI/180)
        CLOSE STRUCTURE
        GOTO 500

300     CONTINUE
C  arm orientation
        OPEN STRUCTURE(LMP)
        SET ELEMENT POINTER(3)
        RTPR(ROT*PI/180)
        CLOSE STRUCTURE
        GOTO 500

400     CONTINUE
C  light orientation
        OPEN STRUCTURE(ARM)
        SET ELEMENT POINTER(3)
        RTPR(ROT*PI/180)
        CLOSE STRUCTURE
        GOTO 500
```

```
500    CONTINUE
       AWAIT EVENT(0, WST, CLASS, DEV)
       IF(CLASS .NE. CHOICE) GOTO 100
       GET CHOICE(ST, CH)
       IF(ST .EQ. NOCHOICE) GOTO 100
       IF(CH .EQ. 4) GOTO 300
       OCH=CH
       GOTO 100


300    CONTINUE
C      STOP option selected
```

The code structure above has been chosen for ease of explanation, clearly optimizations are possible to reduce the number of OPEN STRUCTURE and CLOSE STRUCTURE calls. For example, if the orientation of the same component is being altered on successive cycles through the central loop, it is an unnecessary overhead to close and reopen the corresponding structure. Also, if the orientation of a component is not changed from the value currently held in the structure, it is an unnecessary overhead to replace the corresponding structure element with an identical element.

On each cycle through the central loop, the VALUATOR device is sampled and a new rotation applied to the currently selected component of the lamp. The variable OCH records the current selection. By default it is the lamp base. The input queue is examined on each cycle through the loop (labelled 500) and if there is a CHOICE event in the queue, the event is retrieved from the queue and if one of the base, arm or light is selected, the variable OCH is set accordingly. If the program termination option is selected, appropriate code not shown here will be executed. The AWAIT EVENT function call has a zero timeout so that the program is not suspended awaiting event input on each cycle. The CLASS returned will be NONE until the operator triggers the CHOICE device. In this case the central loop will be executed again without changing the value of the variable OCH and hence the component whose orientation is being controlled.

The VALUATOR device is used in NOECHO mode because in this case adequate feedback is provided to the operator by the movement of the lamp itself.

One problem with this example is that when a new component is selected by the CHOICE device, the rotation applied to it will be the current value of the VALUATOR device on the next cycle through the loop, which if the operator has not altered the VALUATOR device in the meantime will be the last rotation applied to the previously selected object. This can lead to very unsatisfactory interaction. A way to overcome this problem is described in the next section on device initialization.

10.2 INITIALIZATION OF LOGICAL INPUT DEVICES

In Section 10.1.1, the components of the PHIGS logical input device model were described and it was stated that the application program can control some of the characteristics of each logical input device. This control is provided through the device initialization functions. PHIGS provides a pair of initialization functions for each class of logical input device. The functions for LOCATOR, STROKE, CHOICE, VALUATOR and STRING have the form:

INITIALIZE XXX 3
  (WS, DV, initial value, PE, EVOL, data record)

INITIALIZE XXX
  (WS, DV, initial value, PE, XMN, XMX, YMN, YMX, data record)

The pair of functions for the PICK logical input device have an additional parameter, path order, after the data record.

The first two parameters identify the device to be initialized. These are followed by one or more parameters defining the initial value of that type of device. The parameter PE defines the prompt and echo type, as described in Section 10.2.2. For the INITIALIZE XXX 3 functions, the parameter EVOL (an array with six elements) defines the echo volume as described in Section 10.2.3. For the INITIALIZE XXX functions, the parameters XMN to YMX define the echo area for the device (see Section 10.2.3). The remaining parameters define the data record for the device (see Section 10.2.4).

10.2.1 Initial value

In describing the operation of the different operating modes for logical input devices in terms of the PHIGS input model, we have mentioned that when a measure process comes into existence it is initialized to the initial value for the device. The device initialization functions enable the application to set the initial value to which the measure process will be initialized. PHIGS provides a default value if the initialization function is not called.

An example of an initialization function is:

INITIALIZE VALUATOR(WS, DV, VALUE, ...)

When this function is invoked for a particular VALUATOR device, the effect is that the device's measure is initialized to the value specified by VALUE until the initial value is changed by a subsequent invocation of the function.

A good use for initialize is to ensure that the input resulting from one interaction is used as the initial value for the next. This mechanism provides a way to solve the problem raised at the end of Section 10.1.7, where we want an interaction to change the orientation of a component of an object to start from the current orientation. Referring to that example, if the orientation of the lamp, arm and light are stored in variables LMPROT, ARMROT and LHTROT respectively, the code after label 500 could be modified as follows to achieve the desired effect:

```
500  CONTINUE
     AWAIT EVENT(0, WST, CLASS, DEV)
     IF(CLASS .NE. CHOICE) GOTO 100
     GET CHOICE(ST, CH)
     IF(ST .EQ. NOCHOICE) GOTO 100
     IF(CH .EQ. 4) GOTO 1000
     OCH=CH
     GOTO(600, 700, 800), OCH


600  CONTINUE
C base
     IROT=LMPROT
     GOTO 900

700  CONTINUE
C  arm
     IROT=ARMROT
     GOTO 900

800  CONTINUE
     IROT=LHTROT

900  CONTINUE
     SET VALUATOR MODE(WS, DV1, REQUEST, NOECHO)
     INITIALIZE VALUATOR(WS, DV1, IROT, ...)
     SET VALUATOR MODE(WS, DV1, SAMPLE, NOECHO)
     GOTO 100

1000 CONTINUE
C     STOP option selected
```

Note that the current interaction with the device has to be terminated and the device restored to REQUEST mode before the INITIALIZE function can be called. When a new interaction with the device in SAMPLE mode is started, the device's measure will be initialized to the value given by the variable IROT.

The initial value specified by the INITIALIZE function must be a valid value when the function is invoked. The one exception to this is that for the LOCATOR and STROKE devices, a view index may be specified which is undefined when the function is invoked. If the view index is still undefined when a measure process comes into existence, the default view index (0) is used to transform the initial point(s).

INITIALIZE LOCATOR has initial value parameters which specify a view index and the X and Y-coordinates of an initial position. INITIAL-IZE LOCATOR 3 specifies an initial value consisting of a view index and 3D position. The effect of the 2D function is to set the X and Y-coordinates of the initial position to the value specified and to leave the Z-coordinate unchanged. The default value of the latter is implementation dependent. If the Z-value of the initial point is then invalid, the Z-value is set to a value corresponding to the maximum Z-value of the workstation window, which will give a valid position. The INITIALIZE STROKE function has an analogous effect.

It should be noted that some devices may not be able to use the initial value properly, for example for some types of input hardware it may not be possible to initialize the position of cross hairs. In such cases the operator will see the initial echo determined by the device hardware rather than the application program.

10.2.2 Prompt and echo type

In the examples given earlier in this Chapter, several forms of echoing have been used, for example cross hairs for a LOCATOR device and menu for a CHOICE device. The prompt and echo type parameter enables the application program to control the form of prompting and echoing to be used.

Device hardware again poses a problem here in that a particular device may only support a limited range, or indeed only one, form of prompting and echoing. For any logical input device, the prompt and echo type 1 can be specified (parameter PE is given the value 1), for example:

> INITIALIZE VALUATOR(WS, DV, IVAL, 1, ...)

The form of the echo corresponding to prompt and echo type 1 is device dependent and is the *usual* echo for the device. The prompt and echo types for some particular values of PE are given standard meanings by PHIGS and positive values outside this range are reserved for standardization through the Registration process. Zero and negative values of PE have implementation dependent meanings. Not all standardized values of prompt and echo type may be available for a particular device, but when the values are supported, they must have the meanings that have been standardized.

The prompt and echo types that have been standardized by PHIGS are grouped by input class. For all device classes, prompt and echo type 1 is a device dependent technique which must be available (though for the PICK logical input device some guidance is given, see below).

LOCATOR prompt and echo types

2 crosshair cursor intersecting at the current measure

3 tracking cross with its centre at the current measure

4 rubber band line connecting the initial value to the current measure

5 rectangle with one corner at the initial value and the diagonally opposite corner at the current measure

6 a digital representation of the coordinates of the current measure

STROKE prompt and echo types

2 display a digital representation within the echo volume

3 display a marker at each point of the current STROKE

4 display a line joining successive points of the current stroke

VALUATOR prompt and echo types

2 display a graphical representation of the current measure within the echo volume (for example, a dial, a pointer or a sliding scale)

3 display a digital representation of the current measure within the echo volume

CHOICE prompt and echo type

2 prompt using hardware built into the physical device (for example, lights associated with buttons)

3 a display of character strings displayed within the echo volume; the operator selects a string

4 similar to 3, but the operator types in from a keyboard the character string to be selected

5   prompt using a structure named in the CHOICE data record. The structure is displayed in the echo volume and the choice numbers correspond to the pick identifiers in the structure

PICK prompt and echo types

1   highlight the picked primitive for a short period of time using a device dependent technique which must be available

2   highlight the contiguous group of primitives with the same pick identifier as the picked primitive, or highlight all primitives in the structure with the same pick identifier as the picked primitive

3   highlight the whole posted network structure containing the picked primitive

STRING prompt and echo type

1   this is the only type defined in PHIGS

10.2.3 Echo volume and area

For some prompt and echo types it is appropriate for the application program to be able to specify the region of the workstation display in which the echo will be displayed. An example is VALUATOR prompt and echo type 2 which displays a graphical representation of the current measure, for example as a dial or slider bar, within the echo volume.

An echo volume is specified in the INITIALIZE XXX functions by the parameter EVOL which is an array with six components, specifying the minimum and maximum X, Y and Z-coordinates of the volume XMN, XMX, YMN, YMX, ZMN, ZMX in that order. There is a restriction that:

$$XMN < XMX, YMN < YMX, ZMN \le ZMX$$

The echo volume is specified in the device coordinates of the workstation. An echo area in device coordinates of the workstation is specified by the parameters XMN, XMX, YMN, YMX of the INITIALIZE XXX functions with the restriction that:

$$XMN < XMX, YMN < YMX$$

The effect of these 2D functions is to set the X and Y-limits of the echo volume. The Z-limits remain unchanged.

10.2.4 Input data record

The input data record is a mechanism for providing additional control information to logical input devices, which is often dependent upon the prompt and echo type. For example, LOCATOR prompt and echo type 4 is a rubber band line. Control over the linestyle with which the rubber band line is drawn can be provided through the input data record.

The precise form of the input data record is dependent upon the language binding. In Fortran, input data records are a CHARACTER*80 array (DATREC) preceded by the size of the array (LDR), for example:

INITIALIZE VALUATOR(WS, DV, VALUE, PE,
    XMN, XMX, YMN, YMX, LDR, DATREC)

The data record may contain INTEGER, REAL and CHARACTER entities. The routine PACK DATA RECORD is provided by the Fortran language binding to pack data entities into a data record:

PACK DATA RECORD(IL, IA, RL, RA, SL, LSTR, STR, MLDR,
    ERRIND, LDR, DATREC)

DATREC is the CHARACTER*80 array into which the data record is put by PACK DATA RECORD. MLDR is the size of DATREC, and the output parameter LDR is the number of array elements used in DATREC. ERRIND indicates whether any errors occurred in the packing; a value of 0 indicates successful execution. IA, RA and STR contain data (integers, reals and character strings) to be packed into the data record. IL, RL and SL are the number of integers, reals and strings, respectively. For character strings, SL indicates the number of character strings, and the array, LSTR, indicates the length of each string. The strings themselves are arranged in the single array STR.

The Fortran language binding also provides a routine, UNPACK DATA RECORD, which performs the opposite, unpacking, task.

For some logical input device classes, positions in the data record are reserved for specific items of control information. Entries in the data record fall into four categories:

(1) Entries occupying reserved positions in the data record which *must* be interpreted if provided by the application.

(2) Entries occupying reserved positions in the data record which *may* be interpreted if provided by the application.

(3) Entries occupying reserved positions in the data record which are used for control of specific prompt and echo types. A particular logical input device may or may not use some or all of these values.

(4) Entries which provide additional information that is implementation dependent and can be specific to a device class or prompt and echo type.

STROKE, VALUATOR and STRING logical input devices have data record items of the first type:

(1) *STROKE* : the size of the input buffer;

(2) *VALUATOR* : the low and high values of the VALUATOR range;

(3) *STRING* : the input buffer size.

The VALUATOR data record provides the mechanism for defining the range of the VALUATOR logical input device used in Section 9.8 and subsequent examples. The device provides angles in the range 0° to 360°, thus the low value would be set to 0 and the high value to 360. The low and high values of the range are specified by the first two elements in the real array passed to PACK DATA RECORD. The range of a VALUATOR device, DV, could be set to 0 to 360 as follows:

```
IL=0
RL=2
RA(1)=0
RA(2)=360
SL=0
PACK DATA RECORD(IL, IA, RL, RA, SL, LSTR, STR, MLDR,
ERRIND, LDR, DATREC)
INITIALIZE VALUATOR(WS, DV, IVAL, PET, XMN, XMX, YMN, YMX,
LDR, DATREC)
```

The STROKE and STRING logical input devices have data record items of the second type, concerned with editing, but these are beyond the scope of this book.

LOCATOR, STROKE and CHOICE devices have data record entries of the third type, for example for the CHOICE device, prompt and echo type 3, the list of CHOICE strings (menu items) is specified in position 1 of the data record. For prompt and echo type 5, the structure identifier is specified in position 1 and the list of pick identifiers to be associated with choice numbers is specified in position 2.

For more detailed information on input data records, the reader is referred to the documentation of the PHIGS implementation in use. If portability between PHIGS implementations is important, care should be taken in the use of facilities accessed through data records.

10.2.5 PICK path order

The INITIALIZE PICK 3 and INITIALIZE PICK functions have an additional parameter, PORDER, after the data record. This parameter determines the order in which a pick path is to be returned to the application program by the REQUEST PICK, SAMPLE PICK and GET PICK functions. Two values are possible, TOPFIRST and BOTTOMFIRST. The examples in Section 9.7 used TOPFIRST order.

For TOPFIRST order, the structure specified in any pick path item is the parent of the structure specified in the subsequent item. The first example in Section 9.7 was the pick path:

Structure	Pick Identifier	Element Position
WKNV	0	2
DESK	0	1
LG	0	3
BLOT	0	1

The structure WKNV is a parent of DESK, DESK is a parent of LG, and LG is a parent of BLOT.

If the order had been BOTTOMFIRST, the pick path would have been returned in the reverse order:

STRUCTURE	Pick Identifier	Element Position
BLOT	0	1
LG	0	3
DESK	0	1
WKNV	0	2

In this order, the structure specified in any pick path item is a child of the structure specified in the subsequent item. Thus BLOT is a child of LG, LG is a child of DESK and so on.

If only part of the pick path is to be returned by specifying a DEPTH (see Section 9.7) less than the maximum possible, the number of entries returned will be counted from the top so that the set of entries returned will differ depending on whether TOPFIRST or BOTTOMFIRST is defined.

10.3 FURTHER INPUT FUNCTIONS

The discussion of EVENT input has dealt with the case that a single event report is added to the input queue each time the operator fires a trigger. It is possible for more than one event to enter the queue per trigger firing and this is discussed next. The input queue is of finite size and Section 10.3.2 deals with overflow of the input queue.

10.3.1 Simultaneous events

It is possible for any trigger to be shared between a number of logical input devices. A typical example is a LOCATOR and CHOICE device, both of which are mapped onto a multi-button mouse. Clicking any button triggers the LOCATOR device. The CHOICE device is triggered by any button click, and the choice number corresponds to the individual buttons; for a three button mouse, the left-hand button might be choice 1, the centre button choice 2 and the right-hand button choice 3.

Suppose both the LOCATOR and CHOICE device are enabled in EVENT mode. If the operator clicks the left-hand button, two event reports will be added to the input queue: a LOCATOR event report and a CHOICE event report. The former contains the LOCATOR measure when the trigger fired and the latter the CHOICE measure (the choice number corresponding to the button clicked). The two events are referred to as *simultaneous events* because they originate from the same trigger firing. The two events enter the input queue consecutively, but in no particular order.

The function:

INQUIRE MORE SIMULTANEOUS EVENTS(ERRIND, ANYMORE)

enables the application program to discover which events originated from the same trigger action. The parameter ANYMORE can return the values MORE and NOMORE. If the next event in the input queue was generated simultaneously with the last event removed, the value MORE is returned. If the next event was generated by a different trigger firing, the value NOMORE is returned.

10.3.2 Input queue overflow

The input queue is likely to be of finite size in any PHIGS implementation and it is possible that the operator may add events to the queue faster than the application removes them. Thus the input queue may overflow and input data will be lost.

When the input queue overflows, no more event reports are added to the queue until it has been completely emptied by the application program. Feedback would normally be given to the operator that events are not being added to the input queue.

The next time the application program attempts to remove input from the queue after overflow has occurred, AWAIT EVENT will report an error. This can be trapped by replacing the ERROR HANDLING procedure as described in Section 12.6.

Alternatively the inquiry function:

INQUIRE INPUT QUEUE OVERFLOW(ERRIND, WS, CLASS, DV)

can be used. If the error indicator, ERRIND, returns the value 0, input queue overflow has occurred. If the value 257 is returned, input queue overflow has not occurred. Normally this function would be called immediately after AWAIT EVENT. If overflow has occurred, the remaining parameters indicate which logical input device was attempting to add the event report which caused the overflow.

Event reports in the queue when overflow occurs are valid event reports and can be removed in the normal way by calling AWAIT EVENT. Only when the queue is empty (AWAIT EVENT returns the device class NONE), will new events start to be added to the queue. Events can also be removed from the queue using the FLUSH DEVICE EVENTS function described in Section 10.1.6.

10.4 INCREMENTAL SPATIAL SEARCH

Incremental spatial search is a special type of inquiry function on the contents of the central structure store (CSS). It is described in this Chapter because it has some similarities to pick input. The INCREMENTAL SPATIAL SEARCH function searches the CSS from a specified position, looking for a structure element which generates an output primitive which satisfies a spatial search criterion. To satisfy the search criterion, some part of the output primitive must fall within a specified region of world coordinate space.

There are two forms of the incremental spatial search function, a full 3D version and a 2D version:

INCREMENTAL SPATIAL SEARCH 3
(SRPX, SRPY, SRPZ, SDIST, SPTHSZ, SPATH, MCLIPF, SRCHCI,
NFLN, NFLISX, NFLIS, NFLESX, NFLES, IFLN, IFLISX, IFLIS,
IFLESX, IFLES, IPTHSZ, ERRIND, FPTHSZ, FPATH)

INCREMENTAL SPATIAL SEARCH
(SRPX, SRPY, SDIST, SPTHSZ, SPATH, MCLIPF, SRCHCI,
NFLN, NFLISX, NFLIS, NFLESX, NFLES, IFLN, IFLISX, IFLIS,
IFLESX, IFLES, IPTHSZ, ERRIND, FPTHSZ, FPATH)

The parameters SRPX, SRPY (and SPRZ in the 3D function) and SDIST in each function define the search region. SRPX, SRPY, SRPZ is a 3D or 2D position and SDIST is search distance, both expressed in world coordinates. The search region is a sphere in world coordinates; for the 2D function, the position is expanded to 3D by the addition of a Z-coordinate with value 0.

SPATH is the starting path, which defines the position in the CSS at which the search will commence. SPTHSZ is the number of elements in the path. The starting path is defined in a similar way to pick path; it is a list of items, each of which consists of a structure identifier and an element position.

MCLIPF is a flag which can takes the values CLIP or NOCLIP. If the value CLIP is given, any modelling clipping operations defined in the CSS will be applied to primitives before they are tested against the search region. Thus only portions of output primitives not removed by modelling clipping are considered by the search. If the flag has the value NOCLIP, all modelling clipping is ignored.

The parameter SRCHCI specifies a search ceiling index. This index defines a position in the search path. The search will start at the position in the CSS identified by the starting path and will continue until either a structure element satisfying the search is found, or the end of the structure pointed at by the ceiling index is reached.

NFLN to NFLES and IFLN to IFLES specify a normal filter list and an inverted filter list respectively. Each filter consists of a pair of sets of names, the inclusion set and the exclusion set, exactly like the invisibility, highlighting and pick filters. To be considered for testing against the search criterion, a primitive's name set must be accepted by all the filters in the normal list and rejected by all the filters in the inverted filter list.

The binding of the filter lists is rather complicated and will be illustrated by the normal filter list. NFLN is the number of normal filters. The names in the inclusion sets of these filters are specified in the array NFLIS. The array NFLISX is an array of pointers into NFLIS, which specify the element in NFLIS at which each inclusion set ends.

Similarly, the names in the exclusion sets are specified in the array NFLES. NFLESX is an array of pointers to the end of each exclusion set. The inverted filter list is specified in an analogous manner.

ERRIND is an error indicator which has the value 0 if the function terminates successfully. If ERRIND has a non-zero value, the value indicates the reason why the function did not terminate successfully.

FPATH is the found path, which defines the position in the CSS of the structure element generating the output primitive which satisfied the search criterion. The found path is specified in exactly the same way as the starting path. If the search ceiling is reached before an output primitive satisfying the search criterion is found, a null found path is returned.

Spatial search is incremental in that the found path can be provided as a starting path for a further invocation of the function and the search will continue from that point until a further output primitive satisfying the search criterion is found or the search ceiling is reached.

An example of incremental spatial search is given, based on the structure network in Figure 10.6 and the work environment it represents shown in Figure 10.7. The circle at the bottom left-hand corner of the blotter in Figure 10.7 is a 2D projection of the search region.

The primitives representing the large desk have a name set containing the single name NL and the primitives representing the blotter have name sets containing the names NL and NB. The entry +(NL) in the structure network represents the structure element generated by the code:

NMSETA(1)=NL
ADD NAMES TO SET(1, NMSETA)

which has the effect of adding the name NL to the current name set when the structure is traversed.

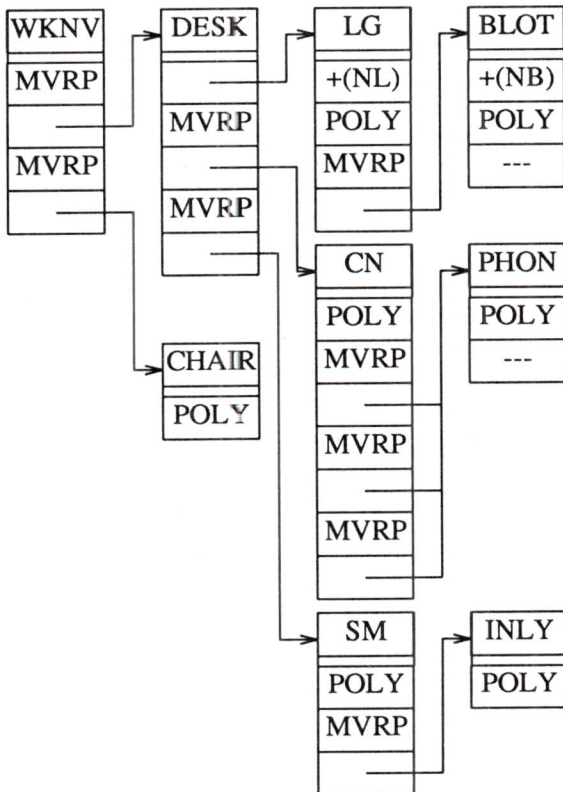

Figure 10.6: *Structure network for Figure 10.7*

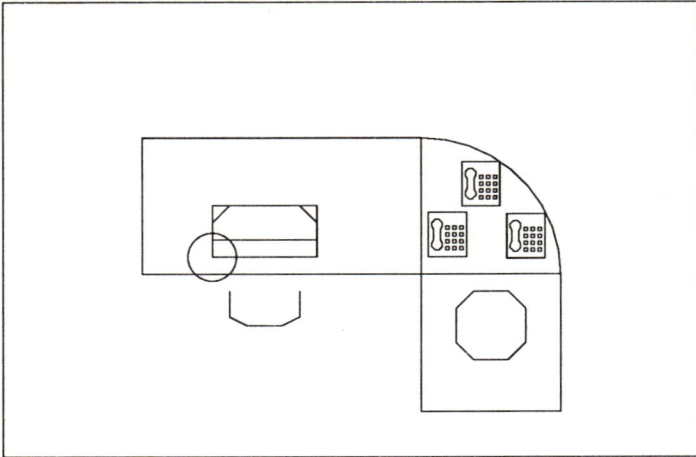

Figure 10.7: *Example of incremental spatial search*

Suppose the incremental spatial search function is invoked with filter lists having the following entries:

Normal Filter List		Inverted Filter List	
Inclusion	Exclusion	Inclusion	Exclusion
NL,NB	EMPTY	EMPTY	EMPTY

and the starting path is:

Structure	Element Position
WKNV	1

Primitives representing the desk and the blotter will be considered by the search because the name sets of each are accepted by all the filters in the normal filter list (none have elements in common with the exclusion list and the desk primitives have NL in common with the inclusion set and blotter primitives have both NL and NB in common), and rejected by all the filters in the inverted filter list (none has any names in common with the inclusion set and so will be rejected). The first position encountered represents the border of the large desk. This falls within the search region and so the found path is:

Structure	Element Position
WKNV	2
DESK	1
LG	2

If the search is restarted using the found path as starting path, the next primitive encountered represents the outline of the blotter. This also satisfies the search criterion and so the found path returned is:

Structure	Element Position
WKNV	2
DESK	1
LG	4
BLOT	2

Here we have assumed that the search ceiling index is 1, so that the search terminates at the end of the structure WKNV.

Suppose in the second case the search ceiling index is 3 (terminate at the end of structure LG) and the filter lists contain the entries

Normal Filter List		Inverted Filter List	
Inclusion	Exclusion	Inclusion	Exclusion
NL,NB	EMPTY	NB	EMPTY

Starting the search after the structure element generating the boundary of the desk, the search fails to find any primitives satisfying the search criterion. This time the primitives representing the blotter fail to satisfy the search criterion because their name sets do not satisfy the filter conditions. The name set (NL, NB) is accepted by the normal filter list. However, this name set is also accepted by the inverted filter list (the name NB is common to the name set and inclusion set) and this fails the condition to be eligible for a search, a primitive's name set must be rejected by the inverted filter list.

11 WORKSTATIONS

11.1 MAIN CHARACTERISTICS

In Section 1.2.3, the concept of a workstation was introduced as the part of a PHIGS system that controlled a specific device. While a great deal of the PHIGS system is concerned with the production of pictures in Normalized Projection Coordinates (NPC) from the traversal of structures, at some stage consideration must be taken of the characteristics of the device upon which the output will appear and from which input is received. This part of the system is called the *workstation* and contains the device dependent code needed to interact with a device.

The standard workstation will have a display surface and a set of input devices attached to it (this is called an OUTIN workstation). A workstation is only allowed a single display surface in PHIGS so if an operator wishes to interact with an application through several display screens, several workstations must be in operation together. PHIGS is designed to allow this and to provide separate control of the pictures displayed on each workstation. Some devices only have the ability to input data (digitizers) or display information (plotters). These are defined as INPUT and OUTPUT workstations respectively. They are categorized differently as these workstations are less complex than OUTIN workstations and so can be optimized differently. Two other workstation categories exist, MO and MI. These workstations do not have a display surface or input devices but, instead, are used to spool information for transmission to a remote device or storage and to read back previously stored graphical information. Their characteristics are implementation dependent and the reader is advised to consult the implementation manual for the PHIGS system being used to find out what has been provided.

PHIGS can be used on a conventional workstation with a bit-map display. If the operator wishes to interact with graphical output in several distinct windows on the display, these will be treated as separate workstations of type OUTIN.

11.2 SETTING UP A WORKSTATION

Before a workstation can be used, the application program has to invoke the function:

OPEN WORKSTATION(WS, CONID, WSTYPE)

This defines a workstation with name WS to be used by the application. Structures can be posted to it as described in Section 2.5 and the result of structure traversal will appear as a picture on the workstation display. The parameter CONID defines the channel that connects the workstation to the application. The way CONID is specified will depend on the language used, the operating system and the type of usage (connecting windows on a display may be different from the way real devices are connected). Again, it is necessary to consult the installation guide for your PHIGS system.

The third parameter, WSTYPE, defines the type of workstation to be connected. A PHIGS implementation will define a set of workstation types that it can handle, effectively the set of devices for which drivers have been written. For each of these, it provides a *workstation description table* containing information about the workstation. For example, it will give the category (OUTIN etc), the size of the display, whether it is a raster device, what aspects of primitives it can handle (for example, the number of linestyles available), what the bundle tables (see Section 4.4) are set to initially, and the input devices it supports. It will also indicate which changes to the display will require the complete picture to be redrawn. Generic workstation types can be defined so that it is not necessary to have a different one for each variant of a manufacturer's range that have similar characteristics.

The execution of OPEN WORKSTATION sets up a *workstation state list* which, initially, contains information drawn from the workstation description table together with standard initialization conditions. The initial bundle settings will come from the workstation description table while the set of posted structures will initially be set to empty. As the session proceeds, the workstation state list will change dependent on what the application does. For example, specific views will be set up for the workstation, structures will be posted to it and input devices will be asked to deliver logical input values.

11.3 WORKSTATION TRANSFORMATION

When a workstation is opened and structures posted to it, the NPC picture created as a result of the viewing operation will be displayed on the workstation such that the NPC unit square in the X and Y-directions will appear as large as possible starting from the bottom left hand corner of the display. For square displays, it will cover the whole display surface while for rectangular displays some display surface will be unused either above or to the right of the area displaying the unit square.

To change the place on the display surface where the output will appear, or to change the size of the area, requires one or more of the following functions to be invoked:

SET WORKSTATION WINDOW
(WS, XWMIN, XWMAX, YWMIN, YWMAX)

SET WORKSTATION WINDOW 3(WS, WA)

SET WORKSTATION VIEWPORT
(WS, XVMIN, XVMAX, YVMIN, YVMAX)

SET WORKSTATION VIEWPORT 3(WS, VA)

In the 2D forms, the area of NPC space defined by the last four parameters of SET WORKSTATION WINDOW is mapped onto the area of the device defined by the last four parameters of SET WORKSTATION VIEWPORT. Initially, the window is defined as though the function:

SET WORKSTATION WINDOW(WS, 0, 1, 0, 1)

had been called and the viewport as though the function:

SET WORKSTATION VIEWPORT(WS, 0, MAX, 0, MAX)

where MAX is the minimum of the device coordinate range in the X and Y-directions.

One major use of redefining the workstation window to viewport mapping is to select some part of the NPC unit square for display. No output will appear outside the workstation viewport.

The display on the device should be an accurate image of the picture in the NPC space. Consequently, no change in aspect ratio is allowed in the definition of the workstation window to viewport mapping. Thus, a circle in the NPC picture will appear as a circle, not an ellipse, on the display surface.

Another reason for limiting the part of the display surface used to display the NPC picture is when space is required to echo input device values so that they do not overlap the displayed picture.

The 3D form of the functions has an array of 6 values as the second parameter. The first four are the equivalent of the 2D parameters defining the area while the last two give the limits in the Z-direction. This allows the mapping of the workstation window to viewport to perform clipping in the Z-direction also. It may also effect how depth cueing or hidden surface calculations are performed.

11.4 DISPLAY UPDATE

The structures posted to a workstation will be traversed and the resulting scene viewed by a transformation specific to a workstation (see Chapter 6 and Chapter 7). The rendering of the primitives on the display surface will depend on the individual attributes and bundle tables as defined by the relevant aspect source flags (see Section 4.5).

Many of the parameters that affect the rendering and viewing of the posted structure can be changed by the application while the structure is posted. Normally, the operator will expect changes to such parameters to occur immediately. This is particularly important if the operator is interacting with what is believed to be the current display. In some cases, it may be less important (for example, if the output is being sent to a plotter). Also, if updating the display takes a long time (the whole picture may need to be redrawn), the operator may prefer to interact with an out-of-date display or one that is poorly rendered.

PHIGS provides facilities for specifying how quickly updates should take place and whether a lower grade of update is acceptable. If changes can be deferred, functions are provided to force an update of the workstation display. These facilities are very dependent on the implementation and the device. Readers should consult the local meanings of SET DISPLAY UPDATE STATE and UPDATE WORKSTATION.

11.5 WORKSTATION CLOSURE

When interaction with a workstation is complete, the application should invoke the function:

CLOSE WORKSTATION(WS)

This ensures that all the output is delivered to the workstation and input received. The workstation state list is also deleted. The function can be used to reset a workstation to its initial values (CLOSE followed by OPEN). It may also be necessary if the application needs to use more workstations in a session than the maximum allowed by the implementation.

12 ENVIRONMENT

12.1 INTRODUCTION

PHIGS is initialized by the function:

OPEN PHIGS(EF, BUFA)

The function must be called before any of the other PHIGS functions described so far can be called. The function is only called once for an invocation of PHIGS.

The parameter EF specifies the name of a file that will be used by PHIGS to return error information to the application program. Error handling in PHIGS is described in Section 12.6. The parameter BUFA defines the amount of memory available for buffer areas. Not all implementations will use this information, and in many cases the buffer area size will be fixed by the implementation.

Opening PHIGS initializes a number of internal variables to default values. For example, the element pointer is initialized to 0 and the edit mode to INSERT. Variables defining the characteristics of a particular implementation (for example the maximum permitted number of open workstations, and the list of available workstation types) are initialized, together with variables which define the characteristics of each of the workstation types supported by the implementation (for example the number of available linetypes).

PHIGS is closed down at the end of a session by the function:

CLOSE PHIGS

The error file is closed, all PHIGS buffers are released, and any other files associated with PHIGS are closed. It should be noted that PHIGS can only be closed after any open structure, open workstations and open archives (see Chapter 14) have been closed.

It is usual for an application to open PHIGS at the start of a session and close it at the end rather than open and close the PHIGS system several times within one session. There are occasions where reopening may be sensible (for example, after error recovery).

12.2 PHIGS OPERATING STATES

As an aid to error handling in PHIGS, the operating state of PHIGS is defined by four variables, each of which has two possible values:

(1) *System State*: this variable can take the values PHIGS open (PHOP) and PHIGS closed (PHCL). Before PHIGS is opened, this variable has the value PHCL. OPEN PHIGS sets the system state to PHOP and CLOSE PHIGS causes the system state to revert to PHCL. Most PHIGS functions can only be invoked when PHIGS is open.

(2) *Workstation State*: the possible values are workstation open (WSOP) and workstation closed (WSCL). The functions OPEN WORKSTA-TION and CLOSE WORKSTATION can affect the value of the workstation state. The value WSOP means that at least one workstation is open and WSCL means that no workstations are open. Most of the functions concerned with workstation activities can only be invoked when at least one workstation is open.

(3) *Structure State*: the possible values are structure open (STOP) and structure closed (STCL). The function OPEN STRUCTURE causes the state to change from STCL to STOP, and CLOSE STRUCTURE changes the state from STOP to STCL. Most of the functions concerned with structures can only be invoked when a structure is open.

(4) *Archive State*: the possible values are archive open (AROP) and archive closed (ARCL). The archive state is similar to the workstation state, the value AROP means that at least one archive file is open and ARCL means that no archive files are open.

Before PHIGS is opened, the state variables are initialized to (PHCL, WSCL, STCL, ARCL). PHIGS defines which state each function can be called in, and which functions cause the state to change.

For example, OPEN PHIGS can only be called in the state (PHCL, WSCL, STCL, ARCL), and changes the state to (PHOP, WSCL, STCL, ARCL). OPEN WORKSTATION can only be called if the system state is PHOP, and any values are allowed for the remaining states. It is immaterial whether other workstations are already open, or whether a structure is open or any archive files are open.

The notation '*' is used to indicate that either value is allowed for a particular state variable. Thus OPEN WORKSTATION is allowed in the state (PHOP,*,*,*) and the resulting state is (PHOP,WSOP,*,*). The functions which create output primitive structure elements in the central structure store, for example, POLYLINE, require that PHIGS is open and a structure is open. The permitted state of these functions is thus

(PHOP,*,STOP,*). The state is unchanged by these functions. Errors will be reported if a function is called in an invalid state.

Readers familiar with GKS should note that there is a strict ordering to the GKS operating states, but there is no such ordering to the PHIGS operating states. This arises from the decoupling of creation and display of graphical output which is fundamental to PHIGS.

12.3 PHIGS STATE LISTS

PHIGS has a number of data structures which contain relevant information about the current state of PHIGS. These data structures are hidden from the application programmer in the sense that values in them cannot be set or tested directly by the application program, but the effect of many of the PHIGS functions is to set variables in these data structures and PHIGS provides functions to inquire the contents of most of these data structures (see Section 12.4).

The data structures are known collectively as the *PHIGS state lists and description tables*. Any reader who has occasion to study the PHIGS Standard itself, will find it useful to understand these data structures.

The state lists and description tables are:

(1) *Operating states*: this consists of four variables which give the values of the system, workstation, structure and archive states as described in the previous section.

(2) *PHIGS description table*: this data structure gives information about the particular PHIGS implementation, and default values. For example, it gives the maximum number of workstations which can be open simultaneously, and the value that will be used for the default values of the aspect source flags. The initial values of many of the items in the PHIGS traversal state list are set from the PHIGS description table.

(3) *PHIGS traversal state list*: the state list maintained by the traverser to record the values of attributes, modelling transformations and modelling clipping volumes during traversal. This state list is different from the other PHIGS data structures in that its contents are completely hidden from the application program; its contents cannot be inquired by the application program. Section 2.5 describes the role of the traversal state list.

(4) *PHIGS state list*: this state list maintains global state information which can be modified and inquired by the application program. Examples of entries in the PHIGS state list include the element pointer, editing mode and name of the open structure. The input queue is also a part of the PHIGS state list.

(5) *Workstation description table*: these contain information about the characteristics of the workstations supported by the particular PHIGS installation. Typical entries in this table include the number of line-types supported by the workstation and the predefined bundles.

(6) *Workstation state list*: these contain information about the workstations that are open. These is one workstation state list per open workstation. Information included in the workstation state list includes the view tables and bundle tables, the workstation transformation and operating mode, echo switch and initialization data for each logical input device supported by the workstation.

The contents of the PHIGS data structures, with the exception of the traversal state list, are accessed by the application program via a set of *inquiry functions*.

12.4 INQUIRY FUNCTIONS

Inquiry functions in PHIGS allow the application program to access the information in the PHIGS data structures. PHIGS also provides inquiry functions to access the central structure store; discussion of these is postponed to Section 12.5.

Inquiry functions are used for a variety of purposes; the main ones are:

(1) to achieve precise results on a particular workstation;

(2) to tailor the application program for particular environments;

(3) to produce library functions;

(4) to recover from errors.

A typical inquiry function has the form:

    INQUIRE EDIT MODE(IND, EDITMO)

PHIGS inquiry functions are defined so that calling them can never generate a PHIGS error. This allows inquiry functions to be called in response to an error condition, without generating further errors. Inquiry functions also have no side effects on the PHIGS state and do not modify any of the PHIGS data structures.

It is clearly possible for inquiry functions to be called in states in which the information being inquired is not available. For example the edit mode is not defined if PHIGS is closed, and so the information inquired by INQUIRE EDIT MODE is not available unless the state is (PHOP,*,*,*). The first output parameter of each inquiry function, IND, is used to indicate whether the information inquired was available or not.

If IND has the value 0 on return, the information inquired, in this case the edit mode, is available, and the remaining parameters return the information. Non-zero values of IND indicate that the information is not available, and the precise value returned indicates the reason why the information is not available. For INQUIRE EDIT MODE, there is only one possible reason, and that is that PHIGS is not in the state (PHOP,*,*,*). The function:

INQUIRE WORKSTATION CONNECTION AND TYPE
(WKID, IND, CONID, WTYPE)

can fail to deliver the information requested if either the operating state is not (PHOP,WSOP,*,*), or the workstation specified by WKID is not open. The values of IND returned enable the application program to distinguish between these two cases.

PHIGS has over 110 inquiry functions, so it is not possible to list them all here. The reader should refer to the relevant PHIGS documentation for further details of these.

One usage of inquiry functions, not mentioned above, is to obtain information from the PHIGS data structures, which is required to be given as arguments to a particular PHIGS function. A typical example (see Section 10.2.1) would be to reset the initial value of a VALUATOR logical input device without changing any of the other characteristics. This can be achieved by using an inquiry function to ascertain the current characteristics of the device, and then calling the INITIALIZE VALUATOR function with a new value for the initial value whilst retaining the other characteristics of the device.

INQUIRE VALUATOR DEVICE STATE(WS, DV, MLDR, IND, MODE, ESW, IVAL, PET, EA, LDR, DATREC)

IF(IND .EQ. 0) INITIALIZE VALUATOR(WS, DV, NEWVAL, PET, EA(1), EA(2), EA(3), EA(4), LDR, DATREC)

IF(IND .NE. 0) GOTO 300

The effect is to set the initial value of the device to NEWVAL. Other characteristics are unchanged. If a value of IND is returned that is non-zero, some error action would need to be taken. It would probably indicate that the function was invoked at the wrong time (the specified workstation was not open or the device was not available). A number of PHIGS functions require more than one value to be set together, and for these the application would need to use inquiry functions or keep a record of the state of the relevant variables if only a subset of the parameters need to be reset.

12.5 INQUIRIES FOR CSS

PHIGS provides functions which enable the application program to inquire the contents of the central structure store (CSS). These functions follow the same pattern as other inquiry functions described in Section 12.4. The CSS inquiry functions are likely to be of most use for library routines, and for ascertaining the contents of a central structure store which has been imported from an archive file (see Section 14.2).

The name of the open structure and the current value of the element pointer can be inquired using the functions:

    INQUIRE OPEN STRUCTURE(IND, ST, SID)
    INQUIRE ELEMENT POINTER(IND, EP)

The status parameter, ST, on the first function returns the value OPEN if there is an open structure and NONE if there is none.

One usage of INQUIRE ELEMENT POINTER is to determine the position of the end of a structure, so that the element pointer can be restored to that position after some other manipulation has been performed. This is not the only way to achieve this, the structure could be closed and reopened, or a label element could be inserted in the structure at the appropriate position, but it can be a useful technique. The example below shows another way to solve the example given in Section 10.1.6.

```
            SET EDIT MODE(INSERT)
            OPEN STRUCTURE(SPMEG)
            POST STRUCTURE(WS, SPMEG, 0.2)
            SET MARKER TYPE(2)
            SET LOCATOR MODE(WS, DV1, EVENT, ECHO)
            SET CHOICE MODE(WS, DV2, EVENT, ECHO)

100     CONTINUE
            AWAIT EVENT(60, WST, CLASS, DV)
            IF (CLASS .EQ. NONE) GOTO 100
            IF (CLASS .EQ. LOCATOR) GOTO 200

            GET CHOICE(ST, OCHOIC)
            INQUIRE ELEMENT POINTER(IND, EP)
            SET EDIT MODE(REPLACE)
            SET ELEMENT POINTER(1)
            SET MARKER TYPE(OCHOIC)
```

```
         SET EDIT MODE(INSERT)
         SET ELEMENT POINTER(EP)
         GOTO 100


200      CONTINUE
         GET LOCATOR(VI, XA(1), YA(1))
         POLYMARKER(1, XA, YA)
         GOTO 100


300      CONTINUE
         CLOSE STRUCTURE


         STOP
C  STOP option selected
```

The variable EP is used to store the position of the end of the structure, whilst the set marker type element at the start of the structure is replaced. After replacement, the edit mode is restored to INSERT and the element pointer to point to the end of the structure.

The function INQUIRE CURRENT ELEMENT TYPE AND SIZE enables the type and size of the structure element at the current element position to be ascertained, and INQUIRE CURRENT ELEMENT CONTENT enables its content to be determined. In the Fortran language binding, element content is returned in an integer array, a real array and a character array. For details of the contents of these arrays for each type of structure element, the reader is referred to the documentation of the PHIGS implementation in use. The contents are standardized by the PHIGS language binding standards.

There are also inquiry functions, INQUIRE ELEMENT TYPE AND SIZE and INQUIRE ELEMENT CONTENT which enable the type, size and content of an element at an arbitrary position in the central structure store to be determined. The element position is specified by two parameters, a structure identifier and an element position. The latter defines the element position within the specified structure.

For illustration, one possible usage of these functions is in conjunction with PICK input. The PICK input device returns the traversal path through the central structure store to the structure element which generated the output primitive picked. These inquiry functions would enable the type of the output primitive and the parameters which define it, to be ascertained.

The function INQUIRE STRUCTURE STATUS enables the status of a particular structure to be ascertained. The values returned indicate whether the specified structure is non-existent, exists and is empty, or exists and is not empty.

There are two functions which enable the relationship of a given structure to other structures in the central structure store to be ascertained.

INQUIRE PATHS TO ANCESTORS returns the paths in the central structure store *which reference* the specified structure. INQUIRE PATHS TO DESCENDANTS returns the paths in the central structure store *which are referenced by* the specified structure. Each PHIGS function returns a list of paths, where each path is a sequence of (structure identifier, element pointer) pairs. This is a similar data structure to a pick path (but without a pick identifier). The element position associated with a structure identifier is the position within that particular structure of the execute structure element which invokes the next structure in the path. For INQUIRE PATHS TO ANCESTORS, the last element of the path is (S,0), where S is the structure whose ancestors are being inquired, and for INQUIRE PATHS TO DESCENDANTS, the last element is (D,0), where D is the deepest descendant in the structure network which contains no execute structure elements. Ancestor and descendant paths can, like PICK paths, be returned in either TOPFIRST or BOTTOMFIRST order.

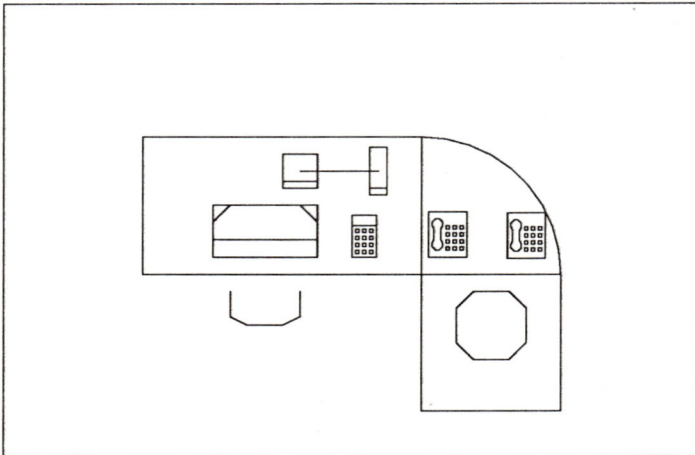

Figure 12.1: *Complete desk*

In the Fortran language binding, both inquiry functions are mapped to subroutines which return a single path, rather than a list of paths. An output parameter specifies how many paths there are, and an input parameter specifies which particular path is to be returned.

These inquiry functions are useful if a library routine needs to explore the structure network it has to operate on. In general, if an application program is creating a structure network itself, one would expect the application to keep track of the network without recourse to inquiry functions.

However, if a structure network is imported from an external source (by an archive file, see Chapter 14), it might be necessary to use inquiry functions to ascertain how and where a particular structure is being used.

For example, consider the structure network in Figure 5.7 (Section 5.4.5), reproduced below in Figure 12.2. The corresponding scene is shown in Figure 12.1.

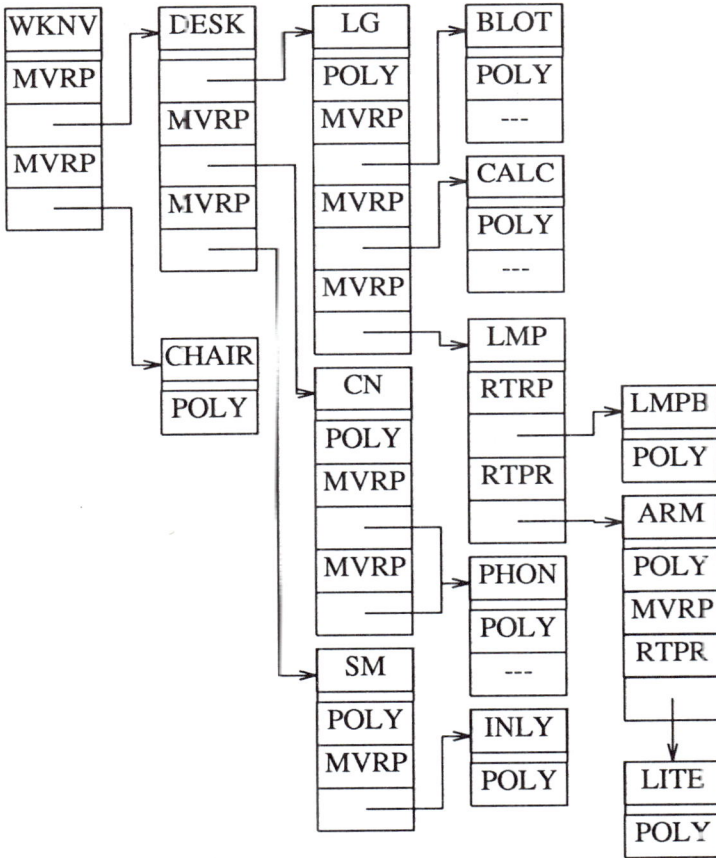

Figure 12.2: *Complete structure network for desk*

The ancestors of the structure PHON are WKNV, DESK, CN but there are two paths through the ancestors to PHON, depending on which of the execute structure elements in CN is followed. The possible paths returned by INQUIRE PATHS TO ANCESTORS are:

Path 1	
Structure	Element Pointer
WKNV	2
DESK	3
CN	3
PHON	0

Path 2	
Structure	Element Pointer
WKNV	2
DESK	3
CN	5
PHON	0

Similarly, an inquiry to determine the descendants of the structure CN, can produce the two paths:

Path 1	
Structure	Element Pointer
CN	3
PHON	0

Path 2	
Structure	Element Pointer
CN	5
PHON	0

The final central structure store inquiry function is the ELEMENT SEARCH function. This function enables an application program to search a specified structure for an occurrence of a specified type of structure element. This function can be useful in conjunction with the INQUIRE ELEMENT CONTENT function for editing structures. The function is:

ELEMENT SEARCH
(SID, SEP, SDIR, EISN, EIS, EESN, EES, IND, ST, FEP)

SID and SEP identify the structure to be searched and the element position from which the search is to start. SDIR indicates whether the search is to be forwards or backwards from this position. EISN and EIS specify an element inclusion set (EIS is an array of EISN elements) and EESN and EES specify an element exclusion set (similarly EES is an array of EESN elements). The remaining parameters are output parameters; IND is the error indicator, ST a status indicator (returning the value FAILURE if an element of the required type is not found and SUCCESS if it is found). FEP points to the position of the element found (if any).

Element inclusion sets and exclusion sets are similar to the inclusion and exclusion sets associated with filters. A structure element will satisfy an element search, if its type is included in the inclusion set, and is not contained in the exclusion set. Using the structure network of Figure 12.2 as an example, an element search:

    EIS(1)=POLYLINE
    EIS(2)=EXECUTE_STRUCTURE

    ELEMENT SEARCH(CN, 0, FORWARDS, 2, EIS, 0, EES, IND, ST, FEP)

will return ST with the value SUCCESS and FEP with value 1, because the first element in the structure CN is a polyline structure element. Calling the function again:

    ELEMENT SEARCH(CN, 2, FORWARDS, 2, EIS, 0, EES, IND, ST, FEP)

will succeed and return FEP with value 3, the position of the first execute structure element in CN.

One application of this function is to locate all elements of a particular type so that, for example, they could be replaced with something else.

12.6 ERROR HANDLING

PHIGS has a well-defined set of errors that will be reported to the application. Readers familiar with GKS will find that the error handling mechanism in PHIGS is very similar to that in GKS, although situations which give rise to errors are rather different. The action of many PHIGS functions is to create structure elements which record the parameters specified in the function call. In many cases, it is not possible to check the validity of the parameters when the function is called, but only when the structure element is traversed. The reason for this is that the environment in which a structure element is traversed (typically the values of the transformation matrices), determines the validity of the parameters. An example is provided by SET CHARACTER UP VECTOR. The parameters to the function are specified in a text local coordinate system and must define a vector of non-zero length. However, it can only be determined at traversal time whether the parameters define a non-zero vector or not (to the precision used by the implementation) because only then is the coordinate system defined.

Because of the diverse ways in which traversal can be implemented, it could for example, be implemented as a process asynchronous from the application program, it would be extremely difficult to handle traversal time errors, and so PHIGS defines default actions to be performed in such cases. For SET CHARACTER UP VECTOR, the default action is to use the vector (0,1) for the up vector and (1,0) for the character base vector.

For situations in which errors are to be reported to the application program, PHIGS uses a mechanism which is very similar to the GKS error handling mechanism. All errors are reported by putting details of the error in the *error file* which was specified when PHIGS was opened.

Typically, occurrence of an error will cause the following information to be recorded in the error file:

(1) *Error number* : a number identifying the error which has occurred.

(2) *PHIGS function* : the name of the PHIGS function that was being executed when the error was detected.

PHIGS defines a standard set of error numbers which are reported by PHIGS functions. When an error has been detected, PHIGS calls the error handling procedure:

ERROR HANDLING(ERRNR, FCTID, ERRFIL)

The parameters are the error number (ERRNR), the function in which the error was detected (FCTID) and the name of the error file (ERRFIL). This function records the error in the error file by calling the function:

ERROR LOGGING(ERRNR, FCTID, ERRFIL)

and then returns to the function in which the error was detected. It is normal in PHIGS for a function in which an error is detected to have no effect on the PHIGS state, in other words, PHIGS ignores the function.

Application programs can turn off error reporting by calling the function:

SET ERROR HANDLING MODE(ERHM)

where the parameter ERHM can take the values OFF and ON. The default value is ON. If the mode is set to OFF, control will not be passed to the ERROR HANDLING procedure when an error is detected and the error will therefore not be reported. This facility would seem to be of limited value. The way it is described in the standard certainly does not imply that error checking is turned off if the mode is OFF. It is error reporting, not error checking, that is disabled.

The application program can provide its own error handling mechanisms by replacing the system supplied error handling procedure.

This application procedure can take any appropriate actions, but to avoid chaos ensuing, there are restrictions on what an application supplied error handling procedure should do. Only ERROR LOGGING, inquiry functions or EMERGENCY CLOSE PHIGS (see below) may be called by an application-supplied error handling procedure. The inquiry functions enable the application program to examine the PHIGS state lists, and so more precise reporting of the circumstances surrounding the error is possible than that provided by the system error handling procedure. It is worth noting that an application-supplied error handling procedure should still call the ERROR LOGGING procedure to record the error before returning control to the function in which the error was detected.

In some situations it will not be possible to recover from an error. The function EMERGENCY CLOSE PHIGS can be called in these circumstances to close the files used by PHIGS in as orderly a manner as possible, and save as much of the graphical information generated (for example in archives) as possible. As noted above, this function can safely be called by an application-supplied error handling procedure, and is used by PHIGS itself in response to certain fatal errors.

13 FURTHER OUTPUT

13.1 INTRODUCTION

The main output primitives and their aspects were defined in Chapter 3. Three other primitives of less importance complete the set available. These are *cell array, annotation text* and *generalized drawing primitive*. Cell array is provided to allow images to be displayed with the other graphical output. Annotation text provides annotations to graphical objects where the transformations to the object are not required on the annotation. Finally, the generalized drawing primitive gives the ability to extend the basic set of output primitives.

13.2 CELL ARRAY

The functions provided are:

    CELL ARRAY(PX, PY, QX, QY,
      DIMX, DIMY, ISC, ISR, DX, DY, COLIA)
    CELL ARRAY 3(CPXA, CPYA, CPZA,
      DIMX, DIMY, ISC, ISR, DX, DY, COLIA)

Cell array defines an image as an array of areas to be given specific colours from the colour table. The parameters up to DIMX define the complete area of the image. DX and DY define how many *cells* the image is to be broken up into in the X and Y-direction. The remaining parameters specify the entries in the array COLIA of dimension (DIMX, DIMY) to be used as the colour index values into the colour table. These specify the colours of the individual cells. Both primitives are planar primitives. The 2D version defines a rectangular array of cells in modelling coordinates on the Z=0 plane while the 3D version defines an array of parallelograms on an arbitrary plane. In both cases, modelling and viewing transformations are applied to the cells so that the grid of cells to be rendered can be quadrilaterals and the various clipping facilities will have been applied to these quadrilaterals.

In the 2D form, the points (PX, PY) and (QX, QY) specify the opposite corners of the rectangle. The cells are numbered with the one nearest (PX, PY) being (1,1) and the one nearest (QX, QY) being (DX, DY).

In the 3D form, the points (CPXA(I), CPYA(I), CPZA(I)) define the 3 adjacent corners of a parallelogram. The point P (I=1) is the equivalent of (PX, PY). The point R (I=2) is the point that defines the X-axis of the parallelogram which extends from P in the direction of R. The point S (I=3) defines the Y-axis of the parallelogram which extends from P in the direction of S. The fourth corner Q is defined as R+S-P. The points PX, PY, PZ) and (QX, QY, QZ) define the opposite corners of the parallelogram. The cells are numbered as for the 2D case.

The remaining parameters allow a part of the COLIA array to be used to define the colour indices associated with the cells. The entries used start at the position COLIA(ISC, ISR). The colour of the (I, J)th cell is defined by the entry COLIA(ISC+I−1, ISR+J−1).

Cell array is unusual in that its geometric and rendering attributes are all provided within the function definition. Only the identification attributes are set globally.

13.3 ANNOTATION TEXT

Annotation text is provided to add labels associated with specific points in the object to be displayed. Normal text could be used for this purpose but, in this case, it would be possible for the text to be rotated through 90° making it visible only from the end on or the perspective transformations applied could make it difficult to read. Annotation text solves the problem by adding the text to the object *after* it has been viewed and its position in Normalized Projection Coordinate (NPC) space established. The functions provided are:

ANNOTATION TEXT RELATIVE(RPX, RPY, APX, APY, CHARS)
ANNOTATION TEXT RELATIVE 3
  (RPX, RPY, RPZ, APX, APY, APZ, CHARS)

The 2D version has the Z-values of the positions set to Z=0.

The *reference point,* RP, defines a point in modelling coordinates to be annotated. This is transformed and projected to produce an equivalent point, RPN, in NPC coordinates. If RPN is outside any of the clipping regions specified by the modelling, viewing, or workstation clips, nothing appears. If not, the annotation text appears at the point RPN+AP. That is, AP defines an offset from the point to be annotated. The annotation text appears with this point as its origin. The text is output in the Z=RPN+AP plane and so appears parallel to the display surface.

Annotation text has a similar set of geometric attributes to normal text (annotation text character height etc) with functions to set each individually. It shares a common text bundle table with normal text.

The attribute ANNOTATION STYLE specifies the visual effect. If set to 1, the annotation text is output by itself. If set to 2, a line is drawn from RPN to RPN+AP as well. This is rendered as though it was defined as a polyline. Other values of ANNOTATION STYLE are implementation dependent (see Section 3.2.3).

13.4 GENERALIZED DRAWING PRIMITIVE

The functions are:

GENERALIZED DRAWING PRIMITIVE
  (N, PXA, PYA, PRIMID, LDR, DATREC)
GENERALIZED DRAWING PRIMITIVE 3
  (N, PXA, PYA, PZA, PRIMID, LDR, DATREC)

The 2D form has the PZA values set to 0. The first set of parameters define N points (PXA(I), PYA(I), PZA(I)) as I goes from 1 to N and these are used in the definition of the generalized drawing primitive (GDP). Other non-positional information associated with the GDP is defined in the data record DATREC of length LDR. This is constructed in the same way as the data record for INITIALIZE VALUATOR described in Section 10.2.4.

PRIMID identifies which of the set of GDP or GDP 3 primitives is required. Little can be said about GDPs as they are implementation dependent. They are provided to allow special primitives such as circles, ellipses, arcs and curves to be defined and implemented. They are allowed to use any of the attributes of the other primitives. For example, a filled area with the points on the boundary defined as markers and some text displayed in the filled area could be defined as a GDP.

The only constraint on the GDP defined is that it must behave like the other primitives under transformation. The geometry of the primitive must be transformed by the modelling and viewing transformations. Consequently, a circle cannot be specified as a single point and a radius value in the data record as this would still remain a circle under transformation. It has to be specified by at least three points so that the appropriate transformations take place.

14 ARCHIVES

14.1 INTRODUCTION

The PHIGS central structure store provides storage for graphical information whilst PHIGS is open. When PHIGS is closed, the Central Structure Store (CSS) disappears and the information contained in it is lost.

Many applications have a requirement to preserve graphical information between invocations of the application program, and the requirement to exchange graphical information between different applications. An application to design work environments, for example, would wish to allow the designer to save the current state of a design and return to it at a later stage. For some applications, it would make most sense to save just the application data structures, but in other cases, where the manipulations performed by the operator have most effect on the CSS, or where generation of the CSS from the application data structures is expensive in compute time, it makes sense for the application to save the CSS contents. It is also useful to build up a library of templates of useful sequences of structure elements that can be edited to perform specific tasks and added to structures using COPY ALL ELEMENTS FROM STRUCTURE (see Section 5.7.4).

PHIGS provides a mechanism for storing structures, called *archive files*. Functions are provided to archive structures from the CSS to archive files and to retrieve structures from archive files into the CSS.

Part 2 of the ISO/IEC PHIGS standard defines the functionality of PHIGS archive files. Essentially the archive file is defined as a sequence of elements of different types, representing the contents of structure elements and control information.

Part 3 of the PHIGS standard defines a representation (or concrete syntax) of the archive file. This follows the same principles as the Clear Text Encoding of the ISO/IEC CGM (Metafile for the storage and transfer of picture description information) standard. Discussion of the functionality and representation of archive files *per se* is beyond the scope of this book. This chapter concentrates on the functions provided by PHIGS for archiving and retrieving structures from archive files.

14.2 ARCHIVAL AND RETRIEVAL FUNCTIONS

Before anything can be written to an archive file, it must be opened. This is done by calling the function:

OPEN ARCHIVE FILE(AFID, ARCFIL)

The first parameter is the archive file identifier, an identifier which is used by subsequent functions to refer to that file. The second parameter is the name of the archive file. Archive identifiers play a similar role to workstation identifiers. PHIGS allows several archive files to be open simultaneously, and again as in the case of workstations, there is an inquiry function which will return the maximum number of archive files which may be open simultaneously.

The function:

CLOSE ARCHIVE FILE(AFID)

closes the specified archive file.

Three functions are provided to archive structures to an archive file:

ARCHIVE STRUCTURES(AFID, N, LSTRID)
ARCHIVE STRUCTURE NETWORKS(AFID, N, LSTRID)
ARCHIVE ALL STRUCTURES(AFID)

The first of these three functions archives each of the structures specified in the list of structure identifiers (N is the number of structures to be archived and the array LSTRID contains the structure identifiers) to the archive file with identifier AFID.

The second archives the structure networks whose roots are specified by the parameters N and LSTRID. As for the previous function, N is the number of structure networks to archive, and the array LSTRID contains the structure identifiers of the roots of each. Using the structure network in Figure 5.7, as an example archiving the two structure networks with root structures CN and LG respectively would archive the structures CN and PHON for the first and LG, BLOT, CALC, LMP, LMPB, ARM and LITE for the second.

The third function archives all the structures in the CSS to the specified archive file. Three analogous functions are provided to retrieve structures from an archive file:

RETRIEVE STRUCTURES(AFID, N, LSTRID)
RETRIEVE STRUCTURE NETWORKS(AFID, N, LSTRID)
RETRIEVE ALL STRUCTURES(AFID)

The first retrieves the specified structures from the specified archive file, the second retrieves the structure networks whose roots are the specified structures and the third retrieves all the structures in the archive file. The effect in each case is to add the structures retrieved to the CSS.

Conflicts may arise, both in archiving structures (the archive file already contains structures with the same names as some of those to be archived), and in retrieving structures (the CSS already contains structures with the same names as some of those to be retrieved). The control provided by PHIGS in such situations is described in the next section.

14.3 CONFLICT RESOLUTION

The function:

SET CONFLICT RESOLUTION(ARCCR, RETCR)

provides the application program with a mechanism for controlling the action to be taken if conflicts arise in archiving or retrieving structures. The parameter ARCCR controls the action on structure archival and RETCR the action on structure retrieval.

The possible values of each flag are MAINTAIN, ABANDON and UPDATE. The value MAINTAIN has the effect that the archival or retrieval operation will only write a structure into the archive or CSS if a structure with the same name does not already exist in the archive file or CSS. A value of ABANDON causes the archival or retrieval operation to be abandoned if a conflict arises, leaves the archive file or CSS in its original state and generates an error. The value UPDATE allows structures in the archive or CSS to be overwritten.

PHIGS does provide inquiry functions which will indicate if a particular operation will generate conflicts. These are described in the next section.

14.4 INQUIRY FUNCTIONS FOR ARCHIVES

PHIGS provides a number of functions which enable the application program to inquire various characteristics of a PHIGS archive file. The function:

RETRIEVE STRUCTURE IDENTIFIERS(AFID, ILS, N, LSTRID)

returns a list of the structure identifiers in the archive file with archive identifier AFID.

The function RETRIEVE PATHS TO ANCESTORS returns the paths in an archive file which reference a specified structure. The function RETRIEVE PATHS TO DESCENDANTS returns the paths in an archive file which are referenced by the specified archived structure. The functions return information as the functions INQUIRE PATHS TO

DESCENDANTS and INQUIRE PATHS TO ANCESTORS described in section Section 12.5. The latter pair of functions provide similar information for structures in the CSS.

14.5 DELETION FUNCTIONS

Three functions are provided to delete structures from an archive file:

DELETE STRUCTURES FROM ARCHIVE(AFID, N, LSTRID)
DELETE STRUCTURE NETWORKS FROM ARCHIVE
  (AFID, N, LSTRID)
DELETE ALL STRUCTURES FROM ARCHIVE(AFID)

The functions delete specified structures, all the structures referenced by specified structure networks, and all the structures in an archive respectively.

The first and second of these functions do not check if the structures to be deleted are referenced from any of the other structures in the archive file, thus some care needs to be exercised in their usage to avoid introducing inconsistencies into the archive file.

15 BINDINGS

15.1 INTRODUCTION

The PHIGS standard defines a set of functions and data types that are independent of any particular programming language. As explained in Section 1.2.2, these functions and data types need to be represented in terms of the facilities of a particular programming language, in order that PHIGS can be used in a standardized way by an application using that language. This is the purpose of the PHIGS language binding standard IS 9593.

IS 9593 is a mult.-part standard, each part of which describes the binding to a particular programming language. Part 1 describes the Fortran binding, Part 2 the Pascal binding, Part 3 the Ada binding and Part 4 the C binding. At the time of writing, only the Fortran and Ada bindings have been published as International Standards. The C binding is a Draft International Standard (October 1990), and the Pascal binding lags considerably behind.

The remainder of this chapter describes the essential features of the Fortran language binding, to the level of detail necessary to enable a programmer to use the functions described in this book, through the Fortran binding. Readers should be aware that the Fortran binding which was eventually standardized, had some significant differences from early drafts. Several of the PHIGS implementations on the market use an early version of the Fortran binding. It is wise to consider which language binding is actually used when purchasing a PHIGS implementation.

15.2 ORGANIZATION OF THE FORTRAN BINDING

The Fortran binding defines a set of Fortran subroutines and parameters which correspond to the PHIGS functions. With the exception of some of the inquiry functions, there is one subroutine per PHIGS function. Inquiry functions are omitted from this chapter, and the reader is referred either to the Fortran language binding itself, or to the documentation of the PHIGS implementation used for details of these.

Table 1 gives the Fortran subroutine names corresponding to the major PHIGS functions and their arguments. The functions are listed in alphabetical order.

In view of the large number of functions described in this chapter, an abbreviated notation is used for describing parameter lists. Each function description consists of the name of the function and a reference to the section of the book in which it is described. The Fortran subroutine name and parameter list appear on the second line. Input parameters are indicated in a roman typeface, and output parameters in italic. Table 2 gives the meanings of the names used in the parameter lists and the corresponding Fortran data types. The names are listed in alphabetical order. In a few instances parameter names with lengths greater than 6 characters have been used in the interests of clarity. This is mainly the addition of the character '3' to distinguish between the parameter names for corresponding 2D and 3D functions. The type ENUMERATION means that the type is a set of enumerated values. As described below, these types are represented as INTEGERs. The italicized names in the right-hand column of Table 2, are the names of the corresponding entries in Table 3, which give the correspondence between these types and INTEGER values.

Dimensions of array parameters are indicated in brackets after the array type, for example:

EVOL   REAL (6)

means that the parameter EVOL is a real array with 6 elements.

The notation used in the earlier chapters of this book substituted variable names for the values of parameters which enumerate a number of possible options, for example, the variables CLIP and NOCLIP were used to represent particular values of clipping indicators. In the PHIGS Fortran language binding, enumerated values are represented as INTEGERs and the language binding standardizes names and INTEGER values for each PHIGS enumerated type. The names will be made available for use by the application, either by means of PARAMETER or DATA statements, the exact details of how the names are included in an application will vary from implementation to implementation. Table 3 gives the correspondence between enumerated types, INTEGER value, Fortran name and the names largely used in the earlier chapters of this book. For the type Element, only the first 5 values are shown. This type gives names to all the PHIGS structure elements, for the remaining values, the reader is referred to the documentation of the PHIGS implementation being used. Enumerated types used only by the INQUIRY functions have been omitted from this table.

Table 1

Function	Page Reference
ADD NAMES TO SET	78
PADS(NSN,NAMSET)	
ANNOTATION TEXT RELATIVE	228
PATR(RPX,RPY,APX,APY,CHARS)	
ANNOTATION TEXT RELATIVE 3	228
PATR3(RPX,RPY,RPZ,APX,APY,APZ,CHARS)	
APPLICATION DATA	109
PAP(LDR,DATREC)	
ARCHIVE ALL STRUCTURES	232
PARAST(AFID)	
ARCHIVE STRUCTURE NETWORKS	232
PARSN(AFID,N,LSTRIDN)	
ARCHIVE STRUCTURES	232
PARST(AFID,N,LSTRIDN)	
AWAIT EVENT	186
PWAIT(TOUT,*WKID,ICL,IDNR*)	
BUILD TRANSFORMATION MATRIX	22
PBLTM(X0,Y0,DX,DY,PHI,FX,FY,*ERRIND,XFRMT*)	
BUILD TRANSFORMATION MATRIX 3	124
PBLTM3(X0,Y0,Z0,DX,DY,DZ,PHIX,PHIY,PHIZ,FX,FY,FZ,*ERRIND,XFRMT3*)	
CELL ARRAY	227
PCA(PX,PY,QX,QY,DIMX,DIMY,ISC,ISR,NROWS,NCOLS,COLIA)	
CELL ARRAY 3	227
PCA3(CPXA,CPYA,CPZA,DIMX,DIMY,ISC,ISR,NROWS,NCOLS,COLIA)	
CHANGE STRUCTURE IDENTIFIER	102
PCSTID(OLDSID,NEWSID)	
CHANGE STRUCTURE IDENTIFIER AND REFERENCES	102
PCSTIR(OLDSID,NEWSID)	
CHANGE STRUCTURE REFERENCES	102
PCSTRF(OLDSID,NEWSID)	
CLOSE ARCHIVE FILE	232
PCLARF(AFID)	
CLOSE PHIGS	213
PCLPH	
CLOSE STRUCTURE	14
PCLST	
CLOSE WORKSTATION	212
PCLWK(WKID)	
COMPOSE MATRIX	101
PCOM(XFRMTA,XFRMTB,*ERRIND,XFRMTO*)	
COMPOSE MATRIX 3	124
PCOM3(XFRMTA3,XFRMTB3,*ERRIND,XFRMTO3*)	

COMPOSE TRANSFORMATION MATRIX   101
    PCOTM(XFRMTI,X0,Y0,DX,DY,PHI,FX,FY,*ERRIND,XFRMTO*)
COMPOSE TRANSFORMATION MATRIX 3   124
    PCOTM3(XFRMTI3,X0,Y0,Z0,DX,DY,DZ,PHIX,PHIY,PHIZ,FX,FY,FZ,
        ERRIND,XFRMTO3)
COPY ALL ELEMENTS FROM STRUCTURE   102
    PCELST(STRID)
DELETE ALL STRUCTURES   104
    PDAS
DELETE ALL STRUCTURES FROM ARCHIVE   234
    PDASAR(AFID)
DELETE ELEMENT   32
    PDEL
DELETE ELEMENT RANGE   33
    PDELRA(EP1,EP2)
DELETE ELEMENTS BETWEEN LABELS   34
    PDELLB(LABEL1,LABEL2)
DELETE STRUCTURE   103
    PDST(STRID)
DELETE STRUCTURE NETWORK   104
    PDSN(STRID,REFHNF)
DELETE STRUCTURE NETWORKS FROM ARCHIVE   234
    PDSNAR(AFID,N,LSTRIDN)
DELETE STRUCTURES FROM ARCHIVE   234
    PDSTAR(AFID,N,LSTRIDN)
ELEMENT SEARCH   222
    PELS(STRID,STRTEP,SRCDIR,EISN,EIS,EESN,EES,*ERRIND,STATUS,FNDEP*)
EMERGENCY CLOSE PHIGS   225
    PECLPH
EMPTY STRUCTURE   104
    PEMST(STRID)
ERROR HANDLING   224
    PERHND(ERRNR,FCTID,ERRFIL)
ERROR LOGGING   224
    PERLOG(ERRNR,FCTID,ERRFIL)
EVALUATE VIEW MAPPING MATRIX   115
    PEVMM(VWWNLM,PJVPLM,*ERRIND,VWMPMT*)
EVALUATE VIEW MAPPING MATRIX 3   131
    PEVMM3(VWWNLM,PJVPLM3,PJTYPE,PJRX,PJRY,PJRZ,VPLD,BPLD,FPLD,
        ERRIND,VWMPMT3)
EVALUATE VIEW ORIENTATION MATRIX   114
    PEVOM(VWRX,VWRY,VUPX,VUPY,*ERRIND,VWORMT*)
EVALUATE VIEW ORIENTATION MATRIX 3   128
    PEVOM3(VWRX,VWRY,VWRZ,VPNX,VPNY,VPNZ,VUPX,VUPY,VUPZ,
        ERRIND,VWORMT3)
EXECUTE STRUCTURE   83
    PEXST(STRID)
FILL AREA   46
    PFA(N,PXAN,PYAN)

FILL AREA 3   46
    PFA3(N,PXAN,PYAN,PZAN)
FILL AREA SET   46
    PFAS(NPL,IXA,PXA,PYA)
FILL AREA SET 3   46
    PFAS3(NPL,IXA,PXA,PYA,PZA)
FLUSH DEVICE EVENTS   191
    PFLUSH(WKID,ICL,IDNR)
GENERALIZED DRAWING PRIMITIVE   229
    PGDP(N,PXA,PYA,PRIMID,LDR,DATREC)
GENERALIZED DRAWING PRIMITIVE 3   229
    PGDP3(N,PXA,PYA,PZA,PRIMID,LDR,DATREC)
GENERALIZED STRUCTURE ELEMENT   109
    PGSE(GSEID,LDR,DATREC)
GET CHOICE   186
    PGTCH(*STAT,CHNR*)
GET ITEM TYPE FROM METAFILE
    PGTITM(WKID,TYPE,IDRL)
GET LOCATOR   187
    PGTLC(*VIEWI,LPX,LPY*)
GET LOCATOR 3   187
    PGTLC3(*VIEWI,LPX,LPY,LPZ*)
GET PICK   186
    PGTPK(IPPD,*STAT,PPD,PP*)
GET STRING   186
    PGTST(*LOSTR,STR*)
GET STROKE   187
    PGTSK(N,*VIEWI,NP,PXAN,PYAN*)
GET STROKE 3   187
    PGTSK3(N,*VIEWI,NP,PXAN,PYAN,PZAN*)
GET VALUATOR   186
    PGTVL(*VAL*)
INCREMENTAL SPATIAL SEARCH   203
    PISS3(SRPX,SRPY,SDIST,SPTHSZ,SPATH,MCLIPF,SRCHCI,
       NFLN,NFLISX,NFLIS,NFLESX,IFLN,IFLISX,IFLIS,
       IFLESX,IFLES,IPTHSZ,*ERRIND,FPTHSZ,FPATH*)
INCREMENTAL SPATIAL SEARCH 3   203
    PISS3(SRPX,SRPY,SRPZ,SDIST,SPTHSZ,SPATH,MCLIPF,SRCHCI,
       NFLN,NFLISX,NFLIS,NFLESX,IFLN,IFLISX,IFLIS,
       IFLESX,IFLES,IPTHSZ,*ERRIND,FPTHSZ,FPATH*)
INITIALIZE CHOICE   194
    PINCH(WKID,CHDNR,ISTAT,ICHNR,PET,XMIN,XMAX,YMIN,YMAX,
       LDR,DATREC)
INITIALIZE CHOICE 3   194
    PINCH3(WKID,CHDNR,ISTAT,ICHNR,PET,EVOL,LDR,DATREC)
INITIALIZE LOCATOR   194
    PINLC(WKID,LCDNR,IVIEWI,IPX,IPY,PET,XMIN,XMAX,YMIN,YMAX,
       LDR,DATREC)

INITIALIZE LOCATOR 3   194
    PINLC3(WKID,LCDNR,IVIEWI,IPX,IPY,IPZ,PET,EVOL,LDR,DATREC)
INITIALIZE PICK   194
    PINPK(WKID,PKDNR,ISTAT,IIPPD,IPP,PET,XMIN,XMAX,YMIN,YMAX,
        LDR,DATREC,PPORDR)
INITIALIZE PICK 3   194
    PINPK3(WKID,PKDNR,ISTAT,IIPPD,IPP,PET,EVOL,LDR,DATREC,PPORDR)
INITIALIZE STRING   194
    PINST(WKID,STDNR,LSTR,ISTR,PET,XMIN,XMAX,YMIN,YMAX,
        LDR,DATREC)
INITIALIZE STRING 3   194
    PINST3(WKID,STDNR,LSTR,ISTR,PET,EVOL,LDR,DATREC)
INITIALIZE STROKE   194
    PINSK(WKID,SKDNR,IVIEWI,INP,IPXA,IPYA,PET,
        XMIN,XMAX,YMIN,YMAX,LDR,DATREC)
INITIALIZE STROKE 3   194
    PINSK3(WKID,SKDNR,IVIEWI,INP,IPXA,IPYA,IPZA,EVOL,LDR,DATREC)
INITIALIZE VALUATOR   194
    PINVL(WKID,VLDNR,IVAL,PET,XMIN,XMAX,YMIN,YMAX,LDR,DATREC)
INITIALIZE VALUATOR 3   194
    PINVL3(WKID,VLDNR,IVAL,PET,EVOL,LDR,DATREC)
INTERPRET ITEM
    PIITM(TYPE,IDRL,LDR,DATREC)
LABEL   30
    PLB(LABEL)
MESSAGE
    PMSG(WKID,MESS)
OFFSET ELEMENT POINTER   29
    POSEP(EPO)
OPEN ARCHIVE FILE   232
    POPARF(AFID,ARCFIL)
OPEN PHIGS   213
    POPPH(ERRFIL,BUFA)
OPEN STRUCTURE   14
    POPST(STRID)
OPEN WORKSTATION   210
    POPWK(WKID,CONID,WTYPE)
PACK DATA RECORD   199
    PPREC(IL,IA,RL,RA,SL,PLSTR,PSTR,MLDR,*ERRIND,PLDR,PACREC*)
POLYLINE   39
    PPL(N,PXAN,PYAN)
POLYLINE 3   39
    PPL3(N,PXAN,PYAN,PZAN)
POLYMARKER   43
    PPM(N,PXAN,PYAN)
POLYMARKER 3   43
    PPM3(N,PXAN,PYAN,PZAN)
POST STRUCTURE   34
    PPOST(WKID,STRID,PRIORT)

READ ITEM FROM METAFILE
    PRDITM(WKID,MIDRL,MLDR,DATREC)
REDRAW ALL STRUCTURES
    PRST(WKID,COFL)
REMOVE NAMES FROM SET   78
    PRES(NSN,NAMSET)
REQUEST CHOICE   173
    PRQCH(WKID,CHDNR,*STAT,CHNR*)
REQUEST LOCATOR   153
    PRQLC(WKID,LCDNR,*STAT VIEWI,PX,PY*)
REQUEST LOCATOR 3   153
    PRQLC3(WKID,LCDNR,*STAT,VIEWI,PX,PY,PZ*)
REQUEST PICK   163
    PRQPK(WKID,PKDNR,IPPD.*STAT,PPD,PP*)
REQUEST STRING   175
    PRQST(WKID,STDNR,*STAT,LOSTR,STR*)
REQUEST STROKE   160
    PRQSK(WKID,SKDNR,N,*STAT,VIEWI,NP,PXAN,PYAN*)
REQUEST STROKE 3   160
    PRQSK3(WKID,SKDNR,N,*STAT,VIEWI,NP,PXAN,PYAN,PZAN*)
REQUEST VALUATOR   170
    PRQVL(WKID,VLDNR,*STAT,VAL*)
RESTORE MODELLING CLIPPING VOLUME   106
    PRMCV
RETRIEVE ALL STRUCTURES   232
    PRAST(AFID)
RETRIEVE PATHS TO ANCESTORS   233
    PREPAN(AFID,STRID,PTHCRD,PTHDEP,IPTHSZ,NELM,*OL,APTHSZ,PATHS*)
RETRIEVE PATHS TO DESCENDANTS   233
    PREPDE(AFID,STRID,PTHORD,PTHDEP,IPTHSZ,NELM,*OL,APTHSZ,PATHS*)
RETRIEVE STRUCTURE IDENTIFIERS   233
    PRSID(AFID,ILSIZE,*NSTRID,LSTRID*)
RETRIEVE STRUCTURE NETWORKS   232
    PRESN(AFID,N,LSTRIDN)
RETRIEVE STRUCTURES   232
    PREST(AFID,N,LSTRIDN)
ROTATE   100
    PRO(ROTANG,*ERRIND,XFRMT*)
ROTATE X   124
    PROX(ROTANG,*ERRIND,XFRMT3*)
ROTATE Y   124
    PROY(ROTANG,*ERRIND,XFRMT3*)
ROTATE Z   124
    PROZ(ROTANG,*ERRIND,XFRMT3*)
SAMPLE CHOICE   183
    PSMCH(WKID,CHDNR,*STAT,CHNR*)
SAMPLE LOCATOR   185
    PSMLC(WKID,LCDNR,*VIEWI,LPX,LPY*)

SAMPLE LOCATOR 3   185
  PSMLC3(WKID,LCDNR,*VIEWI,LPX,LPY,LPZ*)
SAMPLE PICK   183
  PSMPK(WKID,PKDNR,IPPD,*STAT,PPD,PP*)
SAMPLE STRING   183
  PSMST(WKID,STDNR,*LOSTR,STR*)
SAMPLE STROKE   185
  PSMSK(WKID,SKDNR,N,*VIEWI,NP,PXAN,PYAN*)
SAMPLE STROKE 3   185
  PSMSK3(WKID,SKDNR,N,*VIEWI,NP,PXAN,PYAN,PZAN*)
SAMPLE VALUATOR   183
  PSMVL(WKID,VLDNR,*VAL*)
SCALE   100
  PSC(FX,FY,*ERRIND,XFRMT*)
SCALE 3   124
  PSC3(FX,FY,FZ,*ERRIND,XFRMT3*)
SET ANNOTATION STYLE   229
  PSANS(ASTYLE)
SET ANNOTATION TEXT ALIGNMENT   229
  PSATAL(ATALH,ATALV)
SET ANNOTATION TEXT CHARACTER HEIGHT   229
  PSATCH(ATCHH)
SET ANNOTATION TEXT CHARACTER UP VECTOR   229
  PSATCU(ATCHUX,ATCHUY)
SET ANNOTATION TEXT PATH   229
  PSATP(ATP)
SET CHARACTER EXPANSION FACTOR   66
  PSCHXP(CHXP)
SET CHARACTER HEIGHT   66
  PSCHH(CHH)
SET CHARACTER SPACING   66
  PSCHSP(CHSP)
SET CHARACTER UP VECTOR   66
  PSCHUP(CHUX,CHUY)
SET CHOICE MODE   178
  PSCHM(WKID,CHDNR,MODE,ESW)
SET COLOUR MODEL   77
  PSCMD(WKID,CMODEL)
SET COLOUR REPRESENTATION   77
  PSCR(WKID,CI,NCCS,CSPEC)
SET CONFLICT RESOLUTION   233
  PSCNRS(ARCCR,RETCR)
SET DISPLAY UPDATE STATE   212
  PSDUS(WKID,DEFMOD,MODMOD)
SET EDGE COLOUR INDEX   66
  PSEDCI(COLI)
SET EDGE FLAG   66
  PSEDFG(EDFLAG)

SET EDGE INDEX   70
    PSEDI(EDI)
SET EDGE REPRESENTATION   71
    PSEDR(WKID,EDI,EDFLAG,EDTYPE,EWIDTH,COLI)
SET EDGE TYPE   66
    PSEDT(EDTYPE)
SET EDGEWIDTH SCALE FACTOR   66
    PSEWSC(EWIDTH)
SET EDIT MODE   26
    PSEDM(EDITMO)
SET ELEMENT POINTER   26
    PSEP(EP)
SET ELEMENT POINTER AT LABEL   30
    PSEPLB(LABEL)
SET ERROR HANDLING MODE   224
    PSERHM(ERHM)
SET GLOBAL TRANSFORMATION   98
    PSGMT(XFRMT)
SET GLOBAL TRANSFORMATION 3   123
    PSGMT3(XFRMT3)
SET HIGHLIGHTING FILTER   79
    PSHLFT(WKID,ISN,IS,ESN,ES)
SET HLHSR IDENTIFIER   80
    PSHRID(HRID)
SET HLHSR MODE   81
    PSHRM(WKID,HRM)
SET INDIVIDUAL ASF   73
    PSIASF(ASPCID,ASFVAL)
SET INTERIOR COLOUR INDEX   66
    PSICI(COLI)
SET INTERIOR INDEX   70
    PSII(II)
SET INTERIOR REPRESENTATION   71
    PSIR(WKID,II,INTS,STYLI,COLI)
SET INTERIOR STYLE   66
    PSIS(INTS)
SET INTERIOR STYLE INDEX   66
    PSISI(ISTYLI)
SET INVISIBILITY FILTER   79
    PSIVFT(WKID,ISN,IS,ESN,ES)
SET LINETYPE   65
    PSLN(LTYPE)
SET LINEWIDTH SCALE FACTOR   65
    PSLWSC(LWIDTH)
SET LOCAL TRANSFORMATION   21
    PSLMT(XFRMT,CTYPE)
SET LOCAL TRANSFORMATION 3   123
    PSLMT3(XFRMT3,CTYPE)

SET LOCATOR MODE   178
    PSLCM(WKID,LCDNR,MODE,ESW)
SET MARKER SIZE SCALE FACTOR   65
    PSMKSC(MSZSF)
SET MARKER TYPE   65
    PSMK(MTYPE)
SET MODELLING CLIPPING INDICATOR   105
    PSMCLI(MCLIPI)
SET MODELLING CLIPPING VOLUME   105
    PSMCV(OP,NHALFS,HALFSP)
SET MODELLING CLIPPING VOLUME 3   123
    PSMCV3(OP,NHALFS,HALFSP3)
SET PATTERN REFERENCE POINT   52
    PSPARF(RFX,RFY)
SET PATTERN REFERENCE POINT AND VECTORS   52
    PSPRPV(RFX,RFY,RFZ,RFVX,RFVY,RFVZ)
SET PATTERN REPRESENTATION   66
    PSPAR(WKID,PAI,DIMX,DIMY,ISC,ISR,NROWS,NCOLS,COLIA)
SET PATTERN SIZE   51
    PSPA(SZX,SZY)
SET PICK FILTER   168
    PSPKFT(WKID,PKDNR,ISN,IS,ESN,ES)
SET PICK IDENTIFIER   165
    PSPKID(PKID)
SET PICK MODE   178
    PSPKM(WKID,PKDNR,MODE,ESW)
SET POLYLINE COLOUR INDEX   65
    PSPLCI(COLI)
SET POLYLINE INDEX   70
    PSPLI(PLI)
SET POLYLINE REPRESENTATION   71
    PSPLR(WKID,PLI,LTYPE,LWIDTH,COLI)
SET POLYMARKER COLOUR INDEX   65
    PSPMCI(COLI)
SET POLYMARKER INDEX   70
    PSPMI(PMI)
SET POLYMARKER REPRESENTATION   71
    PSPMR(WKID,PMI,MTYPE,MSZSF,COLI)
SET STRING MODE   178
    PSSTM(WKID,STDNR,MODE,ESW)
SET STROKE MODE   178
    PSSKM(WKID,SKDNR,MODE,ESW)
SET TEXT ALIGNMENT   66
    PSTXAL(TXALH,TXALV)
SET TEXT COLOUR INDEX   66
    PSTXCI(COLI)
SET TEXT FONT   66
    PSTXFN(FONT)

SET TEXT INDEX   70
    PSTXI(TXI)
SET TEXT PATH   66
    PSTXP(TXP)
SET TEXT PRECISION   66
    PSTXPR(PREC)
SET TEXT REPRESENTATION   71
    PSTXR(WKID,TXI,FONT,PREC,CHXP,CHSP,COLI)
SET VALUATOR MODE   178
    PSVLM(WKID,VLDNR,MODE,ESW)
SET VIEW INDEX   112
    PSVWI(VIEWI)
SET VIEW REPRESENTATION   116
    PSVWR(WKID,VIEWI,VWORMT,VWMPMT,VWCPLM,XYCLPI)
SET VIEW REPRESENTATION 3   133
    PSVWR3(WKID,VIEWI,VWORMT3,VWMPMT3,VWCPLM3,
        XYCLPI,BCLIPI,FCLIPI)
SET VIEW TRANSFORMATION INPUT PRIORITY   159
    PSVTIP(WKID,VIEWI,RFVWIX,RELPRI)
SET WORKSTATION VIEWPORT   211
    PSWKV(WKID,XMIN,XMAX,YMIN,YMAX)
SET WORKSTATION VIEWPORT 3   211
    PSWKV3(WKID,WKVP)
SET WORKSTATION WINDOW   211
    PSWKW(WKID,XMIN,XMAX,YMIN,YMAX)
SET WORKSTATION WINDOW 3   211
    PSWKW3(WKID,WKWN)
TEXT   54
    PTX(PX,PY,CHARS)
TEXT 3   54
    PTX3(PX,PY,PZ,TDX,TDY,TDZ,CHARS)
TRANSFORM POINT
    PFP(XI,YI,XFRMT,*ERRIND*,*XO*,*YO*)
TRANSFORM POINT 3   130
    PTP3(XI,YI,ZI,XFRMT3,*ERRIND*,*XO*,*YO*,*ZO*)
TRANSLATE   100
    PTR(DX,DY,*ERRIND*,*XFRMT*)
TRANSLATE 3   124
    PTR3(DX,DY,DZ,*ERRIND*,*XFRMT3*)
UNPACK DATA RECORD   199
    PUREC(ULDR,UACREC,IIL,IRL ISL,*ERRIND*,*IL*,*IAU*,*RL*,*RAU*,*SL*,*ULSTR*,*USTR*)
UNPOST ALL STRUCTURES
    PUPAST(WKID)
UNPOST STRUCTURE   17
    PUPOST(WKID,STRID)
UPDATE WORKSTATION
    PUWK(WKID,REGFL)
WRITE ITEM TO METAFILE
    PWITM(WKID,TYPE,IDRL,LDR,DATREC)

Table 2

Parameter	Type	Description
AFID	INTEGER	archive file identifier
APTHSZ	INTEGER	actual size of Nth structure path
APX	REAL	x-annotation offset
APY	REAL	y-annotation offset
APZ	REAL	z-annotation offset
ARCCR	ENUMERATION	archival *conflict resolution*
ARCFIL	INTEGER	archive file name
ASFVAL	ENUMERATION	*aspect source* flag value
ASPCID	ENUMERATION	*aspect identifier*
ASTYLE	INTEGER	annotation style
ATALH	ENUMERATION	annotation *text alignment horizontal*
ATALV	ENUMERATION	annotation *text alignment vertical*
ATCHH	REAL	annotation text character height
ATCHUX	REAL	x-annotation text character up vector
ATCHUY	REAL	y-annotation text character up vector
ATP	ENUMERATION	annotation *text path*
BCLIPI	ENUMERATION	back *clipping indicator*
BPLD	REAL	back plane distance
BUFA	INTEGER	amount of memory units
CHARS	CHARACTER *(*)	character string
CHDNR	INTEGER	choice device number
CHH	REAL	character height
CHNR	INTEGER	choice number
CHSP	REAL	character spacing
CHUX	REAL	x-character up vector
CHUY	REAL	y-character up vector
CHXP	REAL	character expansion factor
CI	INTEGER	colour index
CMODEL	INTEGER	colour model
COFL	ENUMERATION	*control flag*
COLI	INTEGER	colour index
COLIA	INTEGER (DIMX,DIMY)	colour index array
CONID	INTEGER	connection identifier
CPXA	REAL (3)	x-cell parallelogram
CPYA	REAL (3)	y-cell parallelogram
CPZA	REAL (3)	z-cell parallelogram
CSPEC	REAL (*)	colour specification
CTYPE	ENUMERATION	*composition type*
DATREC	CHARACTER *80(LDR)	data record
DEFMOD	ENUMERATION	*deferral mode*
DIMX	INTEGER	dimension of array COLIA
DIMY	INTEGER	dimension of array COLIA
DX	REAL	x-shift vector

DY	REAL	y-shift vector
DZ	REAL	z-shift vector
EDFLAG	ENUMERATION	*on/off switch* edge flag
EDI	INTEGER	edge index
EDITMO	ENUMERATION	*edit mode*
EDTYPE	INTEGER	edgetype
EES	ENUMERATION (EESN)	*element* exclusion set
EESN	INTEGER	number of elements in exclusion set
EIS	ENUMERATION (EISN)	*element* inclusion set
EISN	INTEGER	number of elements in inclusion set
EP,EP1,EP2	INTEGER	element position
EPO	INTEGER	element position offset
ERHM	ENUMERATION	*off/on switch* error handling mode
ERRFIL	INTEGER	error file
ERRIND	INTEGER	error indicator
ERRNR	INTEGER	error number
ES	INTEGER (ESN)	exclusion set
ESN	INTEGER	number of names in exclusion set
ESW	ENUMERATION	*echo switch*
EVOL	REAL (6)	echo volume
EWIDTH	REAL	edgewidth scale factor
FCLIPI	ENUMERATION	front *clipping indicator*
FCTID	INTEGER	function identification
FNDEP	INTEGER	found element position
FONT	INTEGER	text font
FPATH	INTEGER (2,IPTHSZ)	found path
FPLD	REAL	front plane distance
FPTHSZ	INTEGER	found path size
FX	REAL	x-scale factor
FY	REAL	y-scale factor
FZ	REAL	z-scale factor
GSEID	INTEGER	generalized structure element identifier
HALFSP	REAL (4,NHALFS)	list of half-spaces
HALFSP3	REAL (6,NHALFS)	list of half-spaces
HRID	INTEGER	HLHSR identifier
HRM	INTEGER	HLHSR mode
IA	INTEGER (*)	integer entries
IAU	INTEGER (IIL)	integer entries
ICHNR	INTEGER	initial choice number
ICL	ENUMERATION	*input class*
IDNR	INTEGER	logical input device number
IDRL	INTEGER	item data record length
IFLES	INTEGER (*)	inverted filter exclusion sets
IFLESX	INTEGER (IFLN)	array of end indices of inverted filter exclusion sets
IFLIS	INTEGER (*)	inverted filter inclusion sets
IFLISX	INTEGER (IFLN)	array of end indices of inverted filter inclusion sets

IFLN	INTEGER	number of inverted filters
II	INTEGER	interior index
IIL	INTEGER	dimension of integer array
IIPPD	INTEGER	depth of initial pick path
IL	INTEGER	number of integer entries
ILSIZE	INTEGER	size of list (LSTRID)
INP	INTEGER	number of points in initial stroke
INTS	ENUMERATION	*interior style*
IPP	INTEGER (3,IPPD)	initial pick path
IPPD	INTEGER	depth of pick path to return
IPTHSZ	INTEGER	size of path array
IPX	REAL	x-initial locator position
IPY	REAL	y-initial locator position
IPZ	REAL	z-initial locator position
IPXA	REAL (*)	x-initial stroke
IPYA	REAL (*)	y-initial stroke
IPZA	REAL (*)	z-initial stroke
IRL	INTEGER	dimension of real array
IS	INTEGER (ISN)	inclusion set
ISC	INTEGER	index of start column
ISL	INTEGER	dimension of character array
ISN	INTEGER	number of names in inclusion set
ISR	INTEGER	index of start row
ISTAT	ENUMERATION	initial *input device status*
ISTR	CHARACTER *80	initial string
ISTYLI	INTEGER	interior style index
IVAL	REAL	initial value
IVIEWI	INTEGER	initial view index
IXA	INTEGER (NPL)	array of end indices for point lists
LABEL	INTEGER	label identifier
LABEL1	INTEGER	label identifier
LABEL2	INTEGER	label identifier
LCDNR	INTEGER	locator device number
LDR	INTEGER	dimension of data record array
LOSTR	INTEGER	number of characters returned
LPX	REAL	x-locator position
LPY	REAL	y-locator position
LPZ	REAL	z-locator position
LSTR	INTEGER	length of initial string
LSTRID	INTEGER (*)	list of structure identifiers
LSTRIDN	INTEGER (N)	list of structure identifiers
LTYPE	INTEGER	linetype
LWIDTH	REAL	linewidth scale factor
MCLIPF	ENUMERATION	modelling *clipping indicator*
MCLIPI	ENUMERATION	modelling *clipping indicator*
MESS	CHARACTER *(*)	message
MIDRL	INTEGER	maximum item data record length
MLDR	INTEGER	dimension of data record

MODE	ENUMERATION	*operating mode*
MODMOD	ENUMERATION	*modification mode*
MSZSF	REAL	marker size scale factor
MTYPE	INTEGER	marker type
N	INTEGER	array dimension
NAMSET	INTEGER (NSN)	name set
NCCS	INTEGER	number of components of colour specification
NCOLS	INTEGER	number of columns
NELM	INTEGER	element of list of paths
NEWSID	INTEGER	resulting structure identifier
NFLES	INTEGER (*)	normal filter exclusion sets
NFLESX	INTEGER (NFLN)	array of end indices of normal filter exclusion sets
NFLIS	INTEGER (*)	normal filter inclusion sets
NFLISX	INTEGER (NFLN)	array of end indices of normal filter inclusion sets
NFLN	INTEGER	number of normal filters
NHALFS	INTEGER	number of half-spaces in list
NP	INTEGER	number of points in stroke
NPL	INTEGER	number of point lists
NROWS	INTEGER	number of rows
NSN	INTEGER	number of names in set
NSTRID	INTEGER	number of structure identifiers in list
OL	INTEGER	number of paths available
OLDSID	INTEGER	original structure identifier
OP	INTEGER	operator
PACREC	CHARACTER *80 (MLDR)	data record
PAI	INTEGER	pattern index
PATHS	INTEGER (2,IPTHSZ)	Nth structure path
PET	INTEGER	prompt and echo type
PHI	REAL	rotation angle
PHIX	REAL	x-rotation angle
PHIY	REAL	y-rotation angle
PHIZ	REAL	z-rotation angle
PJRX	REAL	x-projection reference point
PJRY	REAL	y-projection reference point
PJRZ	REAL	z-projection reference point
PJTYPE	ENUMERATION	*projection type*
PJVPLM	REAL (4)	projection viewport limits
PJVPLM3	REAL (6)	projection viewport limits
PKDNR	INTEGER	pick device number
PKID	INTEGER	pick identifier
PLDR	INTEGER	number of elements used in PACREC
PLI	INTEGER	polyline index
PLSTR	INTEGER (*)	lengths of each character string entry
PMI	INTEGER	polymarker index
PP	INTEGER (3,IPPD)	pick path

PPD	INTEGER	depth of actual pick path
PPORDR	ENUMERATION	pick *path order*
PREC	ENUMERATION	*text precision*
PRIMID	INTEGER	GDP or GDP3 identifier
PRIORT	REAL	display priority
PSTR	CHARACTER *(*)(*)	character string entries
PTHDEP	INTEGER	path depth
PTHORD	ENUMERATION	*path order*
PX	REAL	x-coordinate of position
PXA	REAL (*)	x-coordinates of points
PXAN	REAL (N)	x-coordinates of points
PY	REAL	y-coordinate of position
PYA	REAL (*)	y-coordinates of points
PYAN	REAL (N)	y-coordinates of points
PZ	REAL	z-coordinate of position
PZA	REAL (*)	z-coordinates of points
PZAN	REAL (N)	z-coordinates of points
QX	REAL	x-coordinate of position
QY	REAL	y-coordinate of position
RA	INTEGER (*)	real entries
RAU	REAL (IRL)	real entries
REFHNF	ENUMERATION	*reference handling flag*
REGFL	ENUMERATION	*reference flag*
RELPRI	ENUMERATION	*relative input priority*
RETCR	ENUMERATION	retrieval *conflict resolution*
RFVWIX	INTEGER	reference view index
RFVX	REAL (2)	x-pattern reference vectors
RFVY	REAL (2)	y-pattern reference vectors
RFVZ	REAL (2)	z-pattern reference vectors
RFX	REAL	x-pattern reference point
RFY	REAL	y-pattern reference point
RFZ	REAL	z-pattern reference point
RL	INTEGER	number of real entries
ROTANG	REAL	rotation angle
RPX	REAL	x-reference point
RPY	REAL	y-reference point
RPZ	REAL	z-reference point
SKDNR	INTEGER	stroke device number
SL	INTEGER	number of character string entries
SPATH	INTEGER (2,SPTHSZ)	starting path
SPTHSZ	INTEGER	number of elements in starting path
SRCDIR	ENUMERATION	*search direction*
SRCHCI	INTEGER	search ceiling
SRPX	REAL	x-search reference point
SRPY	REAL	y-search reference point
SRPZ	REAL	z-search reference point
STAT	ENUMERATION	*input device status*
STATUS	ENUMERATION	*search success indicator*

STDNR	INTEGER	string device number
STR	CHARACTER *(*)	string
STRID	INTEGER	structure identifier
STRTEP	INTEGER	start element position
STYLI	INTEGER	interior style index
SZX	REAL	x-pattern size
SZY	REAL	y-pattern size
TDX	REAL (2)	x-text direction vectors
TDY	REAL (2)	y-text direction vectors
TDZ	REAL (2)	z-text direction vectors
TOUT	REAL	time out
TXALH	ENUMERATION	*text alignment horizontal*
TXALV	ENUMERATION	*text alignment vertical*
TXI	INTEGER	text index
TXP	ENUMERATION	*text path*
TYPE	INTEGER	item type
UACREC	CHARACTER*80 (ULDR)	data record
ULDR	INTEGER	number of elements used in UACREC
ULSTR	INTEGER (ISL)	length of each character string entry
USTR	CHARACTER*(*)(ISL)	character string entries
VAL	REAL	value
VIEWI	INTEGER	view index
VLDNR	INTEGER	valuator device number
VPLD	REAL	view plane distance
VPNX	REAL	x-view plane normal
VPNY	REAL	y-view plane normal
VPNZ	REAL	z-view plane normal
VUPX	REAL	x-view up vector
VUPY	REAL	y-view up vector
VUPZ	REAL	z-view up vector
VWCPLM	REAL (4)	view clipping limits
VWCPLM3	REAL (6)	view clipping limits
VWMPMT	REAL (3,3)	view mapping matrix
VWMPMT3	REAL (4,4)	view mapping matrix
VWORMT	REAL (3,3)	view orientation matrix
VWORMT3	REAL (4,4)	view orientation matrix
VWRX	REAL	x-view reference point
VWRY	REAL	y-view reference point
VWRZ	REAL	z-view reference point
VWWNLM	REAL (4)	window limits
WKID	INTEGER	workstation identifier
WKVP	REAL (6)	workstation viewport limits
WKWN	REAL (6)	workstation window limits
WTYPE	INTEGER	workstation type
X0	REAL	x-fixed point
XFRMT	REAL (3,3)	transformation matrix
XFRMT3	REAL (4,4)	transformation matrix
XFRMTA	REAL (3,3)	transformation matrix

XFRMTA3	REAL (4,4)	transformation matrix
XFRMTB	REAL (3,3)	transformation matrix
XFRMTB3	REAL (4,4)	transformation matrix
XFRMTI	REAL (3,3)	transformation matrix
XFRMTI3	REAL (4,4)	transformation matrix
XFRMTO	REAL (3,3)	transformation matrix
XFRMTO3	REAL (4,4)	transformation matrix
XI	REAL	x-point
XMAX	REAL	x-limit of region
XMIN	REAL	x-limit of region
XO	REAL	x-transformed point
XYCLPI	ENUMERATION	x-y *clipping indicator*
Y0	REAL	y-fixed point
YI	REAL	y-point
YMAX	REAL	y-limit of region
YMIN	REAL	y-limit of region
YO	REAL	y-transformed point
Z0	REAL	z-fixed point
ZI	REAL	z-point
ZO	REAL	z-transformed point

Table 3

Data type	Value	Fortran Name	PHIGS Name
Archive State	0	PARCL	ARCL
	1	PAROP	AROP
Aspect identifier	0	PLN	LINETYPE
	1	PLWSC	LINEWIDTH_SCALE_FACTOR
	2	PPLCI	POLYLINE_COLOUR_INDEX
	3	PMK	MARKER_TYPE
	4	PMKSC	MARKER_SIZE_SCALE_FACTOR
	5	PPMCI	POLYMARKER_COLOUR_INDEX
	6	PTXFN	TEXT_FONT
	7	PTXPR	TEXT_PRECISION
	8	PCHXP	CHARACTER_EXPANSION_FACTOR
	9	PCHSP	CHARACTER_SPACING
	10	PTXCI	TEXT_COLOUR_INDEX
	11	PIS	INTERIOR_STYLE
	12	PISI	INTERIOR_STYLE_INDEX
	13	PICI	INTERIOR_COLOUR_INDEX
	14	PEDFG	EDGE_FLAG
	15	PEDT	EDGE_TYPE

	16	PEWSC	EDGE_WIDTH_SCALE_FACTOR
	17	PEDCI	EDGE_COLOUR_INDEX
Aspect source	0	PBUNDL	BUNDLED
	1	PINDIV	INDIVIDUAL
Clipping indicator	0	PNCLIP	NOCLIP
	1	PCLIP	CLIP
Composition type	0	PCPRE	PRECONCATENATION
	1	PCPOST	POSTCONCATENATE
	2	PCREPL	REPLACE
Conflict resolution	0	PCRMNT	MAINTAIN
	1	PCRABA	ABANDON
	2	PCRUPD	UPDATE
Control flag	0	PCONDI	CONDITIONALLY
	1	PALWAY	ALWAYS
Deferral mode	0	PASAP	ASAP
	1	PBNIG	BNIG
	2	PBNIL	BNIL
	3	PASTI	ASTI
	4	PWAITD	WAIT
Echo switch	0	PNECHO	NOECHO
	1	PECHO	ECHO
Edit mode	0	PINSRT	INSERT
	1	PREPLC	REPLACE
Element	0	PEALL	ALL
	1	PENIL	NIL
	2	PEPL3	POLYLINE_3
	3	PEPL	POLYLINE
	4	PEPM3	POLYMARKER_3
	5	PEPM	POLYMARKER
		. . .	
Input class	0	PNCLAS	NONE
	1	PLOCAT	LOCATOR
	2	PSTROK	STROKE
	3	PVALUA	VALUATOR
	4	PCHOIC	CHOICE
	5	PPICK	PICK
	6	PSTRIN	STRING
Input device status	0	PNONE	NONE
	1	POK	OK
	2	PNPICK	NOPICK
	2	PNCHOI	NOCHOICE
Interior style	0	PHOLLO	HOLLOW
	1	PSOLID	SOLID
	2	PPATTR	PATTERN
	3	PHATCH	HATCH
	4	PISEMP	EMPTY

Modification mode	0	PNIVE	NIVE
	1	PUWOR	UWOR
	2	PUQUM	UQUM
Off/on switch	0	POFF	OFF
	1	PON	ON
Operating mode	0	PREQU	REQUEST
	1	PSAMPL	SAMPLE
	2	PEVENT	EVENT
Path order	0	PPOTOP	TOPFIRST
	1	PPOBOT	BOTTOMFIRST
Projection type	0	PPARL	PARALLEL
	1	PPERS	PERSPECTIVE
Reference handling flag	0	PDELE	DELETE
	1	PKEEP	KEEP
Regeneration flag	0	PPOSTP	POSTPONE
	1	PPERFO	PERFORM
Relative input priority	0	PHIGHR	HIGHER
	1	PLOWER	LOWER
Search direction	0	PBWD	BACKWARD
	1	PFWD	FORWARD
Search success indicator	0	PFAIL	FAILURE
	1	PSUCC	SUCCESS
Text alignment horizontal	0	PAHNOR	NORMAL
	1	PALEFT	LEFT
	2	PACENT	CENTRE
	3	PARITE	RIGHT
Text alignment vertical	0	PAVNOR	NORMAL
	1	PATOP	TOP
	2	PACAP	CAP
	3	PAHALF	HALF
	4	PABASE	BASE
	5	PABOTT	BOTTOM
Text path	0	PRIGHT	RIGHT
	1	PLEFT	LEFT
	2	PUP	UP
	3	PDOWN	DOWN
Text precision	0	PSTRP	STRING
	1	PCHARP	CHAR
	2	PSTRKP	STROKE

INDEX

absolute editing, 26
alignment, 59
annotation text, 39,228
API, 1
archiving, 231
ASFs, 72
aspect ratio, 119,211
aspects, 5,37,65
aspect source flags, 72
attributes, 65

back plane, 127,131,149
base line, 57
binding, 2,235
bottom line, 57
break, 182
bundled, 69
bundled attributes, 69
bundle table, 70

cap line, 57
cell array, 39,227
Central Structure Store, 11
centre line, 57
CGI, 1
CGM, 1
character expansion factor, 55,58
character height, 55,58,66
character spacing, 55,58
character up vector, 56
CHAR text precision, 63
CHOICE, 151,173
CIE colour model, 77
clipping, 104,112,116,148,211

colour models, 76
colour index, 42,76
colour tables, 76
concepts, 2
coordinate systems, 4
CSS, 11
culling, 148
current event report, 186

data record, 178,199
deleting, elements, 32
detectability filter, 78
Device Coordinates(DC), 5,38
DOWN text path, 59

echo, 178,196
echo area, 178,198
echo volume, 178,198
edge bundle table, 72
edge colour index, 53
edge flag, 53
edge index, 70
edge type, 53
edgewidth scale factor, 53
edit mode, 14,25
element pointer, 14,17,25
even-odd rule, 49
event input, 6,152,179,185
EVENT mode, 152,185
exclusion filter, 79,167
exclusion set, 79,167

fill area, 38,46
fill area set, 38,48,53

filters, 78
font 1, 57,63
font 2, 57,63
font specification, 56
Fortran, 2,235
front plane, 127,131,148

generalized drawing primitive,
    39,229
geometric aspects, 69
GKS, 1
GKS-3D, 2
global modelling transformation,
    85,98

half line, 57
half space, 105
HATCH style, 50
hierarchical, 12,83
hierarchy, 83
highlighting filter, 78
HLHSR, 80
HLHSR Identifier, 80
HLHSR method, 51
HLHSR Mode, 80
HLS colour model, 77
homogeneous coordinates, 122
horizontal text alignment, 60
HSV colour model, 77

identification attribute, 78
inclusion filter, 79,167
inclusion set, 79,167
incremental spatial search, 203
individual specification, 65,73
initialization of input devices, 194
initial value, 178,194
input classes, 6,178
input data record, 178,199
input model, 177
input queue overflow, 202
inquiry functions, 216
INSERT edit mode, 14,25

interior, 48
interior bundle table, 72
interior colour index, 49
interior index, 70
interior style, 49,50
invisibility filter, 78

labels, 30
language binding, 2,235
left line, 57
LEFT text path, 58
linetypes, 17,40,41
linewidth scale factor, 40,41
local modelling transformation, 21
local text coordinates, 55,59
LOCATOR, 153
logical input devices, 5,151

markersize scale factor, 44,45
marker type, 44,45
measure process, 177
mixed input modes, 191
modelling, 1
modelling clip, 104
modelling clipping indicator, 106
modelling clipping volume, 105
modelling transformation,
    21,61,84,98
mode setting, 178
mono spaced font, 57
multiple views, 147,156
MVRP, 90

name set, 78
networks, 83
Normalized Projection Coordi-
    nates, 4,38,112,131

oblique projection, 142
open structure, 14
operating modes, 178
operator, 1
orientation, 143

orientation, of text, 59
orthographic projection, 141
output primitive, 4
overlapping views, 157

parallel projection, 127,131,135
pattern array, 52,66
pattern reference point, 51,66
pattern reference point and vectors,
　　52,66
pattern size, 50,51,66
pattern style, 50,66
pattern vectors, 50,52
perspective projection,
　　127,131,142
PHIGS, 2
PHIGS description table, 16,215
PHIGS environment, 213
PICK, 152,162
pick filters, 167
pick identifier, 165
pick path, 163
pick path order, 201
picture, 1,37
picture composition, 86
polyline, 38,39
polyline aspects, 40
polyline bundle table, 70
polyline colour index, 42
polyline index, 69
polymarker, 38,43
polymarker aspects, 44
polymarker colour index, 44,46
polymarker index, 70
posting, 12,15
post list, 16
POST multiplication, 21,22,23,86
PRE multiplication, 21,22,23,86
projection, 6,127,131
Projection Reference Point(PRP),
　　127,131,145
projection viewport, 147
projectors, 127

prompt, 177,196
prompt and echo type, 196

registration, 40
relative editing, 29
rendering, 80
representations, 71
REPLACE edit mode, 25
REQUEST, 152
REQUEST mode, 179
RGB colour model, 76
right handed coordinates, 122
right line, 57
RIGHT text path, 58
root structure, 84
RTPR, 90
RTRP, 90

sample input, 6,152,182
SAMPLE, 152,182
scene, 1,4,37,111
SCPR, 90
shielding, 108
simultaneous events, 202
STRING, 152,175
STRING text precision, 63
STROKE, 151,160
STROKE text precision, 63
structure, 5,11
structure editing, 25
structure elements, 11,13
structure hierarchy, 83
structure networks, 5,83
structure state list, 15

text, 39,54
text alignment, 55,59
text aspects, 55
text colour index, 56
text extent rectangle, 56,57,59
text font, 55
text index, 70
Text Local Coordinates, 55,59

text path, 55
text position, 54,59,61
top line, 57
traversal, 11
traversal state list, 16
traverser, 13,16
trigger, 178

UP text path, 59

VALUATOR, 151,170
vertical text alignment, 60
view culling, 148
view definition, 116
view index, 112,133
viewing, 1,111,124

viewing model, 127
view mapping, 115,124,131
view orientation, 114,127,135
view plane, 127,131,143
view representation, 131
View Reference Coordinates,
    112,125,128,131
View Reference Point, 128,131
view transformation input priority,
    158
view window, 127,131

window to viewport mapping, 139
workstation, 3,65,209
workstation clip, 125,211
world coordinates(WC), 4,37,125